Improving Learning How to Learn

Learning how to learn is an essential preparation for lifelong learning. While this is widely acknowledged by teachers, they have lacked a rich professional knowledge base from which they can teach their pupils to learn how to learn. This book makes a major contribution by building on previous work associated with 'assessment for learning'.

Improving Learning How to Learn is based on the findings of a major development and research project that explored what teachers can do in their classroom practice to help pupils acquire the knowledge and skills of learning how to learn. Specific chapters focus upon:

- values and practices of staff in relation to classroom assessment, professional learning and management practices;
- studies of classrooms which indicate that changes in practice can become ritualised unless teachers develop frameworks for thinking about learning;
- studies of different ways of leading and promoting professional development focused explicitly and consistently on teaching and learning;
- an exploration of the nature of networks and the various ways they support knowledge creation and dissemination;
- how learning how to learn practice is reflected in classroom practice, in teacher learning and in organisational and network learning.

This book will be of interest to all those concerned with improving classroom learning and assessment. A practical companion book, *Learning How to Learn: Tools for Schools*, is also available from Routledge.

Improving Learning TLRP

Series Editor: Andrew Pollard, Director of the ESRC Teaching and Learning Programme

Improving Learning How to Learn

Classrooms, schools and networks

Mary James, Robert McCormick, Paul Black, Patrick Carmichael, Mary-Jane Drummond, Alison Fox, John MacBeath, Bethan Marshall, David Pedder, Richard Procter, Sue Swaffield, Joanna Swann and Dylan Wiliam

Routledge
Taylor & Francis Group
LONDON AND NEW YORK

First published 2007
by Routledge
2 Park Square, Milton Park, Abingdon, Oxon OX14 4RN

Simultaneously published in the USA and Canada
by Routledge
270 Madison Ave, New York, NY 10016

Routledge is an imprint of the Taylor & Francis Group, an informa business

© 2007 Mary James, Robert McCormick, Paul Black, Patrick Carmichael, Mary-Jane Drummond, Alison Fox, John MacBeath, Bethan Marshall, David Pedder, Richard Procter, Sue Swaffield, Joanna Swann and Dylan Wiliam

Typeset in Charter ITC and Stone Sans
by Keystroke, 28 High Street, Tettenhall, Wolverhampton
Printed and bound in Great Britain
by Antony Rowe Ltd, Chippenham, Wiltshire

British Library Cataloguing in Publication Data
A catalogue record for this book is available from the British Library

Library of Congress Cataloging in Publication Data
A catalog record for this book has been requested

ISBN10 0–415–40426–6 (hbk)
ISBN10 0–415–40427–4 (pbk)
ISBN10 0–203–93431–8 (ebk)

ISBN13 978–0–415–40426–6 (hbk)
ISBN13 978–0–415–40427–3 (pbk)
ISBN13 978–0–203–93431–9 (ebk)

Contents

Illustrations

Figures

Tables

Boxes

Contributors

Mary James is Professor of Education at the Institute of Education, University of London and Deputy Director of the ESRC Teaching and Learning Research Programme.

Robert McCormick is Professor at the Faculty of Education and Language Studies, Open University, UK.

Paul Black is Emeritus Professor of Science Education at King's College London, University of London, UK.

Patrick Carmichael is Project Director at the Centre for Applied Research in Educational Technologies, University of Cambridge, UK.

Mary-Jane Drummond has retired from the Faculty of Education, University of Cambridge, UK.

Alison Fox is Research Fellow at the Centre for Curriculum and Teaching Studies, Open University, UK.

John MacBeath O.B.E. is Professor of Educational Leadership, University of Cambridge, UK.

Bethan Marshall is Senior Lecturer in English Education at King's College London, University of London, UK.

David Pedder is Lecturer in Educational Leadership and School Improvement at the Faculty of Education, University of Cambridge, UK.

Richard Procter is at the Centre for Applied Research in Educational Technologies, University of Cambridge, UK.

Sue Swaffield is Lecturer in Educational Leadership and School Improvement at the Faculty of Education, University of Cambridge, UK.

Joanna Swann is Senior Lecturer in Educational Studies at the University of Brighton, UK.

Dylan Wiliam is Deputy Director of the Institute of Education, University of London, UK.

Series editor's preface

The Improving Learning series showcases findings from projects within the Economic and Social Research Council's Teaching and Learning Research Programme (TLRP), the UK's largest ever co-ordinated educational research initiative.

Books in the Improving Learning series are explicitly designed to support 'evidence-informed' decisions in educational practice and policy-making. In particular, they combine rigorous social and educational science with high awareness of the significance of the issues being researched.

Working closely with practitioners, organisations and agencies covering all educational sectors, the program has supported many of the UK's best researchers to work on the direct improvement of policy and practice to support learning. Over seventy projects have been supported, covering many issues across the life course. We are proud to present the results of this work through books in the Improving Learning series.

Each book provides a concise, accessible and definitive overview of innovative findings from a TLRP investment. If more advanced information is required, the books may be used as a gateway to academic journals, monographs, websites, etc. On the other hand, shorter summaries and research briefings on key findings are also available via the program's website at http://www.tlrp.org.

We hope that you will find the analysis and findings presented in this book helpful to you in your work on improving outcomes for learners.

Andrew Pollard
Director, TLRP
Institute of Education, University of London

Acknowledgements

The Learning How to Learn – in classrooms, schools and networks (LHTL) project was supported from 2001 to 2005 by a grant (reference no. L139 25 1020) from the Economic and Social Research Council's Teaching and Learning Research Programme. We are grateful for the opportunity this gave us to research some important questions that have interested us individually and collectively for some time. We are especially grateful to Andrew Pollard (TLRP Director and our critical friend) and to Gary Grubb and Ian Farnden (ESRC Office) who have provided guidance of diverse kinds over these years.

We also give special thanks to David Hargreaves whose idea it first was to bring together research on classrooms, schools and networks, and who was instrumental in developing the proposal with us, although he cannot be held responsible for what we did with it subsequently.

Of course, there are very many other people and organisations that have contributed to our work in very different but important ways, and we want to thank them also. This was a collaborative project distributed across five higher education institutions – Cambridge University, Institute of Education London, King's College London, the Open University and Reading University – and we acknowledge the support that these organisations provided.

Mindful of the fact that film-makers are often better than academics at giving credit to all the people who contribute to the final production, we have attempted to compile our own 'credits' so that readers can see the real scope of a research enterprise such as this. All the people mentioned have played an important part. We name many of them below but if we have missed any, we apologise and thank them also.

First on our list come the 40 project schools, and ten trials schools, with whom we worked, and the hundreds of teachers and pupils who have contributed in some way. Without them there would have been no study. We were constantly amazed at how willing they were to give of their time and expertise at a pressured period in educational history. We cannot name them for confidentiality reasons, but we are indebted to them and have learned so much from them. There is a sense in which we have not 'discovered' new knowledge but have been privileged to find out about, interpret and communicate the knowledge that teachers themselves create.

It is public knowledge that the 40 project schools were located in Essex, Hertfordshire, Medway, Oxfordshire, Redbridge local authorities and the Kent and Somerset Virtual Education Action Zone. Local advisers worked as partners with us and supported schools as local co-ordinators for the project. We thank especially Luke Abbott, Pete Dudley, Tracy Goodway, Jackie Easter, Cindy Ashford, Diane Croston, Jeff Smith, Peter Leech, Wendy Smith, John Ubsdell, Hilary Gerhard, Dorothy Kavanagh, Peter McCarthy, Vicky Coxon, Ron Mehta, Lorraine Dawes and Jessica Chappell.

Other teachers, along with policy-makers and academics, served on our Advisory Group which provided helpful advice and support to us, especially when we had crucial decisions to make. Members of our Advisory Group were: Richard Bartholomew, Tom Bentley, Richard Daugherty, Caroline Gipps, David Hargreaves, Paul Hussey, Neil McLean, Rebecca Parker, Judy Sebba, Margaret Threadgold, Angela Webster and Vanessa Wiseman.

Lots of other people assisted us with the research in important ways:

- *Members of the original team who continued to contribute ideas and help*: Geoff Southworth, Colin Conner, David Frost and Leslie Honour.
- *Statistical advisers*: John Gray and Peter Milligan.
- *Advisers on conducting research with young children*: Elise Alexander and Annabelle Dixon.
- *Readers and reviewers of draft publications*: Eva Baker, Stephen Baron, Peter Blatchford, David Berliner, Sally Brown, Donald Christie, Andy Hargreaves, Erno Lehtinen, John Leach, Ann Lieberman, Carol McGuinness, Donald McIntyre, Terry McLaughlin, Patricia Murphy, Harry O'Neill, David Perkins, Sally Thomas and Chris Watkins.
- *Linked TLRP research fellows*: Robin Bevan and Pete Dudley.
- *Media support*: Martin Ince.
- *Additional data collection*: Dave Ebbutt.

- *Supply of analysed performance data*: Mike Treadaway (Fischer Family Trust, with the agreement of the DfES).
- *Additional data analysis*: Ann-Marie Brandom, Paul Coleman, Jane Cullen and Clare Folkes.
- *Data Entry*: Lidia Pedder and Brian Marley.
- *Transcribers*: Sue Barnard, Brooke Beasley, Linda Bott, Izabela Brodzka, Joan Dadd, Hai Yen Hoang, Shevon Houston, Sue Ingledew, Peggy Nunn, Paula Peachy and Helen Rushton.
- *Website*: Centre for Applied Research in Educational Technologies, Cambridge.
- *Spreadsheet for website*: Elizabeth Moore.
- *Project secretaries*: Carmel Casey-Morley and Nichola Daily.
- *TLRP office*: Lynne Blanchfield, Suzanne Fletcher, Sarah Douglas and James O'Toole.
- *Admin Support*: Katherine Shaw and Tali Kfir.
- *Finance/Contracts*: Barbara Bennett, Lois Davis, Ann Doyle, Ratha Gopal, Steff Hazlehurst, Liesbeth Krul, Lucy Palfreyman, Angela Pollentine, Dot Purdon, Tracey Sendall, Barbara Shannon and Philip Vale.
- *Technical Support*: Rob Bricheno, Matt Ilett and Paul Rogers.
- *Catering and cakes*: Sylvia James.
- *Meeting room arrangements*: Ron Garner, Sue Sadler and Anita Chapman.
- *Sponsorship of a dissemination event for policy-makers*: Nuffield Foundation (Catrin Roberts, Velda Hinds).

This list is tinged with sadness because Terry McLaughlin, Annabelle Dixon and Angela Webster – all brilliant teachers – are no longer with us. We remember them with affection and gratitude.

Part I

What is the issue?

Chapter 1

Promoting learning how to learn through assessment for learning

This book is based on a development and research project that investigated how learning how to learn might be promoted in schools using assessment for learning as a starting point. This chapter sets the scene by exploring the reasons for the growth of interest in learning [how] to learn and describing briefly what the project set out to do. It also clarifies the project's use of important concepts and attempts to answer some questions, such as: What do we mean by learning? What is assessment for learning? What is learning autonomy? What is learning *how* to learn, and is it different from learning to learn? What is the contribution of 'assessment for learning' to 'learning how to learn'?

The importance of learning how to learn in the twenty-first century

The idea of 'learning how to learn', or, more commonly, 'learning to learn', has been around for a long time but it has become especially popular recently because it is felt to be important for lifelong learning in the twenty-first century. The assumption is that in a rapidly developing world in which the creation of knowledge increases exponentially, the crucial resource in 'knowledge economies' is the ability of people to respond flexibly and creatively to demands for new knowledge, skills and dispositions in continuously changing social and economic contexts. Some of what has traditionally been learned at school may become redundant or irrelevant by the time that pupils

* Authored by Mary James with Paul Black, Robert McCormick and David Pedder

enter the workforce; some knowledge may even need to be 'unlearned' as new knowledge supersedes old knowledge. In this context, development of a capability to learn new things, throughout life, becomes essential.

But education for economic growth in increasingly globalised and competitive markets is only part of the story. The benefits and purposes of learning go beyond the enhancement of individual and national economic productivity. This has, of course, been recognised from Plato and Aristotle onwards, although during the 1980s and 1990s both Conservative and New Labour governments in the UK focused on the demands of the economy, reflecting trends elsewhere, especially in the USA. This contributed to the language of markets permeating the world of schools: educational aims and goals became 'targets'; parents became 'consumers'; the curriculum was 'delivered'; and 'choice' was a key value. These concepts are still pervasive but there is growing evidence that they are now being moderated by cross-party concerns for social justice and individual and social well-being – at least at the level of political rhetoric.

This policy shift is illustrated by the fact that the UK Government saw the need to establish a Centre for Research on the Wider Benefits of Learning (http://www.learningbenefits.net/), which has subsequently identified 'social productivity' as a key framework to set alongside 'economic productivity'. Individual health and well-being; family functioning; community cohesion and flourishing; social cohesion, economic growth and equality, are all identified as contributing to 'social productivity'. In other words, learning is seen to benefit the individual, the family, the community and the nation. Feinstein (2006, p. 4) argues:

> In a globalising world with ever increasing levels of technological development and intensification of economic pressures, it is vital that the education system equips children and adults to withstand the economic, cultural and technological challenges they face. Technical and academic skills are essential for this, but . . . so are features of personal development such as resilience, self-regulation, a positive sense of self and personal and social identity. The capability of individuals to function as civic agents with notions of personal responsibility, tolerance and respect depends on these wider features of self as well as on the interaction with others in schools, workplaces, communities, neighbourhoods and through the media and other channels.

This has striking resonance with the Every Child Matters agenda in the UK (HM Government, 2003) which highlights the importance of the following five outcomes of the education system:

- Being healthy
- Staying safe
- Enjoying and achieving
- Making a positive contribution
- Achieving economic well-being.

However, as Feinstein also points out (2006, p. 5) there is a tension between meeting these broad-ranging objectives and focusing on the basic skills and qualifications which have been the major thrust of contemporary policy. It is possible to argue that people who are developing well in these broader terms are better equipped to develop core academic skills, and vice versa, but it is equally possible that these outcomes are in conflict.

Learning how to learn can be thought of as a process of learning which enables the learner to know how best to go about learning other things, including school subjects but also other valued forms of knowledge, skills, attitudes and capability. The development of learning how to learn strategies and dispositions fits well with the idea that education for the twenty-first century should be concerned with building intellectual and social capital for the benefit of individuals and society in a changing world. (We discuss ideas about 'capital' more fully in Chapter 2.) This might explain why, since the turn of the century, there has been a plethora of initiatives concerned with different aspects of learning to learn. For example, in the UK, the Campaign for Learning established an action research project with schools (see http://www.campaign-for-learning.org.uk/projects/L2L/l2lindex. htm), the Economic and Social Research Council (ESRC) funded a seminar series on 'Knowledge and Skills for Learning to Learn' which produced a book (Moseley *et al.*, 2005), and the think-tank DEMOS published the results of a working group in a booklet *About Learning* (DEMOS, 2005). In Finland, researchers at the University of Helsinki developed an instrument to assess learning to learn (Hautamäki, *et al.*, 2002); and, in response to the Lisbon Agreement, the European Commission set up a 'Learning to Learn Expert Group' to make recommendations on the development of an indicator to compare the learning to learn capabilities of 15-year-olds in European Union countries.

The ESRC TLRP Learning How to Learn (LHTL) Project

This book is the result of the work of researchers, schools and local authorities in England, who, stimulated by similar concerns to those described above, worked together from 2001 to 2005 on a major development and research project funded by the ESRC within the UK-wide Teaching and Learning Research Programme (TLRP). Part I of the book provides the background and an introduction to what follows. Part II provides an overview of what we found out, including short case studies from schools that illustrate some of the most interesting developments and issues. Part III summarises the main themes and arguments and draws out implications for practice and policy. A more detailed account of the methods we used to carry out the research can be found in James *et al.* (2006a), although there is also a summary in the Appendix. The book is conceived as a 'gateway' which directs readers to other project publications and resources where more detail can be found on particular aspects of the work.

Background and rationale

While the rhetorical power of learning how to learn (LHTL) was already considerable at the time when we initiated the project, there was little clarity or consensus about what LHTL is, how it can be promoted in classrooms, what challenges it poses for teachers, or how the teacher development that might be necessary can be supported through knowledge creation and sharing within schools and across networks. We wanted to find out more about these issues so we began by articulating a number of assumptions, or premises, derived from our previous research and our reading of existing literature, which we then set out to investigate in our new project.

We identified four such premises. First, we thought that practices likely to promote LHTL would overlap with, and build upon, those associated with assessment for learning (AfL). These include clarifying learning goals and criteria, reflecting on learning, acting on formative feedback and promoting peer- and self-assessment. Members of the research team have considerable experience of research on assessment for learning so we wanted to examine this link, especially the shift from the somewhat teacher-centred approach of AfL to the more pupil-centred approach that learning how to learn implies. We were especially interested in the potential of LHTL to develop autonomous learners.

Second, evidence for the effectiveness of AfL is derived mainly from carefully controlled but small-scale experiments which have involved intensive support to teachers. If these innovations are to be scaled-up and sustained across the system, they will have to grow with much less support. Conditions for the creation and spread of knowledge and practice would be crucial to their successful implementation. We expected that the professional development of teachers and the organisational structures and cultural processes that support and enhance teachers' own learning would be crucial.

This insight led to our third premise: that LHTL should not be seen as an idea with relevance only to the education of pupils, but it should also be central, if it is as powerful as it is claimed, to the learning of teachers, individually and collectively within networks, and to the organisational learning of schools.

Our fourth premise was recognition that LHTL practices, whether applying to pupil or teacher learning, were still novel and would need to be stimulated in most state-maintained schools notwithstanding the fact that, during the course of our work, the Department for Education and Skills (DfES) introduced AfL into its National Strategy frameworks, supported by materials and money for consultants. The results of these initiatives were still unknown so we judged that we needed to do a minimum level of development work, consistent with what was achievable within the normal resources of schools. We expected that the level of engagement of schools with our project would be influential but, in schools where many initiatives interact, we would need to treat this as just one variable among many. Indeed, we were particularly interested in how schools coped with multiple initiatives and whether, for instance, they treated them separately, combined them in some way, or reconstructed ideas from different initiatives into some coherent whole, based on underlying principles. So, we proposed to investigate the way that project ideas 'landed' in schools, what happened to them and why, what we could learn from this about the quality of the ideas, how they were engineered into practice by teachers and schools, and what conditions supported or inhibited effective innovation.

Box 1.1 presents an introduction to assessment for learning.

Box 1.1   An introduction to assessment for learning

The key text is the review of research by Paul Black and Dylan Wiliam (1998a, 1998b), which was commissioned by the UK Assessment Reform Group. The summary below draws on this work, and adds some insights from studies carried out since 1998.

Black and Wiliam analysed 250 studies, of which 50 were a particular focus because they provided evidence of gains in achievement after 'interventions' based on what we now call AfL practices. These gains, measured by pre- and post-summative tests, produced standardised effect sizes of between 0.4 and 0.7 of a standard deviation – larger than for most other educational interventions. Moreover, there was evidence that gains for lower-attaining students were even greater. These findings have convinced many teachers and policy-makers that AfL is worth taking seriously.

The innovations introduced into classroom practice in these studies involved some combination of the following elements.

Developing classroom talk and questioning

Asking questions, either orally or in writing, is crucial to the process of eliciting information about the current state of a pupil's understanding. However, questions phrased simply to establish whether pupils know the correct answer are of little value for formative purposes. Pupils can give right answers for the wrong reasons, or wrong answers for very understandable reasons. Thus, if learning is to be secure, superficially 'correct' answers need to be probed and misconceptions explored. In this way pupils' learning needs can be diagnosed. The implication is that teachers need to spend time planning good diagnostic questions, possibly with colleagues. Pupils can be trained to ask questions too, and to reflect on answers. They need thinking time to do this, as they do to formulate answers that go beyond the superficial. Increasing thinking-time, between asking a question and taking an answer, from the average of 0.9 of a second, can be productive in this respect. So can a 'no hands up' rule which implies that all pupils can be called upon to answer and that their answers will be dealt with seriously, whether right or wrong. All these ideas call for changes in the norms of talk in many classrooms. By promoting thoughtful and sustained dialogue, teachers can explore the knowledge and understanding of pupils and build on this.

Giving appropriate feedback

Feedback is always important but it needs to be approached cautiously because research draws attention to potential negative effects. This happens when feedback focuses on pupils' self-esteem or self-image, as is the case when marks are given, or when praise focuses on the person rather than the learning. Praise can make pupils feel good but it does not help their learning unless it is explicit about what the pupil has done well. This point is powerfully re-inforced by research by Butler (1988) who compared the effects of giving marks as numerical scores, comments only, and marks plus comments. Pupils given only comments made 30 per cent progress and all were motivated. No gains were made by those given marks or those given marks plus comments. In both these groups the lower achievers also lost interest. The explanation was that giving marks washed out the beneficial effects of the comments. Careful commenting works best when it stands on its own.

Sharing criteria with learners

Research also shows how important it is that pupils understand what counts as success in different curriculum areas and at different stages in their development as learners. This entails sharing learning intentions, expectations, objectives, goals, targets and success criteria. However, because these are often framed in generalised ways, they are rarely enough on their own. Pupils need to see what they mean, as applied in the context of their own work, or that of others. They will not understand criteria right away, but regular discussions of concrete examples will help pupils to develop an understanding of quality. In contexts where creativity is valued, as well as excellence, it is important to see criteria of quality as representing a 'horizon of possibilities' rather than a single end point. Notions of assessment for learning as directed towards 'closing

continued

the gap', between present understanding and the learning aimed for, can be too restrictive. This may be especially true in subject areas that do not have a clear linear or hierarchical structure because a 'closing the gap' approach can lead to unexpected outcomes of equal value being ignored.

Peer and self-assessment

The AfL practices described above emphasise changes in the teacher's role. However, they also imply changes in what pupils do and how they might become more involved in assessment and in reflecting on their own learning. Indeed, questioning, giving appropriate feedback and reflecting on criteria of quality can all be rolled up in peer and self-assessment. This is what happened in a research study by Fontana and Fernandes (1994). Over a period of 20 weeks, primary school pupils were progressively trained to carry out self-assessment that involved setting their own learning objectives, constructing relevant problems to test their learning, selecting appropriate tasks, and carrying out self-assessments. Over the period of the experiment the learning gains of this group were twice as great as those of a matched 'control' group.

The importance of peer and self-assessment was also illustrated by Frederiksen and White (1997) who compared learning gains of four classes over the course of a term. The greatest gains were for pupils previously assessed as having weak basic skills. This suggests that low achievement in schools may have much less to do with a lack of 'innate' ability than with pupils' lack of understanding of what they are meant to be learning and what counts as quality.

From 1999 to 2001, a development and research project was carried out by Paul Black and colleagues (2002, 2003) – the King's, Medway and Oxfordshire Formative Assessment Project (KMOFAP) – to test some of these findings in a British context because much of the earlier research came from other countries. Reliable results, in terms of performance measures, became available for 19 of the 24 science and mathematics teachers, in six secondary schools. The mean effect size for this group was 0.34 with a median of 0.27. The reason for this difference was the biasing effect of three high and four negative values which led the research team to conclude that effects crucially depend on the quality of the formative assessment work, a point to which we return in Chapter 3 of this book. Nevertheless, even on the basis of a median effect size of 0.27:

> if replicated across a whole school they would raise the performance of a school at the 25th percentile of achievement nationally into the upper half. At the very least, these data suggest that teachers do not have to choose between teaching well and getting good results.
>
> (Black *et al.*, 2003, p. 29)

In terms of effective formative practice, the KMOFAP team also found peer-assessment to be an important complement to self-assessment because pupils learn to take on the roles of teachers and to see learning from their perspective. At the same time they can give and take criticism and advice in a non-threatening way, and in a language that children naturally use. Most importantly, as with self-assessment, peer-assessment is a strategy for 'placing the work in the hands of the pupils'.

Thoughtful and active learners

These ideas for formative assessment practice have been summed up by the Assessment Reform Group in the following definition of AfL:

> Assessment for Learning is the process of seeking and interpreting evidence for use by learners and their teachers to decide where the learners are in their learning, where they need to go and how best to get there.
>
> (ARG, 2002, pp. 2–3)

The ultimate goal of AfL is therefore to involve pupils in their own assessment so that they can reflect on where they are in their own learning, understand where they need to go next and work out what steps to take to get there. The research literature sometimes refers to this as the processes of self-monitoring and self-regulation. In other words, pupils need to understand both the desired *outcomes*

continued

of their learning and the *processes* of learning by which these outcomes are achieved, and they need to act on this understanding.

Source: This is an edited version of an article in a collection of professional development materials for schools that were developed and tested within the LHTL project (James, et al., 2006b). Versions of these resources are also available on the project website: http://www.learntolearn.ac.uk

Project aims and activity – in brief

Researchers from four universities – Cambridge, London (King's College and the Institute of Education), the Open University and Reading University – came together to carry out the project. They have expertise in assessment for learning, subject teaching, teacher professional development, school leadership and improvement, network analysis and new technologies. All these areas were needed to address the areas of interest to us. The team then worked with 17 secondary, 21 primary and 2 infants' schools from five local authorities (Essex, Medway, Hertfordshire, Oxfordshire and Redbridge) and one Virtual Education Action Zone (Kent and Somerset). (Some 43 schools were originally involved but 3 dropped out early in the project.) The 40 schools provided a balance of urban and rural, large and small, and mono-ethnic and multi-ethnic schools. Performance results in 2000 indicated room for improvement in all of them.

On the basis of our premises (above) we designed a development and research project to advance both understanding and practice of learning how to learn at three levels – in classrooms, schools and networks. Constructing a project on three levels was an administrative convenience because it allowed a division of labour. However, as our work progressed, the boundaries between these levels began to dissolve, both in practice and conceptually, as the discussions in the following chapters will show.

At the beginning of our project, we formulated five project aims that we adhered to throughout. We aimed to do the following:

1. Develop and extend recent work on formative assessment (assessment for learning) into a model of learning how to learn for both teachers and pupils.

2. Investigate what teachers can do to help pupils to learn how to learn in classrooms.
3. Investigate what characterises the school in which teachers successfully create and manage the knowledge and skills of learning how to learn.
4. Investigate how educational networks, including electronic networks, can support the creation, management and transfer of the knowledge and skills of learning how to learn.
5. Attempt to develop a generic model of innovation in teaching and learning that integrates work in classrooms, schools and networks.

These aims are linked in that they relate to a set of hypotheses with the following logic (see Figure 1.1). First, on the right-hand side of Figure 1.1, pupils' learning outcomes, whether defined as academic achievements measured by tests and examinations or as 'soft skills', attitudes and other forms of knowledge or capability, are, at least in part, the result of classroom interactions with teachers, peers and resources. Second, classroom practices are influenced, at least in part, by teachers' and pupils' beliefs about learning, although beliefs can also be an outcome of classroom interactions. Third, these beliefs and practices are, at least in part, outcomes of teachers' professional development, school culture, management practices, and networking opportunities, in which electronic tools may have a role. Engagement with project interventions, such as ours, might also have an impact – indeed, we hoped it would, although we needed to keep an open mind about this. For all these dimensions, background variables, such as school context, teachers' length of experience and pupils' prior learning and achievement, might have an influence and these need to be taken into account also.

These aims and hypotheses guided both our interventions and our data collection and analysis, for, as a development and research project, we needed to engage in two different kinds of activity.

On the development side, we introduced the project ideas to schools in initial Inset sessions, provided optional workshops and feedback from baseline questionnaire results, allocated a small amount of 'critical friend' time to each school, convened meetings for school and local authority co-ordinators, and created a website for the exchange of ideas and materials. Most of these resources are available in a book (James et al., 2006b) and online at: http://www.learntolearn.ac.uk.

On the research side, we observed how project ideas 'landed' in schools, and collected evidence to describe and explain the different

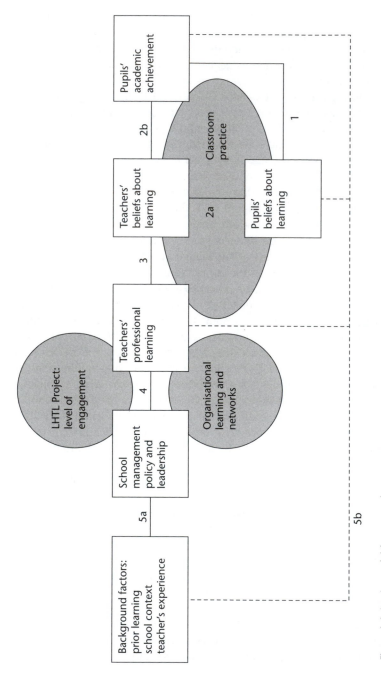

Figure 1.1 Logic model for a causal argument

patterns of implementation and impact. Questionnaires were developed to collect quantitative data on teachers' and pupils' beliefs about learning, staff values and reported practices concerning classroom assessment, professional learning, school leadership and management, and the use of electronic tools. Responses were used to establish a baseline for each school, and change over time in half the sample. School performance data were used as indicators of pupils' academic achievement.

Qualitative data were collected to investigate the links between these measured variables. Indicators of other (mediating) variables, that might have an influence on outcomes, included accounts of policies, initiatives, networks, processes and events derived from classroom observation, interviews, documents and network maps. Again, all these instruments are available on the web site as self-evaluation resources for schools.

We carried out analysis by 'combing' through our data in several different ways. First, we took each dataset, for example, all headteacher interviews or our pupil beliefs about learning questionnaires, and analysed these for patterns within the data across the whole sample of schools. These 'whole sample' analyses produced interesting findings in their own right and these continue to be published in free-standing articles in journals, many of which will be referred to in subsequent chapters. By identifying important factors operating in the settings we were investigating, these analyses also enabled us to relate findings from one dataset with findings from others and to study patterns of association between variables in our 'logic model' (see Figure 1.1). We could do this both for the sample as a whole and for case studies of school and networks, although some incomplete datasets limited the extent to which we could be as systematic as we might have wished. More detail about our research design and methods can be found in the Appendix and in James *et al.* (2006a).

The chapters in this book reflect this analytic framework in their content and organisation. Chapters 3, 4 and 5 present findings across the whole sample for one level: classrooms, schools and networks, respectively. Each tells the story created by analysis of key data pertaining to that context. Chapters 6 and 7, by means of short case studies, show how the variables at two or more levels are related in the context of individual schools. Chapters 8 and 9 then show how some of the dimensions identified across the whole sample exhibit different patterns within and between different schools.

Some of the key ideas we used or developed

Learning

Before we move on to the detail of the empirical findings, we need to consider our first project aim: 'to develop and extend recent work on formative assessment (assessment for learning) into a model of learning how to learn for both teachers and pupils'. This called for some reading and thinking (theoretical work). The meaning of 'assessment for learning', or formative assessment, has been clarified in recent years (see Box 1.1; also Black and Wiliam, 2006) but the project team needed also to clarify what it meant by 'learning how to learn' and to be more precise about how the two concepts, AfL and LHTL, relate. But there is a prior, and very fundamental, question to answer: what do we mean by learning? Both 'assessment for learning' and 'learning how to learn' incorporate the word and the assumption is that we know what we mean when we use it. However, as Box 1.2 makes clear, there exist several different perspectives on learning and we cannot assume that the way one person uses the word is the same as others. Different interpretations are a major source of misunderstanding, not helped by the fact that the word can be used linguistically in so many different ways: as a noun, gerund, present participle or adjective.

Box 1.2 Perspectives on learning

Teaching is based on assumptions about how people learn, although these assumptions are not always very explicit or based on sound evidence. Gradgrind, in Dickens' novel *Hard Times*, believed that children's minds were like little pitchers to be filled full of facts; the job of the teacher was to know a lot of facts and tell them to pupils whose job it was to memorise them. There are still a lot of people who hold this 'folk' perspective, which is more about teaching than learning.

Writers on *learning* theory (e.g. Bredo, 1993; Bransford *et al.*, 1999; Watkins, 2003) often identify three main perspectives. These have acquired a variety of labels but the three most frequently used are:

1.   Behaviourist learning theory.

---

2. Constructivist learning theory.
3. Socio-cultural learning theory.

Common assumptions about learning have their origins in behaviourist psychology which regards learning as a conditioned response to a stimulus. Behaviourism, as its name implies, is most concerned with behaviour, not what goes on in a person's head. Implications for teaching and assessment are: (1) that rewards, or the withholding of rewards, are powerful means to establish desired behaviours; (2) that a complex skill can be taught by breaking it up and teaching and testing the pieces separately; (3) that it is best to learn facts and basic skills first and not try for understanding – that will come later. Although behaviourist theory has fallen out of favour in recent years, many practices associated with it are still widespread.

'Constructivist' theories look at the learning process quite differently and two variants are sometimes identified: cognitive constructivism and social constructivism. Constructivists focus attention on the mental models that a learner employs when responding to new information or to new problems. Learning always involves analysing and transforming any new information. Transformations of incoming ideas can only be achieved in the light of what the learner already knows and understands, so the reception of new knowledge depends on existing knowledge and understanding. This implies that teaching must start by exploring existing ideas and encouraging expression and defence of them; unless learners make their thinking explicit to others, and so to themselves, they cannot become aware of the need for conceptual modification.

Those people who progress better in learning turn out to have better self-awareness and better strategies for self-regulation than their slower learning peers. This implies that students need to understand what it means to learn and they need to monitor how they go about planning, monitoring and revising, to reflect upon their learning and to learn to determine for themselves whether they understand. Such skills enhance meta-cognition, which is an essential strategic competence for learning (see the text below for an explanation of this concept).

Social constructivist approaches extend these ideas, often with reference to the Russian psychologist, Vygotsky, who emphasised

continued

that another important characteristic of learning is that it proceeds by interaction between the teacher (or more expert peer) and the learner, in a social context, mediated by language and promoted by the social norms that value the search for understanding. Wood *et al.* (1976) developed the implications of this for teaching by introducing the metaphor of 'scaffolding' – the teacher provides the scaffold for the building, but the building itself can only be constructed by the learner. In this supportive role, the teacher has to discern the potential of the learner to advance in understanding, so that new challenges are neither too trivial nor too demanding.

Most approaches to assessment for learning have been developed within a cognitive constructivist framework for understanding learning, although Black and Wiliam (2006) have begun to develop a theory of formative assessment drawing on socio-cultural perspectives.

Recent developments in learning theory have come from socio-cultural theorists, including anthropologists, who have observed that people learn through participating in 'communities of practice', like apprentices. Through membership and activity they come to understand what to pay attention to and what counts as quality in a particular group. This is an important consideration for teachers in schools because what is required in one subject, for example writing descriptive prose in English, may not be the same as, say, writing up an experiment in science. The role of experts in guiding novices is important here.

A defining feature of the socio-cultural perspective is that the use of tools and artefacts is seen as enabling people to construct and reconstruct their environments. Such 'mediating tools' can be physical or psychological but language is considered to be the 'tool of tools'. Since tools are the product of social and cultural practices, the intelligence of past and contemporary minds resides in them and knowledge is therefore always distributed – never the creation or possession of a single individual.

The idea of 'distributed cognition' also implies that collective expertise can be more productive than the efforts of individuals alone. The notion that learning involves collaborative problem-solving, and learning through participation in communities of practice, is an important one for teachers in schools and suggests that group work is not an optional extra but essential for learning.

Anna Sfard (1998) points out that underpinning all this theoretical discussion are two key metaphors: a metaphor of *acquisition* and a metaphor of *participation*. Broadly speaking, folk theories, behaviourist theories and constructivist theories are concerned with acquisition of skills, knowledge and understanding (though they each envisage it being achieved by different mechanisms), while socio-cultural theories see learning as embodied in and through participation in cultural activity. However, there is at least one more metaphor for learning that is important, particularly if we value creativity and innovation as a goal of learning. Teachers of creative subjects, for instance, often aim for learners to go beyond the acquisition of skills, knowledge and dispositions, or learning how to practise as others have before them. They hope that their students will produce something novel or original. Indeed originality is the key criterion for the award of PhDs. Thus 'knowledge creation' can be viewed as learning too (Paavola *et al.*, 2004). This third metaphor may be especially important when considering the learning of adults, such as the teachers in the LHTL project who were generating new knowledge about new practices or adapting known practices in new ways.

Nonaka and Takeuchi (1995), for example, describe knowledge construction in terms of moving from implicit to explicit knowledge in a series of cycles, with individuals sharing their knowledge in this process. In the context of developing new practices for assessment for learning, this might explain how teachers, who have developed their own practices, try to make them explicit enough to tell other teachers, who then take these explanations and try to develop them in their own practice until they in turn become part of their implicit knowledge (and 'hidden' from view as it were).

These theories and metaphors help us to look at learning through different lenses and to challenge our taken-for-granted assumptions. Sfard cautions that it is dangerous to show too great a devotion to one particular metaphor. The same might be said of learning theory more generally. Although there are some people who might argue that the different views are logically incompatible, teachers will probably find a practical application at some time for behaviourist, constructivist and socio-cultural theories, and they are likely to use mixed metaphors. Likewise, the LHTL research team took a pragmatic stance and avoided committing to a single

continued

perspective at the outset, although, in the course of the work, and as we moved from considering LHTL by pupils to considering LHTL by teachers and schools, we moved towards a socio-cultural view because of its ability to take account of the many dimensions of the phenomena we were investigating.

Source: This account, which draws substantially on Bredo (1993), is adapted from part of a workshop on 'How People Learn' in James et al. (2006b). A more detailed account of the relationship between teaching, assessment and theories of learning can also be found in James (2006a).

Learning how to learn

The choice of the phrase 'learning how to learn', rather than 'learning to learn', in the title of our project, was deliberate. It drew attention to our primary interest in the development of learning *practices* – the 'how to' of learning. This focus is consistent with the project's starting point in 'assessment for learning': a label for a group of practices that have been shown to help learners to improve their learning. However, a clear understanding of the meaning of learning how to learn (LHTL) was not something with which the project started, and clarification of this concept was our first project aim (see Black *et al.*, 2006, for a more extended discussion). We found LHTL to be a slippery and contested concept with many subtly different meanings.

Interest in, and debate about, learning how to learn, are not new. Robert Dearden, a philosopher of education, around 40 years ago, discussed definitions of the various terms in use. He put forward the idea that:

Learning how to learn is at one stage further removed from any direct specific content of learning. It might therefore reasonably be called 'second-order learning'. There could be many such comparably second-order activities, such as deliberating how to deliberate, investigating how to investigate, thinking out how to think things out, and so on.

(1976, p. 70)

He then explored the possibility that LHTL might be a 'super-powerful unitary skill employable in all first-order learning whatsoever' (ibid.,

p. 70). He rejects this view on the grounds of 'the enormously divergent variety of first-order learning'. This echoes the work of contemporary learning theorists who discuss the learning of writing, reading and numeracy as separate and distinct processes (e.g. Wood, 1998). Such work supports Dearden's conclusion that LHTL marks out 'a family of structures of second-order learning having wide first-order application', a conclusion which distinguishes LHTL from the meaning frequently given to learning to learn.

However, this begs the question of the meaning of 'second-order learning'. The notion of a family is central to Dearden's argument. Some members of this family may be less desirable than others; for example, anything that encourages rote learning without attempting under-standing. Other members may be more desirable, and this leads Dearden to point out that giving salience to LHTL usually leads on to a list that privileges certain practices. Dearden's leading candidate for priority is promoting *learning autonomy*. He argues not merely that this deserves pride of place in the LHTL family, but rather that emphasis on LHTL is justified as an educational policy because of its value for promoting learning autonomy, the latter being seen as above LHTL in the hierarchy of aims. This proposition was important for our project because learning autonomy (see Box 1.3) is a central feature in the LHTL practices which we explored; for example, it was a key factor in our research on teachers' views of classroom assessment practice (see James and Pedder, 2006, and Chapter 4 of this book).

Box 1.3 What is 'learning autonomy'?

The word 'autonomy' comes from Greek and literally means 'self-rule'. It has strong associations with democratic politics and liberal philosophy and usually refers to personal independence and a capacity to make moral decisions and to act upon them. When associated with learning, the term is often used interchangeably with 'independent learning', 'taking responsibility of one's own learning', 'self-determination' and 'self-regulation' (Boud, 1988).

Law (1992, p. 152) expands on this: 'We have some idea what we are talking about when we use it – when our students . . . are acting consciously (not without thought), independently (not compliantly), imaginatively (not routinely) and with commitment (not remotely).'

continued

Ecclestone (2002) has developed a three-fold typology of learning autonomy particularly in relation to the development of assessment for learning in post-compulsory education:

- *procedural autonomy*: command of technical processes in a subject, the requirements of assessment, a body of subject-related 'technical' language and confidence in applying these;
- *personal autonomy*: learners become more self-directing, based on insights into their strengths and weaknesses and their choices for action; they can make informed decisions about their own practice;
- *critical autonomy*: learners relate issues in a subject context to evaluations of, and change in their practice in the light of insights into a broader socio-political and ethical context. Motivation arises from individual and social commitments to a community.

This expansion of the ideas associated with learning autonomy: from an exclusive focus on the individual (the liberal tradition in philosophy and the cognitive tradition in psychology) to incorporate a view of the autonomous learner acting in social context (a socio-cultural perspective) has relevance for our project.

There is, however, a problem that we should mention. As its origins make clear, 'autonomy' is closely associated with western cultural and intellectual traditions. In an increasingly multi-cultural society, it cannot be assumed that all groups of pupils, parents or even teachers will value it equally. Some will come from traditions that may value 'authority' above 'autonomy'. In the end there is a value judgement to be made here. We took the view that promoting learning autonomy was a proper purpose for education.

Our concern for ways of working that might improve learning, what we call 'learning practices', led us away from an exclusive focus on the psychological processes which might underpin such practices. However, there are other definitions, such as the following from cognitive psychologists in Finland, which appear to regard 'learning to learn' as a distinct ability amenable to assessment, with which these researchers are primarily concerned: 'the ability and willingness to adapt to novel tasks, activating one's commitment to thinking and the perspective of hope by means of maintaining one's cognitive and affective self-regulation in and of learning action' (Hautamäki et al., 2002, p. 38). This definition conflates several different ideas. First, it implies a notion of a general-purpose ability, seeing it as something that can be used in different situations. Second, it incorporates attitudinal elements such as 'willingness' and 'hope'. Third, it adds the idea of 'self-regulation'. Fourth, it mentions only the individual learner, ignoring social or collaborative dimensions of learning. Finally, the authors imply, by proposing an instrument to assess their construct, that learning to learn requires conscious attention and *can* be assessed.

These different ideas and definitions stimulated us to ask four specific questions:

1. Is learning [how] to learn separate from learning *per se*?
2. Is learning [how] to learn a higher-order entity?
3. Is learning [how] to learn conscious or unconscious?
4. Is learning [how] to learn an individual property or does it have a social and collaborative dimension?

If we recognise three broad clusters of learning theories (behaviourist, constructivist and socio-cultural – see Box 1.2), the first question only has meaning within a cognitive constructivist point of view. From the perspective of a behaviourist, new learning is no more that an automatic response to a stimulus, while socio-cultural learning theorists argue that the problem-solving process is the focus, and the learning (outcome) that results is often merely incidental (Lave, 1988).

In contrast, constructivists (e.g. Bereiter and Scardamalia, 1989) argue that the goal of problem-solving is to learn concepts and only incidentally to engage in the problem-solving process. This is illustrated in mathematics lessons when 'problems' are set – to provide a 'scaffold' – to teach concepts. Bereiter and Scardamalia also argue that pupils are unlikely to learn unless they are *trying* to learn; they must invest effort into solving the 'given' problem, *and* transfer their learning to those unassigned problems associated with their understanding. The repertoire of strategies that the *intentional* learner employs includes the kinds of things that might be considered as part of the learning process itself, for example, structuring tasks and reviewing learning. However, these are often viewed as 'higher-order strategies' – the ones Dearden was concerned about.

In so far as learning theorists recognise distinct higher-order learning, they use the idea of *metacognition*, which refers to thinking about learning. Some distinguish two elements (Brown, 1981; Phye, 1997):

- knowledge about cognition, i.e. knowing what you know and don't know (such as relating what you are learning to what you already know, realising when you understand something, or not);
- self-regulating mechanisms, i.e. planning what to do next, checking the outcomes of strategies employed, and evaluating and revising strategies.

According to a framework for understanding thinking and learning, developed from a review by Moseley *et al.* (2005), 'strategic and reflective thinking' occupies the highest order.

However, when Bereiter and Scardamalia (1989) discuss intentional learning, they invoke the need for learners to take responsibility, in the sense of consciously choosing the strategy and direction for their own learning. This implies adopting an approach to learning to learn that incorporates general principles of effective learning *per se*, which takes us back to the first question. It is not simply a question of trying to improve learning by adding a separate set of, say, study skills to a learner's repertoire. This is a difficult but important point to get across because the temptation is simply to add a course on study skills to the timetable and believe that this will transform pupils into lifelong learners. A separate course will be just that – separate. What is needed is for learning how to learn practices to permeate the whole curriculum and be integrated into every subject and most lessons so pupils have opportunities to reflect critically and constructively on their learning while they are engaged in learning curriculum content. This approach acknowledges that there might well be different LHTL practices across the various subjects of the curriculum.

Resnick (1989) also emphasises intentionality and that effective learners take responsibility for their learning, referred to as 'agency', which acknowledges that learning is a process that learners have to undertake for themselves. You can support learners but you cannot do the learning for them. As pupils become more skilled in a topic or area, levels of support can be withdrawn. This is as true for higher-level 'strategic thinking and reflection' as it is for the lower-level processes. Often it is the teacher who enacts these higher-level skills by, for example, deciding the main ideas, framing questions to direct attention, evaluating and interpreting texts, and so on. But pupils also need to be engaged at this higher level by being given opportunities to think strategically and reflect on their learning.

In considering this evidence, we came to the conclusion that a separation of learning to learn from the learning process itself, or regarding it as a distinct entity is both hard to justify and unproductive. We came to see a need for a range of elements of learning to be part of any approach to learning how to learn without trying to separate it out as a particular ability or skill.

However, we also came to the view that it is important not to see learning only in terms of individual minds, but also to recognise the importance of the social element in learning (our fourth question). Even such processes as metacognition are developed through collaborative activities. Wood (1998) makes the point that self-regulation is learned through discourse and social interaction and, like Rogoff (1990), he sees adult support serving to mediate metacognition.

Peer collaboration is also an important element of the learning process. The TLRP Groupwork project team (SPRinG) (see: http://www.tlrp.org/pub/documents/BlatchfordRBFinal_001.pdf for a summary), argues that effective group interactions encourage pupils to think about their understanding and that this in turn requires social, communication and problem-solving skills, such as, being able to plan and organise, work out a timescale, brainstorm and to decide what needs to be done collectively and individually. Teachers encourage pupils to reflect on the skills they are developing and, through modelling of reflection, to take responsibility for their own learning. Such an approach enables pupils to become 'metacognitively wise' in relation to working collectively.

The TLRP Groupwork project draws attention to the importance of both 'collaborating to learn' and 'learning to collaborate'. This is a helpful reminder that metacognition, and its centrality to LHTL, need to be understood interpersonally, as a collaborative process between learners, and intrapersonally, at the level of the individual learner. It follows that considering learning to learn in isolation from other aspects of learning may lead to neglect of fundamental changes that may be needed to the learning environment.

The contribution of assessment for learning to learning how to learn

The title of this chapter and the first premise on which the LHTL project was based (see above) make a claim that assessment for learning can contribute to learning how to learn which, in turn, promotes learning autonomy. Following Dearden, this can be conceptualised as a hierarchy of relationships with learning autonomy as the ultimate goal (see Figure 1.2).

But what is the nature of these relationships? Our summary of AfL (Box 1.1) identified four groups of practices that research shows to be effective in promoting learning and achievement: clarifying learning goals and success criteria; eliciting and reflecting on learning through dialogue and questioning; providing formative feedback; and promoting peer- and self-assessment. These help learners to know where they are in their learning, where they are going, and how to get there (the essence of the Assessment Reform Group's definition of AfL, given above). However, the first three of these groups of practices can be teacher-centred: interpreted as things that teachers might be expected to do for their pupils. Learning how to learn, however, is by definition

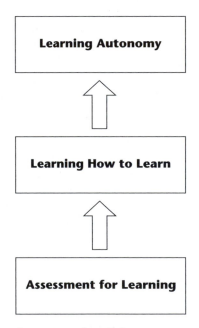

Figure 1.2 Hierarchy of concepts and practices

learner-centred – it is what learners do. In the LHTL project's early development work with schools we encouraged teachers to think about ways of shifting the responsibility for AfL practices to their pupils. For this reason, the project team encouraged peer- and self-assessment, although teachers did not find these practices easy to implement, as the evidence in Chapter 4 will make clear.

As evidence accumulated and our thinking developed, our early assumption that these AfL 'practices' provided a strong foundation for the development of learning how to learn, was reinforced, partly because LHTL can also be regarded as 'practices' to bring about learning. In this sense, AfL is a strategy for accomplishing LHTL, although there may be others. We have never claimed that LHTL only needs AfL.

Thinking about both concepts – AfL and LHTL – also encouraged us to dig deeper to find out what they have in common. Not only did our understanding of LHTL become more sophisticated, but our understanding of the crucial features of AfL became more nuanced. In other words, thinking about one idea encouraged us to think afresh about the other in order to be clearer about the links between them.

In his response to Black and Wiliam's (1998a) review of formative assessment research, Perrenoud argues for a 'reconstruction of the conceptual field' (1998, p. 100). His idea is that formative evaluation (or what we might call AfL) should be concerned with the regulation of *learning processes*. He distinguishes this from the regulation of ongoing *activities* of pupils, which is commonly seen as the principal role of teachers in classrooms. Indeed, he claims that control of activities can actually hinder the regulation of learning if this denies the pupils 'the right to hestitate, make mistakes, reflect, enter into dialogue, and thus learn' (ibid., p.88). Accordingly,

> It no longer suffices to talk, to explain or to show; one needs to take into account the representations acquired and the cognitive functioning of the subject. One needs to accompany him or her in a 'metacognitive' journey, in the form of a dialogue which, being anchored in an activity, separates itself to concentrate on knowledge and the learning process.
>
> (ibid., p. 89)

This discussion, ostensibly of AfL, resonates with our examination of the meaning of LHTL (see above) which led us to regard it as a family of second-order, intentional, learning practices, inextricably linked with learning something, and with both individual cognitive and social dimensions. Strategic and reflective thinking is seen as having priority as the expression of the metacognitive activity and self-regulation that are vital to the development of learning autonomy. It follows that what links AfL to LHTL, and is transferred in the practices, are these deeper ideas associated with a cognitive 'stepping back' from the learning process during engagement with it, in order to reflect on it critically and strategically, often in dialogue with others, and then to 'step back in' to restructure or transform the learning process. This implies that every learning episode should have two dimensions operating simultaneously: learning and regulation of learning. The prize is learning autonomy, because these processes will, eventually, enable learners to understand and control their learning without the help of the teacher.

Of course, this suggestion poses a considerable challenge to learners and to those who support their learning. It makes new demands of both pupils and their teachers in the way they construct their roles and the knowledge, skills and attitudes required to fulfil them. No longer is it sufficient for teachers to set tasks and leave pupils to learn from them as best they might; nor can pupils just do 'stuff' and expect to learn. Such activities are only the raw materials for learning; both teachers and pupils need to see the focus of their productive work as the struggle for learning in the process.

Thus far, we have dealt with these conceptual issues in a rather generic way, and with more reference to the learning of pupils than to the learning, and learning how to learn, of teachers and schools. In the next chapter we examine more closely the implications of these ideas for learners at the different levels identified by our project and discuss whether they are helpful to an understanding of the challenges of spreading innovative ideas and practice beyond the single classroom.

Conclusion

As a result of our deliberations to clarify thinking in the field, and to sort out the issues we needed to research, we concluded that 'learning how to learn' is best understood as referring to a collection of good learning practices, including ones associated with assessment for learning, that encourage learners to be reflective, strategic, intentional and collaborative. These practices may not 'come naturally' but they can be taught in a way to lead pupils (and other learners) to take responsibility for their learning. We judged that evidence from a variety of empirical and theoretical studies supports the view that emphasis should be placed on practices, in both individual and collaborative contexts, that seem to have the potential to promote autonomy in learning. This would seem to be the most secure foundation for lifelong learning.

Chapter 2*

Challenges of embedding and spreading learning how to learn ideas and practice

Well-researched innovations often 'fail' because they are neither fully implemented nor embedded in practice, and the conditions are not right for them to spread beyond individual classrooms or schools. As Fullan (2001) has pointed out, surface 'adoption' of new ideas is not enough to secure or sustain the learning outcomes that are sought. The change process is more complex and the conditions that help or hinder transformations in practice need to be studied. This chapter examines these issues, and particularly their implications for the aspiration to scale up innovations in assessment for learning and learning how to learn within and across schools. It highlights the importance of teachers' own professional learning and the characteristics of schools and networks that support it. It also examines what 'learning how to learn' might mean in the context of teacher learning and organisational learning and the parallels with pupils learning how to learn. This provides the rationale for linking research on classroom practice with research on school improvement and network learning.

Bringing about change in real-world settings

Paul Black and Dylan Wiliam (2006, p. 98) describe assessment for learning as a Trojan Horse in the sense that it offers a practical and concrete way of penetrating the classroom and starting to bring about change in teaching and learning more widely. Pedagogic principles, related to sound learning theory, underpin the ideas but these are not

* Authored by Mary James

made explicit to begin with. What teachers encounter first are suggestions for practices that they might introduce in their teaching in the expectation that these will improve both learning and measured achievement, as was demonstrated in the previous research studies reviewed by Black and Wiliam (1998a). Of course, introducing new practices often changes beliefs so the two are intimately related. Moreover, it is not always the case that practices have to be introduced first: changing beliefs can subsequently change practice. The King's, Medway, Oxfordshire Formative Assessment Project (KMOFAP) (Black et al., 2003) had examples of both. The main point is that developing beliefs and developing practices go hand in hand and successful innovations are unlikely to concentrate on one to the exclusion of the other. (See Chapter 3 for exemplification of this in the context of the LHTL project.)

Initially the LHTL project adopted a similar approach to the KMOFA Project by offering teachers practical strategies to try out in their classrooms, although engagement with underpinning beliefs about learning usually followed, through workshop discussions or discussion of survey results and in interviews with researchers. In contrast with KMOFAP, in our project the ideas tended to be introduced to whole staff groups in their schools, rather than to a small number of selected teachers brought together for Inset days at a university. The reason for this much larger scale (approximately 1,500 teachers had some involvement) was that the LHTL project team wanted to investigate how learning how to learn through assessment for learning might be successfully adopted, implemented, embedded and spread within and across a large number of schools. As Paul Black and his colleagues had shown, the possibility of success on a small scale was not in doubt. What was at issue was whether strategies could be found that would be effective across the system, but without much resource beyond that generally available to schools in England. For example, schools might make use of some of the annual allocation of professional development days, some departmental or team meetings, support from local authority advisers, school improvement partners or consultants, continuing professional development (CPD) and masters courses offered by universities and other training agencies, and support for networking of various kinds.

Authentication of this kind acts as an important 'reality test' for any initiative that may be rolled out nationally as, in a sense, was happening to AfL through the National Strategies in England. Hence the importance of the primary focus of our work on the kind of conditions that enable changes in practice to become embedded in classrooms and schools. As our research progressed, these conditions came to be characterised as barriers and facilitators, or *constraints* and *affordances*. According to Gibson (1979), 'affordances' are 'action possibilities' as perceived by relevant actors. In other words, affordances – and constraints too – are subjective phenomena. This does not deny their objective reality but it emphasises the experiential aspect. We needed to take account of this when we came to interpret our data because our questionnaires and interviews gave us 'perceptions' rather than unambiguous 'facts'.

Nevertheless, two key questions emerged:

1.   How can teachers and schools use AfL to promote LHTL, and especially learning autonomy, in their pupils within learning environments that they perceived as constraining, and what conditions facilitate innovation and change?
2.   In this context, what is the relationship between changes in classroom practice and change in values and beliefs about learning?

Much of the discussion of findings in Part II is framed in response to these two general questions although they answer many more specific questions as well.

In summary, the central feature of the LHTL project was an investigation of the characteristics of schools and networks associated with the implementation of assessment for learning and learning how to learn in classrooms. This required research at three levels in order to investigate the sustainability issues associated with the scaling up of innovations because there is no guarantee that innovations that work on a small scale, in fairly controlled circumstances, with exceptional levels of support, will do so when they 'go wild'. What happens to them, when the initial agents of change 'give away' the ideas, depends significantly on how they land in schools and the conditions for growth they encounter.

Different approaches to scaling up innovation

Currently there is much debate in the UK, and particularly the USA, about evidence-based or, at least, evidence-informed policy-making. Governments have been criticised for ignoring research and, equally, researchers have been criticised for not providing policy-makers and practitioners with the kind of findings they can use and act upon. Some of this criticism has been ill-founded but some has been justified. The problem is often characterised as a need for evidence of what works, which tends to assume that we can know with some certainty which causes produce which effects in which circumstances.

Borrowing heavily from medical research, some people believe that the gold standard is a form of experiment called the randomised controlled trial (RCT) where 'subjects' are randomly allocated to 'treatment' and 'control' groups and the effects are measured and compared. As with drug testing, after a series of such trials, if the treatment group do significantly better than the control group, then the widespread use of the treatment is considered to be warranted. However, in education (and often in medicine too), it is hardly ever this simple because there may be confounding variables that intervene between the treatment variable and the outcome variable. This is particularly so when the experiment is taken out of the laboratory and conducted in real-world settings such as schools. These mediating variables can be crucially important and can relate to differences in the context, input and processes associated with implementation at different sites and at different times.

In the United States researchers are under particular pressure to conduct RCTs in education because the majority of federal funding for research is earmarked for these. In the UK, although RCTs have their advocates (e.g. Gorard, 2006), the debate is less focused on a single methodological approach, perhaps because researchers' funding and recognition are less dependent upon it. The question of what kind of evidence provides the best basis for decisions for major investment in innovation is still a focus of lively debate although there seems more tolerance of 'fuzzy generalisation' which acknowledges an element of uncertainty. Bassey (2001) argues that, in educational research, the best we can claim is that a cause X *may* produce an effect Y, given certain circumstances. Hammersley (2001) goes further and advances the idea that it is only practitioners who can tell us what *will* happen in particular situations, by acting in them. Research findings, and evidence from other sources, can only ever be resources to use in making *judgements* about what *might* happen and what is *probably* the best course of action to take. Over thirty years ago, Lawrence Stenhouse (1975) said much the same thing when he argued that the proposals of curriculum developers need always to be tested anew by teachers in their classrooms. In his view, proposals for change can never be blueprints for adoption, but only hypotheses to be tested in each new setting. However, the 'practice knowledge' thus generated can then be shared and tested in other settings.

This throws an entirely different light on the notion of scaling up but it has a better promise for sustainability as innovations are adapted to changing circumstances. What is sacrificed, however, is any strong view of the need to implement the original idea or practice with total *fidelity*. According to Fullan (2001), implementation, which is a process beyond simple adoption, depends on *people* who are both essential to success but also a source of 'problems'. Thus implementation is hugely difficult and needs itself to be investigated so that lessons can be learned; otherwise all the research that went in to developing an innovation can be wasted.

These insights informed the design of the LHTL project and were the chief motivation for studying how teachers took the ideas from research and attempted to implement them in their different classrooms and schools. When offering ideas for practice, mostly derived from former research or experience of working with other schools, the project team did not insist on faithful replication because we knew that teachers would want to adapt practices. What they chose to do with ideas was a source of particular interest to us for they are indications of teachers' learning , especially that form of learning which, in Chapter 1, we referred to as knowledge creation. For example, we observed many adaptations of a 'traffic light' system originally created as a quick way for teachers to ascertain pupils' confidence in the progress of their learning during lessons (see James *et al.*, 2006b, Part Four, for illustration). Many of these adaptations were ingenious, fit for purpose and offered solutions that might help other teachers in similar circumstances. However, other adaptations were problematic because, for example, traffic lights were being used as proxy scoring systems which undermined the formative intent of assessment for learning. What this revealed, of course, was the extent to which teachers understood the underlying principles of the practices, which reflects the practice–belief relationship identified earlier as a particular issue.

Teacher learning as a key consideration

The 'medical model' approach to scaling up implies that little more is needed than for practitioners to change the prescription when rigorous research has shown a new drug to be effective. The second approach, outlined above, is, however, crucially dependent on the willingness of practitioners to become actively engaged with the innovation, to critically evaluate their existing beliefs and practices in the light of new ideas, to have the motivation, courage and energy to try new things, and to think strategically and creatively about appropriate adaptations or improvements suited to their particular circumstances. In other words, teachers themselves need to learn and teacher learning is usually a condition of change designed to bring about improvements in pupils' learning. Evidence for this association abounds in the education literature and, for example, provides the focus of a special issue of the journal *Research Papers in Education* (volume 20, number 2) published in 2005. This is a collection of five articles from the first TLRP projects to complete and publish their findings. Although they focused on different innovations (in literacy, mathematics, science education, inclusion and pupil consultation), all highlight the importance of teacher learning. According to James (2005, pp. 107–108), the following are shared themes and findings:

1. [Teacher] Learning is both individual and collective and involves both the acquisition of knowledge and skills and participation in social processes. Thus the development of supportive professional cultures within which teachers can learn is vitally important. Within schools, especially secondary schools, the focus is often the department or team. However, the very cohesion of these groups can create insularity and inhibit change. There is a need to provide opportunities for boundary crossings which encourage teachers to learn from others in different networks or communities of practice.
2. Teachers are most ready to accept ideas for change if they resonate with their existing or previous beliefs and experience. However, this does not make them right or appropriate. Teachers need to develop the knowledge and skills to evaluate evidence and the confidence to challenge taken-for-granted assumptions, including their own. This is difficult and it is often helpful to involve outsiders, perhaps researchers from universities or visiting teachers from other schools, in helping teachers to see things differently. Teachers need to be assured that it is acceptable and often fruitful to take risks. Trust is therefore of the essence.

This account makes a number of points relevant to the LHTL project.

First, both acquisition and participation metaphors are used, implying that teacher learning has both dimensions and is both individual property and social practice. The third metaphor of learning as knowledge-creation, which we referred to in Chapter 1, Box 1.2, is not explicitly mentioned. Nevertheless, the reference to teachers learning from others in networks and communities offers this possibility. Within the LHTL project, teacher learning as co-construction of new 'practice knowledge' became an explicit focus and urged us to consider the particular relevance of this third metaphor especially when considering learning through networking (see Chapter 5).

Second, the interplay of beliefs and practice is again emphasised, also the need for teachers to develop skills and dispositions conducive to critical and reflective inquiry into classroom practice, and to developing strategic thinking with an action orientation. Third, the importance of a supportive environment is mentioned: one where teachers are trusted and encouraged to take risks. The culture of schools is a crucial part of such an environment.

This characterisation of teacher learning has many similarities with our conceptualisation of learning and learning how to learn by pupils, as described in Chapter 1. What may be different is that a formal 'curriculum' for teacher learning, as such, is less obvious, and knowledge creation may have a larger role in the learning of teachers than their pupils. However, the promotion of autonomous and ongoing learning through the development of intentional, reflective, strategic and collaborative practices tied closely to the substance of the innovations, in this case assessment for learning, suggests that there is a close correspondence between learning how to learn by pupils and learning how to learn by teachers.

An additional and important feature of the LHTL project was exploration of teachers' learning across levels – in classrooms, schools and networks. We assumed that teachers learn in the interactions they have with pupils, and support staff, within their classrooms. They also learn through formal and informal encounters outside their classrooms but within the school – in meetings, in staff rooms, in corridors, and so on. And they are likely to learn through dialogue with others in the various social and professional networks to which they belong, temporarily or on a longer-term basis. We particularly wanted to investigate new technologies for electronic networking as a means for teachers to develop their practice collaboratively. The possibilities offered by new technologies are considerable, although we were ultimately disappointed (see Chapter 5 and Carmichael and Procter, 2006). It seems that teachers need to develop supportive and trusting social and personal relationships, often in face-to-face encounters, before they are prepared to engage with new technologies to share and develop their practice knowledge. In other words, there is often insufficient social capital to underpin the development of intellectual capital. This idea was crucial to our project for we not only sought to strengthen the intellectual capital of teachers and schools, by offering evidence-informed ideas for new practices, but we encouraged teachers to create new knowledge by mobilising their existing intellectual capital. For this to happen, social capital is also needed (see Box 2.1).

Box 2.1 Social, intellectual and organisational capital

The metaphor of 'capital', borrowed from the field of economics, is often used to explain the quality of communities and organisations such as schools. Material resources, such as buildings and finance, are the most visible form but there are less visible, yet equally important, assets in social, intellectual and organisational capital. Hargreaves (2003a) describes intellectual capital as the knowledge, skills, capabilities, competences, talents, expertise, practices and routines of the individuals in schools. Accordingly,

> The capacity of a school to mobilise its intellectual capital is critical, for this is what fosters new ideas and creates new knowledge, which leads to successful innovation in making the school more effective. Such innovation creates new professional practices so that teachers work smarter, not harder.
>
> (ibid., p. 25)

Social capital creates the environment of trust, mutual respect and reciprocity in which intellectual capital can be created and shared. Hargreaves points out that social capital has both cultural and structural aspects.

> Culturally, social capital consists in the *trust* that exists between the school's members and its various stakeholders; structurally, social capital is the extent and quality of the *networks* among its members – between head and staff, staff and students, staff and partners – as well as the school's networks with external partners. A school that is rich in social capital has a strong sense of itself as a community, with ties to other communities. Such a school understands the importance of knowledge-sharing.
>
> (ibid., p. 25)

---

continued

The concept of *organisational capital* is rather different and, by definition, applies at institutional level. In Hargreaves' account, organisational capital refers to the extent to which the school deploys and increases its intellectual and social capital. This draws attention to the importance of leadership, another important theme in our research.

Ideas about different forms of capital were important to our project and especially to our exploration of teachers learning through networking (Chapter 5) and in our investigation of the interplay of structure and culture in the way schools are managed and led (see Chapter 4), but they are also relevant to the interactions between teachers and pupils in classrooms (Chapter 3). Therefore we do not identify specific forms of capital with any one level; intellectual and social capital are relevant concepts at classroom level, school level and network level.

Can schools learn how to learn?

As with teacher learning there is an extensive literature on organisational learning (see Chapter 4). This literature generally presupposes that the collective learning of the individuals within organisations is more than the sum of the parts and contributes to an embracing culture. Researchers and theorists working in the field of school improvement accept that it is possible to identify and define such cultures. We also take this view, although we are especially interested in *learning* cultures. A key question for the project, therefore, was whether it is possible to think of schools as learning how to learn and whether this, as for teacher learning, has parallels with LHTL for pupils. If this is so, we might expect schools to be proactive, intentional and autonomous in their learning, taking responsibility for building intellectual capital within the organisation through auditing the expertise of the individuals within it and providing opportunities and encouragement for collaborative knowledge creation and sharing. The building of social capital would be an important condition of this, although we regard social capital as more than trust (see Chapter 5).

Reflective and strategic thinking, including critical inquiry as part of self-regulation, would also be important, but not simply in terms of the familiar cycle of plan–do–review. What is required, rather like the metacognitive element of individual learning how to learn, is a metaphorical 'stepping outside' this cycle to render every element of it contestable. Argyris and Schön (1978), theorists of organisational learning, describe this as 'double-loop learning'. In Chapter 4, we use this concept to explain what schools learning how to learn might look like.

Of course, none of this is easy. At the beginning of the twenty-first century, it is still the case that the majority of schools share much in common with those in the nineteenth century. Pupils are still taught subjects, according to a timetable in classes of around thirty, by one teacher sometimes supported by assistants. This makes schools unlike most other workplaces and it presents considerable challenges for building organisational capital. Teachers do not routinely and continuously work alongside one another so that novices learn from experts, and rarely do they have sustained opportunities to inquire into practice and develop new ideas collaboratively. Such events generally have to be planned and supported by resources. Even electronic resources, computers and such like, which now abound in schools, are used principally for teaching and administrative purposes and the shift in perception and practice that is required to realise their potential for professional development purposes needs to be fostered (Carmichael and Procter, 2006). In all these respects, leadership is crucial, whether leadership of the head teacher or more distributed forms of leadership involving, potentially, the whole staff.

What our evidence shows, and will be expanded upon in subsequent chapters, is that leadership of organisational learning how to learn, as with learning how to learn in the classroom, is subject to powerful constraints. Many of these derive from the policy context, at least in England at the time when the LHTL project was carrying out its development and research work. Those schools that refused to be passive but worked – reflectively, strategically, intentionally and collaboratively – on the contradictions to resolve them, showed signs of learning how to learn in much the way that we conceptualised LHTL by pupils and teachers.

How we take up these themes in the chapters that follow

In the chapters that follow in Part II, we explore the themes, arguments and tentative theories developed in Part I. First, we examine these in relation to the findings from analysis of data collected at one level but across our sample of schools. For this purpose Chapters 3, 4 and 5 each focus on one of our project aims. Chapter 3 examines 'what teachers can do to help pupils to learn how to learn in classrooms'. Chapter 4 explores 'what characterises the school in which teachers successfully create and manage the knowledge and skills of learning how to learn'. And Chapter 5 looks at 'how educational networks, including electronic networks, can support the creation, management and transfer of the knowledge and skills of learning how to learn'.

In Chapters 6 and 7 we adopt a different approach and provide short illustrations of how some of the evidence produced for 'level' analyses – classroom, school or network – is related in individual schools. We do not have space in this book to write 'complete' case studies of schools so, in each study, we focus on a single theme. For example, we explore one teacher's trajectory of change in her school and the support she received and contributed to others. Another study poses alternative explanations of high performance by analysing the influence of different initiatives. Leadership is the focus of another study. Decay and growth of innovative practice are the focus of others. In each case, a range of data available for each school, including performance data where relevant, is brought to bear on the chosen issue in order to attempt a rounded and balanced picture. (In these chapters, as in others, according to our confidentiality agreements, we have substituted pseudonyms for the names of schools and personnel, although local authorities are named because these were identified from the start of the project.)

There are dangers, in across-sample surveys, that the complexity is smoothed out in discussion of whole-sample means, or, in school case studies, that within school variation is hidden from view. Chapters 8 and 9, therefore, specifically focus upon some of the between and within-school differences revealed in our data. Chapter 8 examines the evidence for group differences with respect to teachers' classroom assessment practices and values, and Chapter 9 reports some findings from surveys of both teachers' and students' beliefs about learning.

Finally, in Chapter 10, we summarise our key themes and draw out implications for teachers, school leaders, support and inspection agencies, teacher educators and policy-makers. Although the details of our suggestions differ according to the responsibilities of these different groups, they all focus on the priority we ascribe to teacher learning and professional development. This points, again, to the importance of people in the change process and supports the conclusion that, across all levels of our project, it is the development of autonomous learning – in pupils, teachers and organisations – that is crucial. There are no simple technical-rational or managerialist solutions to promoting effective LHTL; it depends on social processes that lead to the transformation of beliefs, values and norms of behaviour i.e. cultural change. Changes in structures can help, as they can also hinder, but they are rarely sufficient in themselves. The challenge is to build intellectual and social capital; hence the importance of professional learning from which much else flows.

Conclusion

If learning autonomy, pursued through the development of learning how to learn and assessment for learning practices, is a desirable goal for the education of pupils, then pupils will need to learn new ways of thinking and acting. This in turn will require their teachers, and those who support them, to think and act in different ways too, especially through enhancing their own sense of agency, by developing skills of critical inquiry and reflection, and through using opportunities to develop and test ideas and share knowledge with others. These changes are not trivial in a climate that discourages risk-taking and penalises failure, so the support of school leaders in creating a climate conducive to innovation is crucial. Both teachers and school leaders need to be supported in this. One potential source of support is professional networks which can be developed to provide opportunities for teachers to create and share practice knowledge in collaboration, thus breaking through the traditional isolation of teachers' work. Perhaps the greatest need, however, is for a relevant framework of policy that promotes a co-ordinated, progressive, coherent, but not restrictive, approach to professional development.

Part II

What does the research tell us?

Chapter 3

Learning how to learn in classrooms

In this chapter we report what we found out in relation to our project aim 'to investigate what teachers can do to help pupils to learn how to learn in classrooms'. As we made clear in Part I, we are interested in both beliefs about learning and about classroom practices, and the relationships between them. Here we use data from interviews with selected classroom teachers, and video recordings of lessons from some of them, to explore in depth the complex iteration between what teachers believe, and the impact this has on what they do. We relate this, briefly, to evidence about the issues from analysis of questionnaires that were explicitly designed to explore the opinions of project school staff about the relationship of their values to classroom assessment practices, although these results are explained in more depth in Chapters 4 and 8. (In Chapter 9, evidence of teachers' general beliefs about learning, derived from responses to another questionnaire, is also reported.)

Changing classroom practice – principles and evidence

We begin by exploring the complex iteration between what teachers believe and what they do. We draw on data collected from two main sources: the first set were interviews with 37 classroom teachers, including 27 for whom the second set, video recordings of their lessons, were also analysed. The observations and interviews were undertaken around the mid-point of the project. (For a detailed description of the methods we used in analysing the data, see Marshall and Drummond, 2006.)

* Authored by Bethan Marshall with Patrick Carmichael and Mary-Jane Drummond

Black and Wiliam have argued that 'Teachers will not take up attractive sounding ideas, albeit based on extensive research, if these are presented as general principles, which leave entirely to them the task of translating them into everyday practice' (1998b, p. 15). For this reason, the King's Medway Oxfordshire Formative Assessment Project (KMOFAP) model, adapted by the LHTL project, emphasised the practical procedures in training sessions with teachers and were, in effect, value-neutral in their delivery. As pointed out in Chapter 2, this is not to say that we did not anticipate change in practice bringing about changes in beliefs, but change in beliefs was not fore-grounded in the way the sessions were conceived. Instead we saw assessment for learning as a Trojan Horse (Black and Wiliam, 2006), which would, by affecting a shift in pedagogic approaches, bring about a complementary change in beliefs. The metaphor is significant. Concealed within the practices of AfL are pedagogic principles which encourage teachers to promote learner autonomy in their pupils (Marshall and Drummond, 2006). Implicit within the metaphor, then, is the idea that these principles are initially hidden from view to ensure the attendant surprise and inevitable triumph when they are finally revealed.

The US-based Capital project (see Coffey et al., 2005), which worked in parallel with the KMOFA Project (Black et al., 2003), took a slightly different approach, however, making the development of teachers beliefs an overt and integral part of their work with practitioners. Underpinning their research was the 'perspective' that,

> Practice is ripe for modification when teachers begin to understand the nature of the gap between their own current actions and the picture they have of themselves as professionals. In the process of becoming the person or professional they want to be, contradictions between beliefs and actions may be confronted, new belief systems may be constructed, existing beliefs deepened, and often times, risks are taken as new actions or behaviours are tried in the classroom'.
>
> (Coffey et al., 2005, p. 170)

The work of the LHTL project highlighted the need to explore these different approaches further.

Lessons from classroom observation: the spirit and the letter of AfL

Box 3.1 outlines the further principles underpinning assessment for learning.

Box 3.1 Further principles underpinning assessment for learning

As outlined in Chapter 1, Perrenoud (1998) characterises AfL as the regulation of learning. For him, the nature of the tasks and activities of a lesson significantly impact on the scope and potential of subsequent interaction and feedback between pupil and teacher as the lesson progresses. He differentiates between those sequences of activity in lessons which he calls 'traditional', which merely allow for the remediation of narrowly prescribed concepts at the end of the sequence of work, and those lessons where the tasks are not 'imposed on the pupils but [adjusted] once they have been initiated' (ibid., p. 88) in order to take the learning forward.

More helpful, however, in establishing and extending the link between assessment and progression towards independent learning are Vygotsky's and Dewey's activity-based approaches to learning. Crucial to appreciating the relevance of their understanding to assessment for learning is the notion of progression toward autonomy (as emphasised in Chapter 1), and the teachers' role in facilitating this through the activities in which they encourage pupils to engage.

Dewey's definition of 'progressive' education as 'high organization based upon ideas' (Dewey, 1966, pp. 28–29) is particularly relevant; the challenge is 'to discover and put into operation a principle of order and operation which follows from understanding what the educative experience signifies' (ibid., p. 29).

Dewey acknowledges that it is a difficult task to work out what kinds of materials, methods, and social relationships are appropriate. In a sense this is what the teachers on the LHTL project were attempting to do. The implementation of AfL and, by extension, LHTL in the classroom, becomes much more than the application of certain procedures – questioning, feedback, sharing the criteria with the learner and peer and self-assessment – but about the realisation of certain principles of teaching and learning.

Enacting principles in practice

What interested us was what the principles, outlined in Box 3.1, looked like in the classroom, so the focus of this section of the chapter explores what we have called the *spirit* of AfL in practice. We have characterised the spirit as 'high organisation based on ideas', where the underpinning principle is pupil autonomy – our defining characteristic of learning how to learn (see Chapter 1). This is in contrast to those lessons where only the procedures (also outlined in Box 3.1), or *letter* of AfL, seem in place. These labels – the spirit and letter – emerged in an attempt to describe the types of lessons we watched. Our usage here has a collo-quial resonance, which echoes something of the differences we are trying to capture.

In common usage, adhering to the spirit, rather than the letter, implies an underlying principle, which does not allow a simple appli-cation of rigid procedure. In contrast, sticking to the letter of a particular rule is likely to lose the underlying spirit it was intended to embody. Any crude polarisation is, however, unlikely to capture the complexity of the way in which teachers implement changes in their practice. However, comparing two types of lessons may give a better under-standing of what the spirit of AfL looks like in practice.

Discussing a lesson, which captures the spirit of AfL, in conjunction with one that follows the letter, helps highlight the way in which lessons can either promote or restrict learner autonomy. Table 3.1 gives brief outlines of the main activities in two such contrasting English lessons, each with a Year 8 class. The outlines refer to the activity of 'model-ling' criteria. In English lessons it is common practice to start a lesson with a 'model', or example of a piece of work, which is used to illustrate what will subsequently be required of the pupils themselves at another point in the lesson. In other words, a model is used as a way of eliciting or communicating criteria. The extent to which this successfully acts as a means of sharing the criteria with pupils is discussed.

What is evident at first glance is that the lessons share much in common. Both Tracy, from Elm High School (see Chapter 7), and Angela, from Hawthorn School (see Chapter 7), ask pupils to engage with pre-twentieth-century texts, a requirement of the National Curriculum in English. In Tracy's lesson, pupils were looking at a letter they had written, based on a Victorian short story; in Angela's they were asked to consider a dramatic rendition of a nineteenth-century poem that they had begun looking at in the previous lesson. Both lessons had the potential for pupils to engage with the question of what makes

Table 3.1 The letter and the spirit of AfL – classroom indicators

A: Letter (Tracy)	B: Spirit (Angela)
Yr 8 Lesson A – pre-twentieth-century short story	Yr 8 Lesson B – pre-twentieth-century poem
Teacher models criteria by sampling examples from the text she wishes them to correct	Class draw up list of criteria guided by teacher
Pupils correct text	Teacher and assistant perform poem
Teacher checks answers with whole class	Pupils asked to critique performance
Pupils correct each other's work	Pupils rehearse performance
	Pupils peer-assess poems based on criteria
	Pupils perform poems based on criteria

for quality in a piece of work – an issue which is difficult in English and hard for pupils to grasp (see Marshall, 2004a, 2004b). Both Tracy and Angela adopt familiar procedures associated with assessment for learning (see Box 1.1 in Chapter 1): sharing the criteria with the learner and peer and self-assessment as a means to this end. These two activities – modelling and peer assessment – are linked; in both lessons, the modelling activity at the start of the lesson appears to be designed to help pupils know what to do when they peer-assess.

Tracy modelled the criteria for the eventual peer-assessment activity by giving pupils a piece of writing that was full of technical errors (i.e. spelling and punctuation). They were asked to correct it on their own while she went around the class monitoring their progress. All these interchanges revolved around notions of correctness and there was little scope for anything other than closed questions. The second activity in Tracy's lesson centred, again, on the teacher checking whether or not the pupils had found the errors in the text. The feedback involved pupils volunteering where they had found a mistake and the correction they had made. Occasionally they missed something in the text and Tracy would go back until a pupil identified the missing error and corrected it. Similarly, on the small number of occasions when a pupil got the answer wrong, Tracy would pause and wait for another pupil to volunteer the right answer. In this exchange the teacher adjudicated questions of correctness with no opportunity for the pupils to extend the narrowly defined scope of the task. Pupils then went on to peer-assess one another's work.

Angela modelled the criteria for peer-assessment differently. She began the lesson by asking the pupils to draw up a list of criteria for performing a poem. Suggestions all came from the pupils while she probed, challenged and polished their contributions. For example:

Pupil: You could speed it up and slow it down.
Angela: Yes – pace, that's very important in reading [teacher then writes the word 'pace' on the board].

Angela and the classroom assistant then performed the poem to the class and invited pupils to critique their performance based on the criteria. A similar form of probing took place in these exchanges also:

Pupil: It [the performance] was boring.
Angela: What do you mean boring?
Pupil: There wasn't enough expression in your face when the poem was being read or in the reading.
Angela: So what could I have done to make it better?
Pupil: You could have looked and sounded more alarmed.
Angela: Like this? [strikes a pose]
Pupil: Not quite.
Angela: More like this? [strikes another pose]
Pupil: Yeah.

These three tasks in Angela's lesson – the creation of the criteria, the performance of the poem and the application of the criteria to Angela's and the assistant's performance – governed both the pupils' thinking about what was needed when they acted out the poem themselves and the peer assessment of those performances.

Two crucial but subtle elements differentiate these lessons: the potential scope of the tasks; and the opportunities these afforded for current and future pupil independence. Although it is hard to separate out the various aspects of the lessons, as they overlap, it is possible to use the labels – 'making learning explicit', 'promoting learning auton-omy' and 'performance orientation' – taken from the factor analysis of the LHTL staff questionnaire (see Chapter 4) as a way of organising the analysis. For example, with regard to 'making learning explicit', the scope of the task in Tracy's lesson was considerably more restricted in helping pupils understand what quality might look like, focusing instead on those things which were simply right and wrong. Pupils in Angela's lesson, on the other hand, engaged both in technical considerations, such as clarity and accuracy, as well as the higher-order, interpretive concepts of meaning and effect. In addition, the modelling of what was required in Angela's lesson ensured that pupils went beyond an imitation of that model because it challenged them to think about the variety of ways they might enact their interpretation of the poem.

The sequence of activities guided the pupils in Angela's lesson towards 'learning autonomy', a key concept in our theoretical analysis of the concept of learning how to learn (see Chapter 1). In addition to encouraging the pupils to create their own criteria, the tasks helped them to think for themselves about what might be needed to capture the meaning of the poem in performance. In Tracy's lesson, the AfL procedures, alone, were insufficient to lead to this key beneficial outcome of Angela's lesson.

Pupils in Angela's lesson, therefore, also began to engage in the more complex issues of any performance, be it oral or written. That is, the pupils were asked to explore the relationship between the meaning of a product and the way in which that meaning is expressed: between form and content. This leads us to the final element, which we labelled 'performance orientation'. Crucially, Angela always described the tasks as opportunities for the pupils to improve their performance. In this way the activities had an open, fluid feel which corresponded with the notion of promoting pupil autonomy. It reinforced a sense of limitless progress whereby assessment is always seen as a tool for changing future performance rather than for judging what has been done already. In the main this was done by creating tasks designed to enable children to enter the subject community 'guild' (see Sadler, 1989). Performance in Tracy's lesson, by contrast, comprised a finite act, conforming to a fixed, identifiable, measurable notion of correctness in which issues of quality went undiscussed.

Lessons from interviews: the importance of incremental and task-oriented views of learning

So how might we understand why teachers, such as Angela, are able to put into practice the spirit of AfL? If trying to make sense of lessons is an untidy business, relating what occurs in these lessons to the teachers' beliefs about learning is even messier and affords few neat correspondences between teachers' beliefs and their practices. Quantitative data from the LHTL staff questionnaires indicate (see Chapters 4 and 8) that teachers do not all negotiate the pressures of the performance culture (that leads to a performance orientation) in the same manner. Within a development and research project such as LHTL, they progress and change in how they relate their values to their practice. So the positions taken around the mid-point of the project, when the videos and interviews were carried out, should not be seen as fixed in any way, merely an indication of the point of trajectory (see Coffey *et al.*, 2005).

In analysing the interviews we looked especially at those teachers for whom we had video data and focused on two aspects: their views on the promotion of learning autonomy, as this element had been central to the critique of the lessons; and their views on what might impede learning taking place.

Two interesting issues arose out of these teachers' interviews. The first is the extent to which they value pupil autonomy as an explicit aim of their teaching; the second is the extent to which the teachers hold themselves responsible, rather than either external circumstances or characteristics of pupils, for any impediment to children's learning. All those teachers, identified through the observations of the videos as capturing the spirit of AfL, spoke, more than other teachers, of the value they placed on pupil autonomy. When asked about impediments to learning, they tended to proffer, as the first or second explanation, their own responsibility for motivating or helping pupils to learn. The rest, while mentioning the importance of pupil autonomy in varying degrees, identify external factors when considering barriers to learning.

One way of understanding the differences between the way in which teachers respond is to use Dweck's (2000) distinction between performance goals and learning goals, which relate to underlying 'entity' or 'incremental' theories of intelligence (see Box 3.2).

Box 3.2 Dweck's theories of motivation and development

Psychologist Carol Dweck (2000) identifies two contrasting but co-existing views, held by pupils, which have profound effects on their motivation to engage with learning. The first view is defined by 'performance' or 'ego-involving' goals which are about 'winning positive judgments of your competence and avoiding negative ones . . . to look smart and avoid looking dumb' (ibid., p. 15). The second view is about a desire to get smarter by learning new skills, mastering new tasks, or understanding new things. This view is characterised as having a learning, mastery or task orientation. Dweck points out that 'an overemphasis on performance goals can drive out learning goals . . . and foster a helpless response' (ibid., p. 16). This concept of 'learned helplessness' is a powerful one.

A performance goal is about measuring ability, while a learning goal is about mastering new things, so implicit in this distinction are different views of intelligence. Dweck relates these two goal orientations to what she calls incremental versus entity theories of intelligence. Broadly speaking, those who hold an entity theory see intelligence as fixed; but those who hold an incremental view tend to believe that intelligence is 'malleable' and learnable – you can become smarter if you focus on the task in hand. Those who focus on the task are more able to learn from the experience the task has given them, and improve as a result; while those who are ego-involved are most concerned with how they appear to others. The learning of this latter group can be impeded by focusing on issues such as their view of their own ability or the circumstances in which the task is undertaken.

AfL and theories of goal orientation

We found that those teachers who capture what we have called the spirit of AfL share what might be described as a learning or task orientation underpinned by an incremental view of intelligence. This is made manifest by the way in which they look to their own practice to understand how well the pupils in their class did or did not learn, rather than attribute this to any cause external to themselves, such as the fixed intelligence of pupils or the pressures of policy prescription. At its most simple, these teachers are able to describe the type of activities in which a teacher would have to engage in order to ensure an environment in which pupils learn. Drawing on an example of how pupils often come to class distracted, one teacher explains,

> Obviously if you're going to get them to actually turn that around, you want to be making sure that they're focused and that they're concentrating. So getting them interested in what you're doing is clearly something that has got to happen. They're not going to learn if they're bored . . . The teacher also needs to make sure that everyone's kind of engaged.
>
> (Simon, teacher, Vine School, secondary)

Simon's comments may seem to be stating the obvious, yet very few teachers interviewed made the role of the teacher in creating conditions of learning this explicit. Moreover, implicit within his observation is also the converse: if pupils are bored or not concentrating, then it is both the teacher's fault and responsibility to change the situation.

Another teacher reflects on the way the quality of the tasks set in lessons can impede learning. Again, by implication, the teacher can improve what happens by altering the task:

> The idea [is] that sometimes you prepare the lesson, which isn't appropriate for the pupils. It's over their heads, or it's too easy, and that sometimes prevents learning from taking place, or meaningful learning . . . You might be able to control the situations so they complete the task but they haven't actually learnt anything because it's too complicated and they didn't get the hang of it, or it was too easy and it was something they could dash off.
>
> (Fran, teacher, Redwood High School, secondary)

The possibility that reflection on what has occurred can bring about beneficial change is most clearly expressed by Angela, the teacher of the Year 8 class whose lesson was described above. Underlying the way she conducted her English lesson was a strong conviction that her job was to make the pupils in her classes less passively dependent on her, and more dependent on themselves and one another. Unlike Tracy, Angela thought of learning as centred on a move towards greater pupil independence. Running like a *leitmotif* through her interview is her claim that, 'If I've taught a lesson, then I'll go over it, reflect, think, what could I do better next time?' Again, 'So I do a lesson with one and then I think, okay, how could I improve that for the next time?', and:

> But it depends, sometimes it's just a thought and sometimes [I] actually kind of go back over the scheme of work, look at the lesson

plan and write notes to myself for next time. So it depends on what it is really and how severely bad it went.

(Angela, teacher, Hawthorn High School, secondary)

Not all Angela's reflections are negative: 'I suppose you say what do you do better, but you can also say, what went well.'

There is an apparent irony in the way these teachers feel the fault lies with them, if learning is not taking place, yet are keenest to promote independence in their pupils. But it appears to be an important relationship. Evident in each of these teachers' comments is the idea that nothing in the classroom is fixed or beyond their control. For Angela, for example, it is the place where she needs to learn about how well she has done in relationship to the task she set herself – to promote pupils' learning. In this way her approach, and those of the teachers like her, echo the importance Dweck (2000) attaches to learning goals and incremental intelligence. All lessons give Angela, for example, experiences from which she can refine and develop her craft for the benefit of the pupils, whom she believes to be capable of learning. It is this essentially progressive process – the possibility that all performance and knowledge can be developed – that Angela wishes her pupils to understand. In this way there is a synergy between her concept of independent learning, and of the formative process for her pupils, and the way she approaches her own teaching and indeed her own learning. This is evidence for the parallels between learning how to learn for pupils and learning how to learn by teachers which we proposed in Chapter 2.

Teacher interviews: evidence of a constraining performance culture

The group of teachers described above, however, proved the exception. Only around 20 per cent of the teachers observed captured what we have called the spirit of AfL and held correspondingly incremental or task-oriented views of learning. Significantly, perhaps, this percentage coincides with findings from analysis of the LHTL staff questionnaire data, described more fully in Chapters 4 and 8, which also show one cluster of teachers who are different. About 20 per cent of over 1,200 teachers surveyed have almost no gap between what they value in terms of promoting learning autonomy and what they report as practised.

Yet one of the most striking features of these questionnaire data, gathered at school level, is the way that, for the rest of the teachers (around 80 per cent), there are marked gaps between what they value and the practice they report, in relation to the three factors mentioned earlier: making learning explicit; promoting learning autonomy; and performance orientation. Most of this group of teachers believe more strongly in promoting learner autonomy than claim to practise it; and they practise performance orientation more than they believe in its value. Only on the factor labeled 'making learning explicit' was there any consistent degree of correspondence between what teachers value and what they practise. What such quantitative data cannot reveal, however, is why this might be so. The qualitative data collected by the project was, partly, intended to illuminate the findings from the questionnaires. Thus, it is to interviews with a group of teachers, who express concerns about such values–practice gaps, that we now turn our attention.

What emerges from the interviews with the majority of teachers is what might be called a culture of performance. Drawing on Foucault, the French post-structuralist theorist, Stephen Ball (2003) describes what he calls the dominance of performativity within the culture of schools. There is a sense in which our data tell a similar story because Ball's characterisation describes the context in which the teachers in the LHTL project work. But our interviews lend Ball's narrative a significant sub-plot, which, to extend the metaphor for a moment, affects the main action – the learning that takes place within schools. The interviews with these LHTL teachers make reference beyond the institutional managerial structures, which Ball considers, and begin to unpick how and why teachers believe this performance-orientated culture has an impact on their effectiveness as teachers, and their pupils' ability to learn.

We coded our transcriptions of 37 interviews with 'focal' teachers. Of 16 major coding categories, one was 'performance orientation' (140 quotations) and another was 'barriers to pupil learning' (366 quotations). When we looked at the coincidence of these two major categories, we found three further sub-categories that are important to understanding how teachers feel constrained by the circumstances in which they work. These are 'curriculum coverage', 'national testing' and 'tick-box' culture. (To understand what we mean by 'constrained', see Box 3.3.)

Box 3.3 Distinctions between tension and constraint

In Chapter 2, we noted that 'affordances' and 'constraints' refer to the way people perceive and interpret their experience of living in the world. Woods *et al.* (1997) have explored the concept of 'constraint' further in their studies of teachers' lives in school. In analysing primary teachers' accounts, they chart progression from the experience of being faced with *dilemmas*, through *tension*, to *constraint*. They define tensions as 'the product of trying to accommodate two or more opposing courses where choice is limited or circumscribed' (ibid., p. 21). Constraints, on the other hand, are, 'Structural, in the sense that they are beyond personal resolution within the immediate context. Constraint implies compulsion, forced repression of natural feelings' (ibid., p. 21). Moreover, these constraints are not simply practical; they also constitute what Woods and his colleagues call an 'assault on values' (ibid., p. 84).

Tension is produced in circumstances where teachers are significantly limited in their choices in resolving dilemmas. But where they feel that there is little choice at all, they experience constraint. The idea that constraints cause an assault on value is important for our work as it potentially helps us understand the values–practice gaps that we identified.

Curriculum coverage

One theme running through the teacher interview data is a sense of the time pressure that arises from curriculum coverage:

> Well, the curriculum can interfere in as much as you are pushed for time to get through things and therefore, often it's a race against time . . . and you feel sometimes a slower pace for certain areas would be more useful but we haven't got the time allocated for it.
>
> (Alison, teacher,
> Pear Tree Church of England School, primary)

This teacher's use of the metaphor of a race is implicit in many of the teachers' comments about the pressure of curriculum coverage. They frequently talk in terms of movement: about 'rush' and 'pace' in relation to the quantity of material to be covered. A secondary teacher observes, 'There is too much to cover and there is the expectation, certainly with the National Numeracy Strategy, for the level of pace that is difficult to maintain.' And from a primary teacher, 'the curriculum is so full, you're expected to cover so much in such a short time, that you feel it's got to be pacey. You've got to go, go, go.' In this, they echo the teachers in the original KMOFAP work, who also noted the way time pressures inhibited their initial attempts to introduce AfL (Black, *et al.*, 2003).

Alongside the pressure of time sits the prescriptive nature of the curriculum. While some teachers see the value in the National Curriculum, they still feel constrained by the level of prescription:

> I think that the curriculum can be quite restricting sometimes . . . you know, there are areas in there to encourage independent learning and study. The fact that you have to stick to the curriculum and do all these set topics in a specific time can be quite restricting.
> (Georgina, teacher, Mulberry School, secondary)

An infants teacher comments:

> I don't think the curriculum as it stands is helpful. I think we needed it at the time . . . I think schools were sort of doing their own thing . . . and now you know full well that all children will be doing the same thing.
> (Melody, teacher, Aspen Infants School)

One secondary teacher put it very strongly indeed:

> I think we . . . have quite a Maoist idea of education which is 'we all do this, we all follow this curriculum, we all follow the set pattern, we all follow this set structure in the classroom. We have a starter, we have a session, we have a plenary. We must include this, this, this and this.' And while that is right to a certain degree, it undoubtedly inhibits your ability to put your personal style and personal stamp upon a lesson and it inhibits your ability to change what you're teaching to the group that you're teaching it to.
> (Hayden, teacher, Garland Tree Science and
> Technology College, secondary)

This repetitive litany lends Hayden's reflections a rhythmic, patterned quality reminiscent of the kind of un-personalised rote learning the list evokes. His concern about the effect this has, not only on his own teaching but also on those of the pupils, is shared by other teachers. Differentiation appears to suffer in a number of ways. Pace can interfere with a desire to make the curriculum appropriate to the needs of learners: as one primary teacher puts it, 'You find [you're] constantly moving on to the next set of learning objectives for the children . . . we have to give a curriculum that fits our children not fit the children to the curriculum.'

Curriculum coverage and pace (interpreted as speed rather than rhythm and balance) also inhibit opportunities for the pupils to consolidate their understanding. The race metaphor is again in evidence. In terms reminiscent of Dweck's (2000) ego-involved goals, one teacher describes pupils who are keen to be 'the first to finish' rather than slowing down and engaging with the work. More importantly, perhaps, the teachers worry that it prevents pupils exploring ideas for themselves: 'In the main we're trying to put too much into the curriculum and not allowing the children to explore and enjoy a fewer things and make stronger links . . . we're galloping through.'

National tests and examinations

Teachers show even more marked concern for pupils' learning when they discuss the impact of the tests, particularly the way they perceive them to inhibit pupils' ability to learn independently. Indeed, almost all the explicit references to barriers to pupils becoming independent and autonomous learners come in connection with testing. For example, one secondary teacher observes, 'What do they do to help themselves to learn when they are forced to learn things, literally learn things by rote, like, for tests?'

Such a culture can lead to passivity in the pupils, or what Dweck calls 'learned helplessness'. One secondary teacher imagines pupils as saying: 'I'm leaning back in my chair so teach me what I need to know.' Another describes ambitious pupils as wanting to be 'spoon-fed'. Others question whether long-term learning can be achieved through drilling for tests while acknowledging its short-term efficiency as a way of passing exams. One secondary teacher concludes, 'I've written down "learning versus testing" . . . I think that assessment impedes learning. There is so much emphasis on it at the moment.'

The tensions that teachers experience, between meeting the demands of the testing regime and encouraging pupils to be independent or autonomous learners within this system, are palpable. An interpretation that this goes beyond tension and becomes constraint (Woods *et al.*, 1997) seems justified by teachers' reflections on the powerful external pressures which restrict their scope for action. As one teacher explains:

> We move and we snapshot areas and we do it because we have an exam at the end of it and we have to cover areas that have to be examined. But that stops learning. That stops developing their love of learning . . . I think we have driven so hard to achieve certain results that teachers are judged on results, that we push for results. And results sadly, at GCSE, are about knowledge and under-standing . . . important reflective attitude and analytic attitude, you will get nowhere unless you have knowledge and understanding.
>
> (Hayden, teacher, Garland Tree Science and Technology College, secondary)

Another teacher holds a similar view:

> The ethical dilemma is simply the fact that you are continually teaching to try and get good results in exams and things and we know that there's a whole lot of other stuff that might be in there that's really good learning . . . they're not going to get kids through the exams. And you know we need to get the balance right between pushing them towards the exam and learning in general.
>
> (Molly, teacher, Fir Tree School for Girls, secondary)

Each of these observations illustrates the way teachers feel constrained by what they perceive as the limits of the examinations. They are torn by an obligation to get the best results for their pupils and the sense that in so doing they are short-changing them. Their responses are redolent of the concept of constraint as defined by Woods *et al.* (1997). This sense of constraint, experienced by the teachers interviewed, meant that they felt impelled to adopt pedagogies, and make decisions about their use of time, which went against their professional judgement of best practice. This feeling extends right down into early years education:

> I think when they come to us, we're immediately testing them. And this whole issue with testing is a really big one. But obviously with SATs starting when they're so young now, I think that's already become part of the culture. Now I'm not sure it should be there, but

that's just my personal view. Because I think you're putting pressure on kids at a very young age. But when you are looking at GCSE results and you're looking at that background, how you get from A to B, then of course you have to go down that route.

(Melody, teacher, Aspen Infants School)

Melody's 'personal view' and values appear as a mere parenthesis to the system in which both she and her pupils operate. The tension can be compounded by a sense of the valueless nature of the tests themselves:

We have to work to the best we can to see that our students achieve the best they can at the exams. I don't see it's the best way of assessing, sitting in a room and seeing if they can answer questions over two one-and-a-half hour slots or whatever it is. Is that the fairest way to test someone's mathematical ability? I'm not convinced.

(Nigel, teacher, Lime School, secondary)

Tick-box culture

All but one of the frequent references to tick boxes or checklists provide evidence of Ball's (2003) culture of performativity. These are regarded as bureaucratic and external impositions on teachers' working conditions and bear little resemblance to indicators of a learning organisation expounded by MacBeath and Mortimore (2001). The one exception is in a comment from a secondary teacher who introduced a target checklist with her pupils: 'The target checklist was something because of learning to learn [the project] but also I do try to think of what I can and to help the kids.'

Generally the use of tick lists with pupils can be seen as part of the performance culture. Ticks are, after all, symbols of both completion and correctness. The elision between the apparent benefits for pupils and performance is evident in this teacher's explanation of why she introduced them:

They can choose their targets and they can be aware of what I'm looking for, as in, you know the reason why we're doing this is because the literacy strategy says that for a certain level you have to be able to do these . . . They are really proud as well when they get to tick stuff off.

(Tracy, teacher, Elm High School, secondary)

A primary teacher makes the connection between ticks and performance clearer: 'They tend to monitor how many ticks they've be given as an achievement record [laughs], which really isn't important at all.' Indeed, some teachers see this tendency of pupils as an impediment to their learning: 'There are misconceptions about learning. They have a certain tick-box mentality. If they've done something they can tick it off their list and forget about it.'

Significantly, most references to tick-boxes do not even mention learning. While they are clearly related to both the pressure to cover the curriculum and testing – 'we're galloping through and ticking off' – they seem more overtly connected to school bureaucracy and paperwork. For most teachers this detracts from what they feel to be the purpose of their job: 'I feel under pressure to press on and make sure I've covered everything and I've ticked all the boxes, whereas actually, what I'd like to do, is go back and teach something again.' This primary teacher adds, 'I sometimes feel I'm teaching in order to tick boxes . . . whereas actually I just want to get on with using the assessment to teach the next bit [.] but I'm ploughing through the paperwork'.

Connected with bureaucracy is accountability as a manifestation of performativity. Again this detracts from teaching and learning. One primary teacher, commenting on 'a lot of form filling as evidence', explains,

> It is starting to get so that everything has to be recorded and assessed in one form or another [.] we are expected, in each subject to have literally a list of the children and ticks next to them whether they can do this, this and this. And it can be, you know, just really time-consuming and, in a way, I feel most of the time unnecessary as well [.] the time that you spend filling these in surely it can be put to better use in identifying children with problems and then, you know, meeting those needs where they are, rather than filling out loads of paperwork just to say – oh, this child hasn't done this.
> (Len, teacher, Sycamore Primary School)

Conclusion

The research undertaken, through observations in classrooms and interviews with classroom teachers, illustrates the difficulty of effecting change. Teachers are very willing to trial and take on board new ideas and techniques but the circumstances in which they work, and the beliefs they hold, impact on the way they implement change. Our evidence suggests that certain sets of beliefs more readily support what we have called the spirit of AfL than others. In particular, teachers who hold task-oriented and incremental views of learning are better equipped to deal with external pressures experienced as constraints.

These findings call into question traditional methods of professional training and development where very little attention is paid to the beliefs that teachers hold. The implication is that beliefs and practices need to be developed together. Advice on specific classroom practices may be useful, in the short term, but continuous and progressive professional development will have more lasting value. This is likely to involve encouraging teachers to re-evaluate their beliefs about learning, the way they structure learning tasks and activities during lessons, and the nature of their classroom roles and relationships.

Our research also has implications for the policy context and implies a need to ameliorate the constraining effects of over-emphasis on curriculum coverage, teaching to tests and the impact of a pervasive tick-box culture. Our data were collected between 2002 and the end of 2004 and some policies have changed (slightly) since then. Further research will be needed to tell whether new policies and climates for change create better conditions for teachers and pupils to pursue the goals of learning how to learn.

Chapter 4*

Schools learning how to learn

As we saw in Chapter 3, a key focus of our classroom-based research was on teachers' use of assessment for learning to engender autonomous learning by their pupils, and how they created the conditions that supported the development of such learning practices. We also discussed aspects of the environment in which teachers and pupils work that are perceived to help or hinder them. Asking teachers to find ways of promoting learning autonomy within an already exacting pedagogy places serious demands on their professional expertise and raises a critical question. How do teachers support their pupils in developing greater independence in their learning and decision-making while at the same time ensuring that they meet demands for curriculum coverage and preparation for tests and exams? One thing was certain at the outset of the project: teachers would not be able to shoulder the responsibility for promoting learning how to learn (LHTL) in their classrooms alone. They would need help and support, much of which would necessarily come from within their own schools.

With this as our premise, we focus, in this chapter, on the organ-isational conditions that support teachers in promoting LHTL, and on the nature of help and support that would enhance LHTL in their classrooms. What would characterise the quality of leadership which fosters a commitment to the principles and practice of LHTL? What kinds of systems, structures and cultures shape and support the promotion of LHTL within and across classrooms? These were key questions that developed through the course of our research with schools. An initial assumption that guided our approach was that if schools are to promote LHTL, they need to develop the processes and practices of learning organisations.

* Authored by John MacBeath, David Pedder and Sue Swaffield

Chris Argyris and Donald Schön's (1978) concept of 'double-loop learning' offered us a lens through which to view the process of learning at school level, as we indicated in Chapter 2. Through ongoing critical inquiry, they argue, an organisation can develop new ways of thinking about the quality of its members and the nature of individual and shared learning. Applying this concept to our study, it implied an ability and disposition on the part of school staff to stand back from the conduct of classroom learning in order to reflect more deeply on their experiences, to learn more about themselves, individually as well as collectively, through the activities in which they were participating (see Box 4.1). John MacBeath (2006) argues that while this might be characterised as a form of self-evaluation, it goes beyond the formulaic, single-loop approach, advocated by the Office for Standards in Education (Ofsted), for example.

Box 4.1 Double-loop learning

The notion of double-loop learning comes from a business context but is applicable in a range of situations: in schools, in classrooms and at the level of the individual learner. School pupils very often apply a single-loop strategy – make a mistake, correct mistake, then move on. A double-loop strategy would be to learn how to learn more effectively. At the organisational level a school learns through mistakes, and successes, but with a capacity to learn how to embed the bigger lesson learned into the working practices and thinking of the school. This is how Argyris and Schön (1978: 2–3) describe the process:

> When the error detected and corrected permits the organization to carry on its present policies or achieve its present objectives, then that error-and-correction process is *single-loop* learning. Single-loop learning is like a thermostat that learns when it is too hot or too cold and turns the heat on or off. The thermostat can perform this task because it can receive information (the temperature of the room) and take corrective action. *Double-loop* learning occurs when error is detected and corrected in ways that involve the modification of an organization's underlying norms, policies and objectives.

The double-loop learning process adopts a critical stance to what Massey (1998) refers to as 'the way we do things around here' and raises questions such as 'what are we noticing about the process of our learning as a school?' and 'how can we learn more about ourselves as a learning community?' This approach mirrors an individual's metacognitive processes, as discussed in Chapter 1, and relates to the concept of 'critical autonomy' (see Box 1.3). Our hypothesis was that in a school committed to deep critical inquiry, more reflective and self-critical learning by pupils would also develop as teachers became more able to 'double-loop' their practice, while encouraging their charges to do the same. We believed that as pupils became more reflective and critical with regard to their own and one another's learning, teachers' learning would benefit too. We worked with a range of different sources of evidence to explore these hypotheses.

In the account that follows, we examine first our baseline data, that is, the results of our analysis of questionnaires administered to all staff and interviews with head teachers and co-ordinators of the LHTL project in the schools, at the beginning of our work with them in 2002. We then move on to look at our evidence of change based on similar data collected in the same schools, though not necessarily from all of the same teachers (some had changed), towards the end of the project in 2004. These analyses gave us insights into influential school conditions for bringing about change.

School conditions influential in the promotion of learning how to learn

Relationships between different kinds of practices in schools

In 2002, 1,212 staff completed a survey questionnaire: the 'staff questionnaire' referred to in Chapter 3. (Further details of sampling, procedures and findings can be found in Pedder, 2006.) Drawing on the data from these questionnaires, we explored relationships between three kinds of practices in schools: (1) classroom assessment practices; (2) teachers' professional learning practices; and (3) school management practices and systems. Our reading of previous research led us to expect that this would help us to develop a better understanding of the organisational conditions that foster the promotion of LHTL.

One approach was to use factor analysis, a statistical process for reducing a large number of individual questionnaire items to groups of cognate items which can be represented as a single 'factor'. Each factor refers to a grouping of practices which are linked together through some shared characteristic. We summarised the characteristics of each grouping of practice for each of the three main areas of interest as follows.

Our first main area of interest was learning how to learn at the classroom level through teachers' incorporation of assessment for learning practices (see James and Pedder, 2006, for more detail). We identified three salient groupings of practice which we describe as:

- *Making learning explicit*: eliciting, clarifying and responding to evidence of learning; working with pupils to develop a positive learning orientation.
- *Promoting learning autonomy*: a widening of scope for pupils to take on greater independence over their learning objectives and the assessment of their own and one another's work.
- *Performance orientation*: a concern to help pupils comply with performance goals prescribed by the curriculum through closed questioning and measured by marks and grades. (This definition shares much in common with Dweck's (2000) definition of performance goals, discussed in Chapter 3.)

The second area of interest was teachers' professional learning (see Pedder *et al.*, 2005, for details). Here we identified four salient groupings of practice which we describe as:

- *Inquiry*: using and responding to different sources of evidence; carrying out joint research and evaluation with colleagues.
- *Building social capital*: learning, working, supporting and talking with one another.
- *Critical and responsive learning*: through reflection, self-evaluation, experimentation and by responding to feedback.
- *Valuing learning*: both their own and pupils' learning.

For our third area of interest, school management practices and systems (see Pedder and MacBeath, forthcoming), we identified the following four groupings of practice which we describe as:

- *Deciding and acting together*: involving staff in decision-making and using their professional know-how in the formulation and critical evaluation of school policy.
- *Developing a sense of where we are going*: clear communication by senior management of a clear vision and the fostering of staff commitment to the whole school, based on good working knowledge among staff of school development priorities which they view as relevant and useful for learning and teaching.
- *Supporting professional development*: providing formal and informal training opportunities so that teachers, for example, can develop skills to assess their pupils' work in ways that move them on in their learning, and to observe learning as it happens in the classroom.
- *Auditing expertise and supporting networking.* Information is collected on practices that staff themselves think they do effectively, and on informal teacher networking in which they play an active role. Teachers are supported in sharing practice with other schools through networking.

We analysed these groupings of practices together (through regression analysis) to explore relationships among them (see Pedder, 2006, and James and Pedder, 2005, for more detail). Figure 4.1 illustrates the inter-relationship of factors that we found are most salient in fostering the promotion of LHTL within classrooms. Where the boxes are linked by lines and arrowheads we found an association that is statistically significant.

What is striking about these relationships is the importance of the 'Inquiry' grouping of practices. The 'Inquiry' group reflects a range of classroom-based approaches to collaborative teacher learning and it is these that appeared to be most directly and powerfully associated with LHTL in the classroom through 'Promoting learning autonomy'. The importance of learning autonomy, in relation to LHTL, was discussed in Chapter 1 (see also Black *et al.*, 2006).

What also struck us were the patterns of relationship between organisational strategies, on the left side of Figure 4.1, and the classroom practices on the right-hand side. It appears from our data that organisational strategies such as 'Developing a sense of where we are going', 'Supporting professional development' and 'Auditing expertise and supporting networking', have an indirect influence on learning how to learn at classroom level (represented by the factors 'Promoting learning autonomy' and 'Making learning explicit'). In other words, school management practices do not have a direct impact on classroom

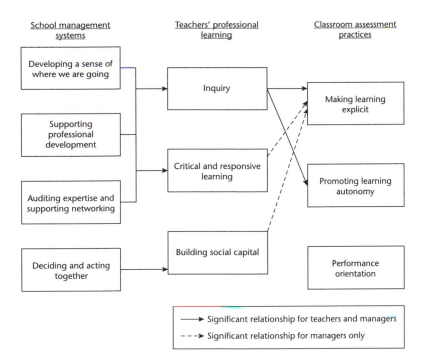

Figure 4.1 Organisational conditions that foster successful classroom promotion of learning how to learn

practices; they are mediated by the 'Inquiry' group of professional learning practices. This has important implication because it suggests that school leaders who want to promote LHTL in classrooms need to focus management on enabling inquiry approaches to professional learning in their staff.

Trust and quality of relationships among teachers are reflected in the 'Building social capital' factor. Reflection and modifying practice in light of feedback from colleagues and pupils are reflected in the 'Critical and responsive learning' factor. Neither factor shows direct associations with LHTL in the classroom through 'Promoting learning autonomy'. However, managers' responses indicate direct associations between these two factors and 'Making learning explicit'. Our data show no significant associations between school management system factors (on the left side of Figure 4.1) and teacher learning factors (in the middle of Figure 4.1) on the one hand and, on the other hand, the classroom practice factor, 'Performance orientation' (on the right side of Figure 4. 1). These particular findings are difficult to interpret but they reinforce the importance of teachers learning through inquiry, and management support for this, for promoting learning autonomy in the classroom. They also suggest that an emphasis on performance orientation in the classroom is disconnected both from professional learning and from organisational learning, which would support the evidence and argument presented in Chapter 3.

The analysis so far has helped us to examine the relationships between different groups of *practices* found in schools. The next section explores what practices teachers *value* and what they see as already in place, and the gaps between aspiration and current practice.

Values–practice gaps in 2002

Figures 4.2, 4.3 and 4.4 show the importance school staff attach to the sets of practices described above (values), and what they reported to be practised at the time when we conducted the baseline survey. In the bar charts, values are shown by the grey bars and practices are shown by the white bars.

Classroom assessment

Figure 4.2 shows that teachers tended, in 2002, to place highest value on 'Making learning explicit'. 'Promoting learning autonomy', although positively valued, had a lower mean value. 'Performance orientation' was valued least of all. With regard to current practice, 'Making learning explicit' aligned more closely with teachers' values than did 'Promoting learning autonomy'. This appeared, at the outset of the project, to reflect something of the difficulty teachers experience in encouraging independent learning, which may, in part, be explained by responses to the 'Performance orientation' grouping of items. While ascribing relatively low value to this, practice scores were relatively high, suggesting that teachers felt constrained to focus on performance goals, even when this was out of step with the importance they placed on such practices. This finding is congruent with the qualitative evidence reported in Chapter 3. (It is discussed in greater detail in James and Pedder, 2006.)

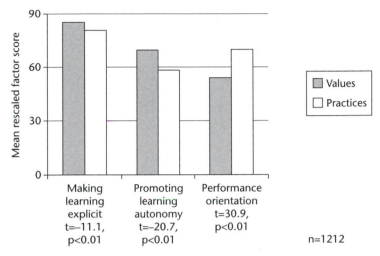

Figure 4.2 Dimensions of classroom assessment: values and practices, 2002

Teachers' professional learning

Figure 4.3 shows that of the four professional learning factors, 'Valuing learning' was perceived to be practised most as well as valued most. Not only did teachers tend to place high value on pupils' capacity for learning but apparently viewed themselves as learners too. Particularly striking were their responses to the items under 'Building social capital'. High mean values scores suggest that teachers derived benefit from opportunities to engage with their colleagues outside of the classroom. They placed particular emphasis on open discussion among their peers, as to what and how they were learning, and the bonds of trust that arose from disclosing professional problems to one another. They also placed high value on practices included in the 'Critical and responsive learning' grouping, including reflection, self-evaluation, experimentation and responding to feedback from pupils and colleagues

What struck us as interesting was that, although teachers appeared to be happy and committed to exchanges with colleagues *outside* of their classrooms, there was less evidence of their readiness to learn alongside colleagues *inside* their classrooms (see further discussion in Pedder *et al.*, 2005). Carrying out joint research and evaluation, team teaching and consulting pupils are all examples of classroom-based collaborative teacher learning practices that were grouped together in

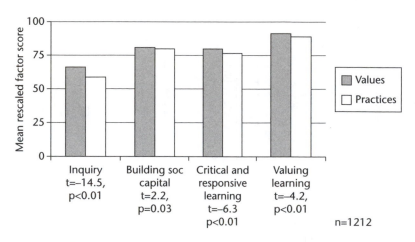

Figure 4.3 Dimensions of teachers' learning: values and practices, 2002

the 'Inquiry' factor. However, teachers told us, in interviews, that although they placed high value on these elements of inquiry, this was not typical of their practice. This is an important finding in itself. It becomes crucial when considered alongside the importance of these learning practices in our model of the organisational conditions that foster classroom promotion of LHTL (see Figure 4.1).

School management practices and systems

Figure 4.4 shows that in 2002 there was a striking imbalance in the relationship between teachers' values and perceived practices with regard to all four dimensions of school management at the outset of the project, in 2002.

While teachers tended to place high value on 'Deciding and acting together' they recorded much lower mean scores for levels of perceived practice. Similar patterns of high value scores but much lower practice scores were evident for the group of practices under 'Developing a sense of where we are going' and for 'Supporting professional development'. 'Auditing expertise and supporting networking' were lower than for the other three dimensions both in respect of value and practice.

These trends of low levels of practice and large values–practice gaps for all four dimensions of school management say something about the challenges faced by schools, at the beginning of our project, in developing a shared vision, supporting teachers' learning, and in fostering a

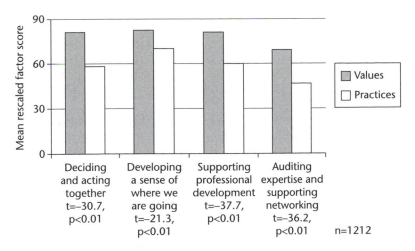

Figure 4.4 Dimensions of school management systems: values and practices, 2002

culture of participation in school decision-making. They also suggest to us that, in 2002, promoting LHTL would benefit from placing much greater emphasis on the active and systematic management of schools' knowledge resources – what in Chapter 2 was described as intellectual capital. (Management practices and values are explored further by Pedder and MacBeath, forthcoming.)

The baseline questionnaire data reported here suggest that the challenges involved in developing and incorporating LHTL practices in classroom lessons represented a significant challenge to the resources, time and expertise of teachers in the schools who took part in the survey in 2002 (32 of our total sample of 40 schools – a different questionnaire was administered to the remainder). If the level of challenge was low, then teachers' practices and values would have been in much closer alignment than our data reveal. The same can be said of the challenges faced by school leaders who set about developing systems and approaches to embedding LHTL practices throughout their schools.

The task of encouraging spread and uptake of those practices, which are shown to promote LHTL, places considerable demands on school leaders. They need strategies that support teachers in incorporating AfL practices, leading to the promotion of LHTL, and which embody the spirit and not simply the letter (see Chapter 3). But, as school leaders know, it is not simply a matter of teachers incorporating new practices but also having the creativity and flexibility to adapt their pedagogy within their own classroom contexts and developing the learned habits of their pupils. So the leadership challenge is further extended to address this issue with recognition of the risks involved. This emerges clearly as one of the hallmarks in the relationships among innovative classroom practices, leadership and organisational learning – the focus of the next section.

The data from the 2002 baseline survey therefore provided us with both puzzles and a challenge. The puzzles were to understand more fully what lay behind these responses and how they actually played out in practice. The challenge, for the research team, was to ascertain to what extent a commitment to an LHTL approach could help to reframe thinking and practice and open classroom doors wider, both literally and metaphorically.

Extended interviews with head teachers and school LHTL co-ordinators, conducted also at the outset of the project in 2002, provide an opportunity to explore in depth some of the puzzles about teachers' professional learning and school leadership presented by the survey evidence. The strongest messages from the interview transcripts were related to the following themes:

- the influence of the policy environment;
- the relationship between structural and cultural approaches to change;
- conceptions of leadership associated with embedding an LHTL approach.

The policy environment

The emphasis on a performance orientation revealed in the survey was also evident in interviews with head teachers (as it was in the interviews with classroom teachers discussed in Chapter 3). When invited to describe their schools, and their current development priorities, head teachers' accounts tended to be framed by policies within which an LHTL approach had to be accommodated. In the forefront of their concerns were National Strategies, testing, performance tables and Ofsted inspections. The degree to which these head teachers embraced, or offered critique of, the policy environment could be seen as a spectrum, with most adopting an ambivalent or selective approach somewhere between compliance and subversion. (A more detailed discussion of the head teachers' perspectives can be found in MacBeath,

2008.) Across the spectrum of views was a common expression of initiative overload:

> We've been absolutely bombarded by government initiatives. Some are very good and some are awful, but we've got so caught up in it and we're all very obedient now and we all do as we're told [although] I still think children learn an awful lot of rubbish at school that is totally unnecessary to them as people.
>
> (Nell, head teacher, Oak Infant School)

This reference to 'doing what we're told' revealed, among many of the heads, an ambivalence about policy initiatives. There were policy imperatives which appeared to offer little 'wiggle room'. Some heads viewed these as a constraining straitjacket; others welcomed the structure and direction that they provided. While, for some, LHTL did not appear to present a conflict with the main thrust of policy, others spoke of the struggle to resolve what they saw as inherent tensions (see Woods *et al.*, 1997, and Chapter 3) between the kind of exploratory, and intellectually subversive, approach that learning how to learn implied, and a highly prescriptive curriculum and set of teaching strategies. From the perspective of the research team, the implications of an LHTL culture of inquiry, reflection and collegial learning did not sit easily within a high-pressure, high-stakes performativity agenda. Our task was to explore with schools the extent to which these inherent tensions could be resolved.

What became clear from baseline interviews with head teachers and school co-ordinators was just how deeply embedded, in thinking and practice, were performance levels and attainment targets; as one head teacher put it: 'a topic of endless discussions'. It is hardly surprising that there was a similarly high emphasis in the classrooms. Targets were made visible on classroom walls, stamped on front of books, reviewed at the start of lessons, reinforced and highlighted at every opportunity.

The prevalence of language to do with targets and levels, monitoring, standardisation and consensus contrasted sharply with the absence of terms such as dialogue, dissent, disagreement, or conflict. It seemed as if these forms of interaction were viewed as negatives to be avoided, and not part of a discourse among professional colleagues through which decisions about 'a sense of where we are going' or 'acting together' (two of the survey factors) could be made. In twelve head teacher interviews selected for more in-depth analysis (see MacBeath, 2008), conflict is mentioned only in relation to children, or in one case as a management style which 'heads off' potential conflict. 'Dissent' is not in the lexicon of policy and improvement. 'Dialogue' is mentioned in four interviews, in each case referring to exchanges between teachers and pupils in order to set targets – an instrumental use.

In these initial interviews the way in which head teachers framed the discourse pointed repeatedly to a conflation of teaching with learning. In discussion about learning, head teachers frequently referred more to what the teachers were doing, or to teacher intention, rather than to pupil activity or learning, resulting in an awkward straddling of the two ideas.

It is within this policy context and its dominant lexicon, constructed predominantly with reference to the external validation of practice and measures of success, that the pursuit of an approach to embedding LHTL (the focus of following sections) was set. How schools managed the tensions between external pressures and the risk-taking inevitable in developing new ways of working, and between prescribed teaching approaches and an openness to learning, revealed much about the nature and conduct of leadership. (We turn to the leadership issues in a later section.)

Embedding a LHTL approach

Analyses of interviews from the head teachers in twelve schools chosen for more intensive study (chosen simply because these schools had the most complete data) led us to characterise embedding strategies, at the early stage of the project, as leaning towards a structural approach, on the one hand, and a cultural approach, on the other. (The case studies in Chapters 6 and 7 provide examples: see Hawthorn High School for an approach favouring structure, and Hazel Primary School tending more to the cultural approach, although both have elements of each.) In making this distinction we are aware of the interplay of these approaches. Paul Willis (1983) reminds us that schools produce culture as well as reproducing it; they do so through their responses to large-scale structural reform as well as through introducing new structures and building unique cultures of their own. In attempting to disentangle the interplay of structure and culture, we were afforded a picture of how schools envisaged the institutionalising of LHTL at school and classroom levels.

While all the project schools used both structural and cultural approaches to embedding LHTL, the conception of change described by some heads could clearly be located within the former. Elements of classical organisational theory, as described by Max Weber (1961), include a clearly defined organisational structure with identified roles, linking mechanisms between roles, and clear communication patterns. There are specific tasks with explicit lines of authority leading, within a traditional school hierarchy of responsibility, to a downward flow of decision-making from senior leadership to classroom teachers and classroom assistants. These aspects were apparent in a number of head teachers' accounts, and were portrayed starkly by one in these terms: 'So there's a few core things that come from me and senior team that they're not for ownership . . . and if you don't submit to that, it's not really a place to work' (Anna, head teacher, Mulberry secondary school). Other heads envisaged embedding more in terms of a cultural shift in which values and systems of belief change over time, through persuasion and support. Changing cultures, it was said, required a more extended time frame, exemplified in the use of the horticultural metaphor; change was portrayed as an organic growth and nurturing process. The term 'bedding in' was used to describe a settling down of ideas and practices into a new soil where they take root over time and with watchful tending:

> What I'm trying to do is step back and let different things run. And that does seem to be working. So that's what I see as a learning organisation. People take the initiative in a non-hierarchical way; people reflect on what they're doing; they share that practice.
>
> (Ed, head teacher Redwood High School, secondary)

These conceptions of structural and cultural change contained within them assumptions about the role and impact of leadership and the creation and nurturing of organisational learning (see Box 4.2).

Box 4.2 Organisational learning

Can organisations learn? This is the question that has been explored by theorists and researchers, stemming from a concern that an organisation, such as a school, for example, tends to be less intelligent than its individual members. This is because it does not have the capacity, or intelligence, to identify, nurture and sustain its internal, often hidden, resources, which some call its 'organisational capital' (see Hargreaves, 2003a, and Chapter 2). When there is a synergy among a staff, multiplying rather than diminishing individual intelligence, a school may be described as a learning organisation. It is described in the following terms by Leithwood and Aitken (1995, p. 63):

> A 'learning organisation' involves a group of people pursuing common purposes (individual purposes as well) with a collective commitment to regularly weighing the value of those purposes, modifying them when that makes sense, and continuously developing more effective and efficient ways of accomplishing those purposes.

Conceptions of embedding and organisational learning were put to the test when, in 2004, after LHTL development work had been under-way for three years, we administered the staff questionnaire a second time and conducted follow-up interviews with project co-ordinators in schools.

Changes from 2002 and 2004

Values and practices reported in questionnaire responses

When we administered the staff questionnaire in 2004, we compared teachers' responses with responses in 2002. These comparisons provided us with evidence of shifts in classroom practice, or at least in teachers' perceptions of classroom practice (see Pedder, 2006, for a detailed account).

For example, in relation to 'Promoting learning autonomy', while mean values scores had remained more or less the same, practice was reported to have increased, if only on a modest scale, across the sample as a whole. This coincided with a reported decrease in prac-tices associated with 'Performance orientation'. The high levels of practice for 'Making learning explicit' that were reported in 2002 had been maintained, and slightly enhanced, and the values–practice gap was smaller.

With regard to teachers' professional learning, levels of practice showed modest increases across all dimensions; however, there was a marked increase in levels of practice reported for the 'Inquiry' factor. This was very encouraging because, as we made clear earlier (see Figure 4.1), the set of practices represented by this factor appears to be crucial in mediating the impact of organisational strategies on promotion of learning autonomy. In other words, if promotion of learning autonomy is the ultimate goal of learning how to learn, as we argued in Chapter 1, then teachers' learning how to learn through inquiry is the crucial condition. And school management strategies need to promote this, otherwise they risk being ineffective.

While scores for 'Inquiry' practices in 2002 had been the lowest of all teacher learning scores, interviews revealed that teacher collaboration on classroom-based approaches was beginning to play an increasingly important role in embedding LHTL in the classroom both in relation to 'Making learning explicit' and 'Promoting learning autonomy'. It would be attractive to us to claim that this change was directly attributable to innovations associated with the project. We believe that this is indeed evidence of the influence of project ideas, but we acknowledge that in the 'real world', where many initiatives interact, other developments are also likely to have contributed (see the case study from Eucalyptus Junior School, in Chapter 6 for an illustration of interacting initiatives).

Important and encouraging changes were also identified in the organisational strategies that schools were developing. For example, there were marked increases in the mean practice scores for 'Auditing expertise and supporting networking' and for 'Supporting professional development' – two factors important for the development of inquiry-based approaches in teacher learning. Such increases were achieved while sustaining and increasing levels of practice for 'Developing a sense of where we are going' and 'Deciding and acting together'.

However, for all four dimensions of school management, while values placed on these by teachers were sustained, by 2004, practices were still markedly behind levels of values. This suggests that, although the level of practice was improving, there was still a way to go to meet teachers' aspirations. This implies that a considerable level of challenge remains in the efforts of schools to implement organisational strategies that are able to promote and sustain LHTL practice in classrooms.

These general findings, aggregated across all schools in our sample, are illuminated by insights from interviews with school co-ordinators conducted in 2004. (In Chapter 8, we examine some of the within and between school differences that analysis of our staff questionnaires reveal.)

Embedding: part two: co-ordinator interviews in 2004

Two plus years down the line there was little in our various sources of evidence to suggest that embedding strategies favoured by individual schools at that time had undergone fundamental transformation. However, what the data do suggest is that, despite widely differing approaches to embedding, whether leaning to a structural or cultural view, staff attitudes to learning, assessment and learning how to learn had shifted considerably.

There were schools in which interviewees attested to significant change in practice, fashioned through being clearly mandated and closely monitored. A description of the embedding of assessment for learning from one secondary school co-ordinator illustrates an unapologetic top-down approach to change:

> In terms of assessment for learning, we've got a policy which is very, very directive. You must carry out peer or self-assessment once a term. You must not use grades. You must, you know – it's very, very prescriptive. But how you do that in the classroom and what you do as a department to deliver it is probably down to the department. What we were aiming for in the policy was that any kid could go to any lesson over a term and expect to get a diet of whatever.
>
> (Sally, co-ordinator, Hawthorn High School, secondary)

While this approach is a deliberate attempt to change the school culture, it is one that that had been seen to work primarily through structures and hierarchy to achieve its purpose. This contrasts with other less impatient approaches to embedding, which embody a view that it is a longer-term cultural shift. Changing habits of thinking about learning was seen as needing a more extended time frame, although advocating patience creates a tension in relation to the quality of current pupils' experience.

Along with the horticultural metaphor, mentioned earlier, other metaphors used to describe the process of cultural change had a culinary reference – 'the bubbles in the oil'. A learning how to learn approach was 'constantly bubbling away'. Embedding was depicted as a slow simmering – a constant informal presence in the background of school life:

There's very informal stuff going on in the staff room, people talking about things. I was photocopying this morning and someone said, 'I've tried this technique and that really works.' So there is that sort of thing going on and I think it goes on a lot and I think that's because in the school there is a learning culture here.

(Sally, co-ordinator, Hawthorn High School, secondary)

In another secondary school the co-ordinator described the ongoing nature of the process as 'change and develop and adapt and change and develop and adapt'. This suggests a gradualist approach, seeking to develop beliefs and practices together and iteratively (see the discussions of learning in Chapters 1 and 2), as against a more explicitly behaviourist approach which holds that hearts and minds will follow in the wake of being required to behave differently.

Although structural and cultural approaches may be portrayed in stark theoretical contrast, in practice, there was a considerable degree of common ground among schools in the adoption of strategies which used committed leading teachers to move the school forward. In head teacher and co-ordinator interviews there were frequent references to 'the thinkers', 'the innovators', 'the change agents', and the 'champions' whom heads rely on and 'use' to foster a climate of change. In some cases these people enjoyed no formal status but, more commonly, they occupied a middle leadership role. In secondary schools, departmental heads or departments as a whole were seen as spearheading change. The leading edge departments, or 'those at the sharp end', tended to be seen as those that had been involved most centrally in the National Strategies, offering a core of changed practice and modelling which extended outward to other departments.

Not all schools, however, focused change initiatives at departmental level. Some schools set up cross-departmental teaching and learning groups or working parties to develop and test ideas, devise policies, feed back to senior leadership teams and lead professional development. Some groups included members of staff with no formal status, for example, newly qualified teachers, who were seen to have the commitment and enthusiasm to take new ideas forward. While these accounts contain a hint of a welcome for diversity and challenge to the everyday practice, the latitude for 'dissent' or radical reappraisal of mainstream orthodoxy tended to remain a more open question. (These issues are discussed in greater depth in Swaffield and MacBeath, 2006.)

Lessons for leadership

Responses to the policy context and approaches to embedding reveal the nature of leadership – an issue that was infrequently addressed in interviews but disclosed in the sub-text. Leadership was thought about in two main ways: as residing within the province of the head teacher or senior leadership team, whose singular vision carried staff with them; or as more dispersed forms of leadership in which initiative was exercised by a range of staff. The following two quotes, one from a secondary head, the second from the head teacher of an infants school, illustrate the different conceptions about the exercise of leadership:

> This policy has got a lot of me in it. It's largely me . . . That wasn't from the staff, that was from myself . . . It was quite brutal. It was tough. It was me.
>
> (Brian, head teacher, Hawthorn High School, secondary)

> I have always believed in bottom-up management, I've always believed that the whole team has something to say and I think there is nothing worse than working for top-down management where nobody has any input.
>
> (Nell, head teacher and co-ordinator, Oak Infants School)

Yet despite this polarity of approach to leadership both schools engaged fully with the project, and, as attested to by questionnaire responses and in interviews, had made considerable advances both in their thinking and reported practice. It may be tempting to attribute the different styles to types of schools (secondary and infant), or to the gender of the head teachers, but we found no consistent pattern across all the schools. Nor did we find evidence to suggest that 'strong leadership' needed to be highly visible, 'brutal' or 'tough'. (A case study of an approach to strong leadership in Hawthorn High School can be found in Chapter 7.) One secondary school co-ordinator referred to the leadership wisdom of the deputy head, seeing embedding strategies as coming 'through his vision of how to take things forward as a whole school', a vision that was realised in a quiet, unassuming manner. This resonates with the findings of Collins' (2005) extended study of corporate leadership, which found strong leadership to be characterised by self-effacing modesty combined with a passion for the health of the organisation.

There were frequent references to leading by example and modelling of behaviour. For some this was quite subtle, but other approaches to modelling were more explicit and directive, such as 'modelling hopefully great lessons through our training'. In this school, staff training sessions were structured around objectives, starters and activities catering for different learning preferences, and a plenary for feedback and evaluation, holding up for emulation by all an exemplary model of what a lesson should look like.

A number of heads and co-ordinators found that leading by example, listening to and acknowledging differences, and adopting a 'softly softly' approach, were not in themselves sufficient. One school co-ordinator found 'pushing from behind' (as she put it) could often prove frustrating. Having described herself as 'very much a person who likes to keep a reasonably low profile', she went on to acknowledge that she had learnt a need to sometimes be a 'louder, pushier person'. This resonates with accounts from others, both primary and secondary, who found that their preferred style of encouragement, persuasion, consultation, and expecting desired practice to simply evolve, did not always result in desired change throughout the school: 'General reminders and putting articles under their nose will not make it happen. To make it happen, I have to be more demanding of the people around me and more specific in my expectation' (Judy, head teacher, Willow Park, secondary).

Engaging the whole staff rather than just the enthusiasts, and so impacting on all pupils, was a challenge faced by many leaders, particularly in the second and third years of the project. The response in a number of such schools was a change in leadership style to become more directive, effecting a cultural shift aligned with structures which engaged everyone in the embedding of an LHTL approach. For example, a number of secondary schools started with working groups consisting of volunteers, or carefully chosen teachers, who tried out new approaches in their classrooms, perhaps contributing to the formulation of a new policy. Subsequently, everyone was required to participate in a series of workshops or department meetings focusing on LHTL.

School leaders found themselves having to deal with a tension between teachers' autonomy and the desire for consistency, while respecting the entitlement of all pupils. One response was for the senior leadership team to establish parameters, or principles, to which everyone was expected to adhere, while allowing some freedom within them. Such structurally mandated change does, however, create resistance and head teachers found themselves having to find ways to deal with dissent, which tended to be seen as reactionary rather than informed and an opportunity for creative debate.

In contrast to the expectation that teachers would adhere to a prescribed set of principles and procedures, there were school leaders within our sample who expressed the belief that you cannot force people to change, and indeed that a directive approach could be counter-productive.

> I don't think we can impose things on people. If you say, 'You will do this immediately', the people . . . who are less co-operative, who are stuck in their ways, are just going to pull down the shutters and you are not going to get what you want . . . If you start by being dictatorial they don't respond because they have all these other pressures . . . That sort of approach to management . . . evokes this culture of people in corners bitching and arguing about it.
>
> (Helen, co-ordinator, Deodar Primary School)

One source of challenge and informed 'dissent' were the project critical friends, one attached to each school, who were able to act as mirrors to 'the way we do things around here'. The intention was that they should help schools move forward in their thinking and practice. The next section discusses what we learned about their roles and impact.

The role and impact of critical friendship

As Chapter 2 explained, one of the aims of the project was to consider issues associated with 'going to scale' – how an innovation could be spread among many schools without intensive support and intervention. A defining feature of critical friendship within the LHTL project was its 'light touch'. Each critical friend, a university academic, had a half-day per term for each school for the first two years, and moved to a 'response mode' only for the third year. Each critical friend was initially attached to three or four schools, although personnel changes resulted in some of them taking on more schools as the project progressed.

Critical friends brought with them a variety of previous experiences, for example as a critical friend within other projects, as a researcher, as a former local authority adviser, or as tutor on initial teacher training courses. Each came to the task with their own conceptions of their role and body of skills. Their key remit was liaison between the schools and the universities and, together with the project's contracted researchers, who collected most of the data, they were the face of the project within schools, encouraging commitment, engagement, reflection and critique. It was generally critical friends who conducted the initial whole-school presentation about the project, and in some cases they also led subsequent training using project workshop materials. They fed back data from analysis of the baseline questionnaire, usually to the school's senior leadership team, with the intention that the findings would inform the focus and direction of future development. This was intended to encourage critical reflection on the findings and discussion of how they fed into the school's plans for taking forward LHTL. Another of the tasks of critical friends was to help school staff make the connections between the three 'levels' of the project – classroom, school and networks. A number of the critical friends, when interviewed about their work, stressed the importance of listening, which forced the schools' co-ordinators to formulate and articulate their ideas. The analogy was the sounding board, or mirror, to aid reflection: 'a kind of sounding board . . . Someone who will listen to you while you formulate your ideas . . . Hold up a mirror to another person in terms of their practice or ideas so that they can examine them critically' (critical friend).

There was general agreement among the critical friends that a key element of the role was asking questions. One commented that, 'Critical friendship for me is asking the right questions at the right time.' The 'right' questions were perceived as those that probe, have a critical edge, or provoke thinking – qualities also acknowledged by school co-ordinators: 'She [the critical friend] asked a lot of critical questions that made me think a lot deeper than perhaps I had' (Janice, deputy head teacher, Aspen Infants School). These conceptions align with an aspect of Costa and Kallick's definition of a critical friend as someone 'who asks provocative questions' (1993, p. 50).

Other elements of the role commented upon by critical friends include: to 'present an alternative interpretation of the evidence'; to compare practices with underlying principles or statements; or to raise awareness of contradictions.

> I asked for some examples and then I fed back to them about the extent to which I didn't think it was fulfilling the kind of things that we were saying about questioning in relation to assessment for learning. It was trying to help them to see what they were doing against the principles that underpinned assessment for learning.
>
> (critical friend)

Another critical friend spoke of raising school colleagues' awareness of contradictions, a reference to the concept of double-loop learning with which we framed learning how to learn at school level. Critical friends also assisted school developments by providing co-ordinators with relevant materials, literature and web sources, and shared practices and approaches from other schools.

> [The co-ordinator] expressed interest in the ideas that underpin the project so I made sure I fed her articles: have you read this? Have you read that? And there were times when we met we'd kind of engage in a conversation about the sense she made of the articles . . . So I think the role of the critical friend is to continually remind them where these ideas come from. They're not just things that have . . . come out of the ether; they're evidence informed.
>
> (critical friend)

Through analysis of the interviews with critical friends, school co-ordinators and the web-based logs, we were able not only to gain insights into the activities of critical friends within the LHTL project but, more importantly, into the affordances and hindrances to critical friendship – which in many cases proved to be two sides of the same coin. A common understanding of the role, shared by school co-ordinator and critical friend, including the limitations and possibilities, aided the relationship. However, the context of the project added additional elements (such as project liaison and initial training) to what would normally be considered the core of critical friendship (asking questions, providing data, stimulating reflection). At the same time the light touch conditions limited the critical friends' activities quite significantly.

The involvement with schools was often more sustained by other people connected to the project, particularly local authority advisers who were able to provide training, support and facilitate networking with other schools. The researchers, who conducted in-depth interviews with key school personnel and observed in classrooms, were often afforded a better view of the school and its key decision-makers than critical friends. Indeed, both researchers and local authority advisers were viewed, by some teachers within the project, as critical friends, although they were not formally designated as such. This created tensions for the designated critical friends and school co-ordinators alike, with some critical friends, for example, concealing their sub-stantive and training expertise, and some co-ordinators not knowing how best to use their critical friend, especially in the third 'response only' year.

Trust, an essential condition for successful critical friendship, was both assisted and hindered by the fact that the critical friends were university personnel, a number with international reputations. Some schools were initially very excited to learn that they were to have 'x' as their critical friend, anticipating that they would benefit from considerable contact with that person, but then found that the relationship was very circumscribed. For others the perceived high status of the universities, and a perceived mismatch in power, proved problematic.

The limitations on the critical friends' time allocated for each school constrained the quality of their activities as well as frequency of contact. It was difficult for them to build up detailed knowledge and understanding of the school, the practices, personnel or issues, which limited their ability to engage in detailed discussion, questioning or critique. Some critical friends felt constrained by not having access to classroom practice, or having to couch their questioning in general rather than specific terms. The large geographical distances involved, and the tight structuring of many schools, meant that critical friends were unable frequently to 'drop in', which would have helped build up their knowledge of the school, while at the same time they would have become more of a 'familiar face around the place'. In many respects the advisers, who were the project's co-ordinators at local authority level, were in a better position to do this although their time was often equally circumscribed by financial considerations.

Despite these constraints, critical friends were in some cases able to provide the challenge that really assisted a school in learning how to learn. However, the 'light touch' characteristic, which meant there were minimal opportunities for critical friends and school colleagues to work together, restricted very considerably the contribution of the critical friends. It seems that there is a limit to how light a critical friend's touch can be, yet still be effective. In the 'real world' where resources are limited, the question is whether creative ways can be found to provide critical friendship of sufficient quality to make it worthwhile. In her more detailed discussion, Swaffield (2007) argues that the recent introduction in England of School Improvement Partners for schools, may be inadequate to meet this need.

Conclusion

Embedding learning how to learn at classroom, school and network level was a highly ambitious project, embarked on in a policy climate in which there were increasing demands on school staff, together with raised, and often inappropriate, expectations of school leadership. The tensions between the performativity agenda and the agenda of change implicit in LHTL were to provide a running theme through the project. The questionnaire responses to the factor we described as a 'performance orientation' were highly revealing in the direction of the gap they exposed between what teachers said they valued and what they said they actually did. They valued making learning explicit, learning autonomy and collaborative work, although to differing degrees, but, as interviews revealed, believed that such aspirations were not easily achievable within current constraints.

Yet within these tight parameters, schools were generally successful in moving thinking and practice forward. Not unexpectedly, impact varied widely among schools, dependent on their level of engagement with the project, the support of critical friends (in different guises), the demands of Ofsted and other sources of immediate pressure. Perhaps most significantly it was the quality of leadership which made LHTL a widely shared, and genuinely owned priority for teachers. While this was brought about in very different ways it was ultimately down to a school's capacity to create space for school staff to reflect on and share aspects of their practice; to engage in a new form of learning discourse in and out of classrooms. Taking such practices forward so that they align with teachers' values, particularly those relating to promoting learning autonomy, appears to be the key long-term challenge for organisational change of the kind that supports sustainable innovation in the classroom through LHTL.

Chapter 5

Learning through networking

If *all* schools are to develop new practices, such as those associated with assessment for learning (AfL) and learning how to learn (LHTL), they need to move away from sole reliance on methods of professional learning that involve teachers working in close physical proximity with one another. Chapter 4 focused on how schools develop their own strong internal communities; here we consider how these communities can benefit by developing networks and networking. We propose that learning how to learn, in this context, involves: learning to network; recognising the existing networks of people who work in schools; and actively promoting the building of such networks. This applies in relation to networks and networking *within* schools, and to networks and networking *between* schools.

As part of our study we investigated the role of electronic tools in networking. We found that electronic networks are not well used in relation to knowledge-creation and knowledge-sharing by teachers, but we are optimistic, as were our project schools, that one day they might be important.

Context

During the lifetime of the LHTL project, educational networks became the subject of much discussion, nationally; indeed, considerable funding went into their establishment, most notably through the establishment of networked learning communities (NLCs) supported by the National Centre for School Leadership (NCSL). The experience of these

* Authored by Robert McCormick, Alison Fox, Patrick Carmichael and Richard Procter

NLCs was drawn upon by the DfES Innovation Unit in setting up Primary Learning Networks, and by Hargreaves (2004) in launching networks of secondary schools through the Specialist Schools and Academies Trust. All these initiatives were taken *after* we had embarked on our project, but before we completed it. Before this time there had been so little research on school networks – our project is, we believe, the first substantial study – that we incline to the view that the imperative to implement ran ahead of the production of the empirical evidence that might properly inform such innovation. The argument for school network development tended to be based on literature from the business world, and especially IT companies, on the assumption that their experience would transfer, broadly, to the school sector (see Hargreaves, 2003a and 2004).

At an earlier point, while we were developing our project proposal, the government created Virtual Education Action Zones (VEAZ), to allow schools that were dispersed over a large geographical area to work together. The funding for this initiative went in part to provide ICT resources to the schools and to enable them to use these for collaborative work. We deliberately included schools from one of these VEAZs in our sample so that we could investigate electronic networking although, as the work progressed, we became interested in networks and networking more generally, which is the focus of this chapter.

Networks as a basis for knowledge-creation and sharing

In Chapter 1 we noted the use of a range of metaphors of learning (see Box 1.2), and, in Chapter 2, we remarked on the importance of the 'knowledge-creation' metaphor when discussing teacher learning. This metaphor is helpful when thinking about situations where experienced teachers develop new practice, and ideas about practice, as in the area of assessment for learning (AfL). One element of such development is what has been called 'networked expertise'. As Chapter 2 indicated, this concept takes us beyond individual teachers and schools, to consider how their expertise can benefit from the world outside the school. This is not a new idea, as the examples below indicate.

Examples of networking

Example 1   Relationships developed from various events

Two deputy heads, in different local authorities, after meeting on more than one occasion and for different reasons, found they had many things in common. They decided to develop a professional relationship:

Deputy head: We're very interested in how they're doing it. They're very interested in how we're doing it, so vice versa . . .

Researcher: How did you find out about that, and how were you starting to communicate?

Deputy head: Well, that was through email; mail, phone, meeting, and attendance at another event, then at an LHTL [project] event . . .

Researcher: So you met in another context too?

Deputy head: Yeah.

(Ben, co-ordinator, Mulberry School, secondary)

Example 2   Talk in the spaces of formal meetings

Researcher: So are the gaps [spaces] between things as important . . . as the agenda and the formal aspects of the meeting?

Head: Yeah, I think so because . . . it's often those set meetings that are the points of contact that generate relationships that can spin into other areas of interest and so on and so . . . we might find it could even come up in the formal business of the meeting that, say, a school has had a certain approach to something and you just flag it up and catch that a bit later and say, 'I was interested in that, could I come and have a look?', you know, 'Can we have a talk about it?'.

(Alan, head teacher, Hebe Church of England
Primary School)

Example 3   Opportunities afforded by formal presentations

I go out to talk about school councils to other schools and always mention learning [how] to learn in the presentation that I do, which often gets people thinking, 'Oh, what's that then? – never heard of that'. And of course that just raises awareness.

(Daphne, co-ordinator, Oak Infants School)

Example 4 Picking up ideas at conferences

A school co-ordinator (Kate, Juniper Primary School) talks of staff who, returning from a conference, say:

> 'Oh, we went to this conference and this was suggested and it's really good, and some of us are going to go away and try it.' So we have had little pockets of teachers trying things out . . . especially in areas that haven't yet become part of the whole-school approach.

She also noted how things picked up might feed into staff development.

> We've had a couple of people going [to conferences] and then they've come back and they've done an INSET after that. We've fed back to the whole staff as well. So you're bringing in different ideas and different perspectives.

Example 5 Visits to other schools

> I have got an AST [advanced skills teacher] teacher and she is making all sorts of contacts in local schools that are hers, but are relevant to the rest of us because she brings back ideas.
>
> (Amy, head teacher, Dove Tree Community
Primary School)

Most of these examples will be familiar, and unremarkable. However, they illustrate some important elements of school networking, and indeed networks:

- They are usually based on face-to-face contact, or at least start that way.
- They can involve informal contacts, even at formal occasions.
- They can take the form of just a mention, or a one-way communication, at a presentation or conference.
- They can be from an external expert.
- They can be from a visit to a school.

As we will show, these all relate to important dimensions of networking and networks. First, though, we explore what is special about the idea of a network.

Why networks?

Most professional development for teachers involves teachers working together. At its best, as the evidence in Chapter 4 suggests, this involves collaboration, especially work in one another's classrooms. Some people (see Veugelers and O'Hair, 2005) view networks as based on groups of teachers from different schools meeting regularly and working together on common problems. These form the communities of practice, mentioned in Chapter 1 (Box 1.2); their members learn together by participating in joint activity. The 'participation metaphor' of learning is relevant in this context. In this chapter, however, we especially want to explore what networks and networked expertise might have to offer to 'knowledge creation'. There are good reasons for this, relating to the practicality of involving all schools in knowledge creation and sharing.

Chapter 2 emphasised how important it is to have innovations that can be scaled up for all schools, not just those that benefit from large inputs of external support or resources. Under the many pressures facing schools, only a minority of teachers are likely to be prepared to get involved in intensive and regular work with teachers in other schools. Trying to do this within one school can be difficult enough. Even where teachers are willing, there are practical difficulties and costs involved. One of the networked learning communities (NLCs) that we studied decided that it would enable all its teachers to visit another teacher in another school within the network. It funded this from a budget allocated by the National College for School Leadership (NCSL), but the cost was sizeable for even one afternoon's visit for every teacher from nine primary schools and one large secondary school. (Interestingly, the secondary school was funded to allow its teachers to visit one another within the school.) Even this level of provision was not enough, however, because many teachers did not have the time to make arrangements to visit another school. Eventually the NLC appointed an administrator to arrange the visits. This illustrates the point that when external funding is not present, it is unlikely that worthwhile initiatives, of this kind, can be sustained. However, it is also important that schools are able to benefit from external contacts and expertise, and to overcome isolation, even when they feel they are expert because, as Wenger *et al.* (2002, p. 149) point out, a strong sense of competence can lead to an unbending commitment to established canons and methods. Here, again, there is a dilemma to be faced and a tension to be resolved.

What are networks and what is networking?

We use a modification of an existing definition of networking to clarify the nature of networking and networks: 'The . . . establishment and use (management) of internal and external links (communication, interaction, and co-ordination) between people, teams or organisations ("nodes") in order to improve performance' (van Aalst, 2003, p. 34). This captures three important elements of a network: the nodes, the links and implicitly the 'traffic' that flows through these links. Links involve communication, interaction, and co-ordination. Not all networks are complete or bounded, which suggests that they should not be seen as 'entities'. For example, a teacher or a head teacher in a school will be part of a variety of networks, some formal, and related to their job, and some informal and perhaps related to their social or non-school life. Looking at networks from the perspective of the person (the subject) within them, rather than attempting to examine them as objects from an external viewpoint, is described as taking an 'ego-centric' view of networks. This is the view we took in our research.

The NLCs, mentioned above, are manifestations, in England, of current ideas about how school networks could work. These communities were set up to link a group of schools around a common focus, such as AfL. A number of LHTL project schools joined such NLCs shortly after the start of the project, which gave us an opportunity to study them. One approach might have been to analyse the links among all the teachers in such an NLC, assuming that together they formed a complete network. However, this was impractical, so we chose to look at particular individuals' ego-centric views of their personal networks. These revealed, not a single network, but various perceptions of multiple networks woven across the NLC.

The evidence from innovative companies in the field of business indicates that external networking is important (Hakkarainen *et al.*, 2004). But so too are internal networks and networking, where developing a community might be more feasible and appropriate. This was the case in Juniper Primary School, one of our project schools (see Example 6 below).

Another example of networking

Example 6 Juniper Primary School

This is a small school with explicit policies to develop the kind of community that reflects the collaboration indicated in Chapter 4:

> I think as a collective body, we're all responsible for each others' professional development in a way, aren't we? We kind of all feed into it and, especially for my role, I've been very responsible for their professional development.
>
> (Kate, co-ordinator, Juniper Primary School)

> I think [the buddies] are a supporting role [and are] a way in which we have actually promoted that, so that [policies] bed in faster than if people are just left to sort of think about it. But then there are still things that every so often you throw up and you think, 'Oh, we thought they had understood that and they haven't', so you then have to go back and say, 'Actually, we do it like this, you know' and you have to not be frightened to say that.
>
> (Barbara, head teacher, Juniper Primary School)

This sense of community extended to all staff, including new and supply teachers, teaching assistants, parents and indeed pupils; for example, pupil voice was emphasised through a school council. As part of our data collection on networks, we asked the head teacher to draw a map or picture of what, and with whom, the school communicated. Barbara had an above average number of internal links, compared to other heads (see Figure 5.1), although she drew numerous external links also. Together these indicated a strong sense of an internally-engaged, yet outward-looking, school community based on trust.

Networks and social capital

Hargreaves (2003b) highlights *trust* in his ideas on social capital, which we discussed in Chapter 2. To reiterate:

> Culturally, social capital is the level of *trust* between head and staff and among the staff, between staff and students and among the student body as a whole. Structurally, it is the extent and quality

of the internal networks, such as networks of teaching teams as well as informal networks of friends. A school that is rich in social capital has a strong sense of itself as a community, but also has many external networks with ties to other communities.

(Hargreaves, 2003b, p. 8)

As Hargreaves points out, both internal and external networks and networking matter and the two dimensions need to be balanced. On the one hand, a school that only considers the outside links is in danger of under-rating the difficulties in communicating, internally, any externally gained knowledge. This was made clear to us in secondary schools (or large primary schools), where external networking was extensive. For example, in one secondary school the LHTL co-ordinator admitted that, although the school had teachers who were recognised nationally for AfL practice (i.e. who were important in the school's external links), there remained problems in spreading good practice throughout the school. The problem lay with internal networking; the group of teachers promoting AfL in the school did not have sufficiently strong links to the heads of faculties, who could support and promote change.

On the other hand, notwithstanding the importance of internal networking, a preoccupation with internal links can reduce the outward-looking nature of the school. This can limit experience of new practices and inhibit the creation of new knowledge because there is too little challenge to the status quo (a point made in relation to critical friends in Chapter 4). We had respondents who depicted their school's communications with very few, or sometimes no, indication of external links.

Hargreaves' point about the importance of external networks is therefore relevant to our argument, although we are less sure that it is 'ties to other communities', as such, that matter. We found that few schools mentioned 'communities' in their depictions of links external to the school, except where they were the 'local community' such as a local ethnic community, or other schools. They were more likely to mention individuals or groups or agencies, mostly designated by role (see Fox *et al.*, 2006, for a detailed account).

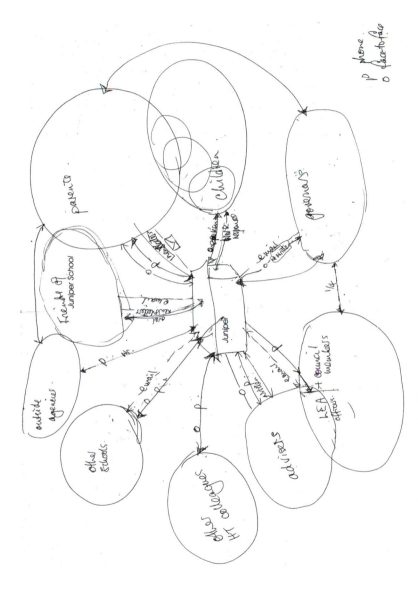

Figure 5.1 Map drawn by the head teacher (Barbara)

Box 5.1   An introduction to network theories and their investigation

Castells (2000) is a major network theorist, although his focus is on networks involving new technology. He provides an important classification of layers of networks that include electronic elements. The first layer is the electronic network itself: what we might call the *electronic map*. Layer 1 describes the electronic connections and how various servers, server systems and exchanges, inter-relate and switch electronic traffic around. The second layer is concerned with mapping networked resources such as web pages: what we call the *information map*. This offers the potential to make resource discovery more efficient and effective. This is the kind of analysis that *Google* uses for its search engine. A third layer is concerned with the use of the network by actors and groups: what we would call the *actor map*. Who people turn to for advice or ideas on practice is an example of this.

The most common form of analysis relating to networks is social network analysis (SNA), which focuses on the third level – the actor map. This is a general methodology based upon the study of the relations among a set of actors. It focuses on the relationships between actors and not their attributes. (An international network for SNA can be found at http://www.insna.org/ – accessed 20 January 2007.)

The most usual form of SNA is the *complete analysis*, which typically can be used for a company. Companies are often regarded as bounded networks. In these settings everyone in the company can be asked to give information on their relationships with others in the organisation. Palonen *et al.* (2004), for example, asked all the members of a Finnish telecommunications company to describe the nature of the relationship they had with all other people in the same company. They asked the following questions to express this relationship:

- Who do you go to for advice?
- Who do you go to for new information?
- Who is the worker with whom you are having discussions outside work-related matters, who you have trust in?
- Who is a collaboration partner of yours?

From this they were able to draw diagrams that illustrated the connections among people in the organisation, and in particular which people were well connected and who less so. From such data, and interviews with the individuals, a variety of network concepts emerged that allowed the network to be analysed in terms of the nature of the networks and their likely effectiveness.

See McCormick and Carmichael (2005) for a further discussion of network theory.

LHTL and networking

Chapter 1 discussed what learning how to learn might mean for pupils, indicating that, although it was possible to see it as a second-order family of learning practices, it had to be closely related to the process of learning 'something'. Chapter 4 developed this idea further with reference to 'double-loop learning', which is, in a sense, the organisation's second-order learning. In this chapter we push this idea further again and ask what LHTL might be in relation to links among schools, or with other external people and bodies, in relation to networking. We examine this question by considering:

- how individuals learn to network;
- how schools and school leaders learn to recognise networks and create networking opportunities;
- how schools can think about the resources that might flow around a network (the traffic);
- how networks of schools are created.

In our view, all these aspects contribute to learning how to learn in and through networks and networking.

Learning to network

Two characteristics of LHTL, related to metacognition (discussed in Chapter 1), were 'knowing what you know' and being aware of your learning processes so that you can self-regulate, i.e. plan what to do next and evaluate and revise strategies. In networking terms this would mean trying to understand when networking is taking place and what might be possible to learn from the various kinds of links. Some of that learning will be through teacher collaboration and work in a community of practice, as in the following example of a head teacher describing the links between a Beacon school and partner schools:

Head teacher: Now we're more clear that the purpose of these links is to bring about improvement here and in other places. That's the purpose, and then sustained links, where there's a focus on changing classroom practice, are the way to go. Therefore deeper links over a longer period of time are more important than . . .

Researcher: And deeper in what meaning?

Head teacher: Deeper in the sense we maintain the contact over a longer period and the focus is on the classroom.

(Ed, head teacher, Redwood High School, secondary)

This contrasts with links that led to teachers at a presentation (in Example 3 above) to 'pick up on AfL' through a one-off, almost casual, link. Certainly linkage was not sustained, or made with people who were known, and only an 'awareness' was communicated. Similarly, at a conference, a teacher might hear an idea or an example of practice and take it back for further work with colleagues at school (Example 4 above). Thus, LHTL with regard to networking means recognising the *strength* of a link, and understanding that a link that is neither well established nor intense – what we would call a *weak link* – can nevertheless be useful. Thus hearing a good idea from a national speaker at a conference is a *weak link*, but it can lead to important developments of practice through, for example, inspiring teachers to act.

In contrast, *strong links* are reciprocal and allow complex, context-bound, and tacit knowledge to be exchanged (see Table 5.1 for a comparison of strong and weak links).

Strong links are illustrated in the context of an NLC, where sustained groupings are formed across schools:

[T]he links that are being established between a very small research group, who kicked off the assessment for learning thing, then the link between them and the teaching and learning styles group has just really grown in strength . . . then that's just kind of gone over to heads of department meetings because we've actually got a lot of heads of department representing their department at the teaching and learning styles group now, more than ever. At one of the last meetings I counted up how many people who attended the meetings were heads of department and it was high. Whereas it's not intended to be that; it can be anybody. It doesn't matter what their experience is . . . but the fact that when you compared the make-up of the group from, say, a year ago to now, heads of department kind of wanting to come to that group . . . So from this small core thing to, then, the teaching and learning styles group, and then that's having an influence over other areas of the school. That's really important.

(Alice, co-ordinator, Redwood High School, secondary)

Table 5.1 Comparison of strong and weak links (adapted from Hakkarainen *et al.*, 2004, p. 75)

Characteristics	Strong links	Weak links
Information flow	Reciprocal information	Non-redundant and often asymmetric information
Nature of knowledge exchanged	Usually complex	Simple and accurate
Form of knowledge	Often non-codified or tacit	Often codified
Relationship to the knowledge environment	Context-bound, i.e. a part of a larger knowledge structure	Often context-free and independently understandable
Type of communication	'Thick' and encapsulated, including chunks and expert terms	'Thin' and easy to understand

Our respondents, who recognised both strong and weak links, also distinguished between the *strength* of links and their *value*. They suggested that there were strong links that were of little value and, more significantly, weak links of high value. For example, low value was attributed, by leaders in a primary school, to links with government agencies with respect to a raft of recent initiatives. Kate, the project co-ordinator at Juniper Primary School, articulated this idea of value:

You can have a strong [valued] link with somebody that you don't have a quality relationship with. I think it's probably just maybe the role . . . there's also an element within yourself of satisfaction, isn't there? Which links you find the most satisfying.

This idea of value is important in learning about networks and networking, because evaluations of the value of links enable teachers to make strategic decisions – by becoming aware, teachers may choose to develop different kinds of links. The value of weak links stems from their ability to introduce new ideas (to overcome the 'established canons and methods' referred to earlier), and to make connections to other people, which may lead to closer, strong ties eventually. Such links might therefore be for information (Castells' layer 2) or about relationships (layer 3). The following account of a meeting of head teachers shows how both can occur:

We'd get a school or a head teacher or a maths subject leader to come up and talk about what they've been doing in their school and so that has led to situations where somebody may have then approached the person afterwards and said, 'Well, just tell me a bit more' or 'Could I have a copy of . . .?' or 'Can I come and pay a visit?' and so on.

(Redbridge local authority co-ordinator/adviser)

This provides an 'LHTL agenda' for continuing professional development (CPD) in relation to networking by highlighting the need to become aware and cultivate network links of a variety of kinds (of strength), and to be clear about which are most valuable. Learning *about* networks, and *to* network, are both important and involve the acquisition of cognitive understanding and learning to participate (Sfard's, 1998, two metaphors of learning – see Chapter 1). Those who study innovative IT companies that create and share new knowledge, have argued that this agenda should also be part of the curriculum for pupils' learning (Hakkarainen *et al.*, 2004). Here we are arguing that it should be part of teacher learning too.

However, learning about networking and through networking, extends beyond individual teachers. Hargreaves (2003b, see the quotation on pp. 95–96) indicates the importance of the social capital of a school's staff, which he argues can be used to mobilise its intellectual capital. We consider this collective aspect below.

Learning to recognise networks

As we pointed out earlier, a school does not have a single network, rather it, potentially, has access to all the networks that individuals have, both personally and as part of their role in school. Thus, leaders need to take an *ego-centred view* of networks if the school is to benefit from the social and intellectual capital of all its members. This means finding out about individuals' views of the networks that are important to them. These may include the school as a network, any organised network of which the school is a part (such as an NLC or local authority cluster), and all the personal and unique links that individuals possess (and are willing to talk about, for there are issues of intrusion and privacy to consider).

Our evidence tells us that the networks of individuals may differ considerably, even when they work together. For example, we had two respondents from the same school whose representations of their school's network(s) did not coincide, even though there were common elements. Reasons for such differences may include their experience of different network links or because they inhabit different roles and therefore perceive them differently. (Later we discuss how such representations are obtained.) If head teachers are interested in exploring networks, the first ego-centred view they might examine is their own.

Informal links and networks

A common element in head teachers' networks is informal contacts made at formal meetings (see Example 2 above). (Fox *et al.*, 2006, and Carmichael *et al.*, 2006, provide more detailed accounts of the theory and evidence on which the following discussion is based.) Some of these informal links are built up over long periods of time in a school or a local authority, as indicated by Hilary, a head teacher: 'I think just the fact the people you know. I mean at least three of the heads here have been my deputies. So . . . you keep in contact with people, they phone you, you phone them' (Hilary, head teacher, Deodar Primary School). These are *embedded links*: embedded because they are personal and involve friendship. Another example was a set of informal links formed round a group that played football:

I have actually established a whole link and group of friends through playing football basically. Obviously the more formal meetings too, but the informal discussion that goes on has been far more productive . . . because you basically tend to be like-minded individuals sharing my views.

(Sam, head teacher, Alder Primary School)

In this case, school roles and formal events were not necessarily important. More usually, however, head teachers build links with one another in *affiliation networks*, which they are then able to use when they need help:

I would then ring people and ask, 'What do you do with so and so?' or you know, 'Have you ever had to deal with whatever?' . . . Yes, it is partly because I have been around for a while so that I probably know most of the longer standing heads reasonably well.

(Barbara, head teacher, Juniper Primary School)

Being aware of these links and networks is only one consideration. Links and networks need to be sustained and activated, even created, if that doesn't seem too instrumental a view of how social relationships are handled. Our study of particular schools, such as Juniper Primary School, where we were able to investigate the networks of both a head teacher and an LHTL project co-ordinator, indicated important differences in their informal networks. When someone is given a role, such as a co-ordinator of an activity with relationships outside of the school, they will of course have existing links and networks, especially if they already have a leadership role (e.g. as a deputy head teacher). Ken, from Beech School, illustrates this:

Actually there's a couple of other informal things which have started recently which I'm finding very useful which are just informal discussion groups . . . where there are four either deputy heads or assistant heads who are in a similar position to me, and we meet once a half term just to discuss various issues . . . I find those really useful, listening to people who are trying to tackle the same sort of problems that we are trying to tackle here.

(Ken, co-ordinator, Beech School, secondary)

They will also find new links that come with the role, especially if they are linked to a project like ours or to other initiatives from outside the school. Thus the LHTL co-ordinator in Juniper Primary School was able to build new links (see Figure 5.2), which were different from those

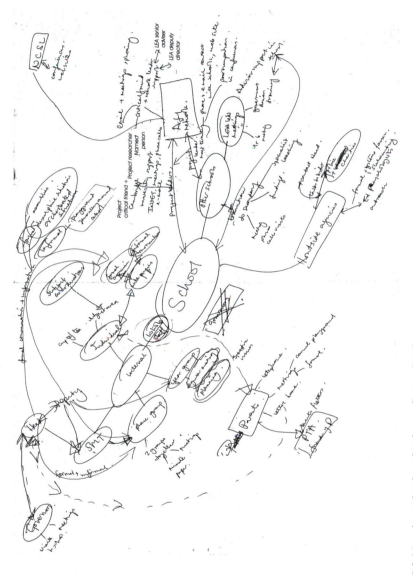

Figure 5.2 Map drawn by the school co-ordinator (Kate)

of her head teacher (see Figure 5.1). She had to develop these links and was able to use them to help the school. This was aided by the school's membership of an AfL NLC, which helped her to establish and maintain new links beyond the school's internal networks, giving her a greater range of resources and expertise upon which to draw.

By linking the school to new networks, the co-ordinator at Juniper Primary School formed a *bridge* from the school to these networks and other external sources of expertise. This is a familiar function fulfilled by any teacher who goes out of school to a meeting, inservice activity or conference and reports back (as in Example 4). This form of bridging tends to be relatively passive, although it will involve some active selection of what to report. Head teachers do this kind of selection routinely with information and materials that come into the school. In the case of the LHTL co-ordinators in project schools, the bridging was to expertise, ideas and practice. The co-ordinator at Juniper Primary School, for example, saw her role in the AfL network as *mediating* between school and the network. She was able to list a range of individuals, their roles as participants, leaders and 'supporters' of the NLC, and the media used to maintain communications with them. She also identified NLC events as a basis for establishing links with other schools; here she could 'pick things up from other schools' and feed them back to her colleagues. Sharing was reciprocal, as she indicates in the following statement (referring to two elements of AfL practice – see Box 1.1 in Chapter 1): 'So we've presented stuff about the "success criteria" . . . and shown some of the practice that we've done and . . . things that have worked . . . or that haven't worked. We did the same with "feedback"' (Kate, co-ordinator, Juniper Primary School). These sorts of developments gave the school access to expertise and practice within the local network (the NLC), but also to the NCSL, which organised the NLCs. Similarly, Kate bridged to those involved in the LHTL project.

Sometimes the bridging is not at the level of relationships (Castells' layer 3), but at the informational level (layer 2), for example, through collecting a list of names and telephone numbers of key people. These contacts to key people involve more than list-making, however; they usually embody personal or role links that can be activated to gain more information for the school. The person holding the information therefore has a *gate-keeping* role. The following quotation provides a detailed account of a school-based gatekeeper (the head teacher) 'bridging' with a gatekeeper from an external agency, which led to further links and new practice:

I had pretty much a social conversation with [Johnny Stanton, local authority co-ordinator who went on to join the NCSL] that this was an area of interest. [Johnny] obviously latched on and was very enthusiastic, and that provided us with some contacts which we . . . hadn't known about and out of it all we have opened, of course, the links with the National College [NCSL] . . . We used it to run our own programme in induction week, which we are currently reviewing for next year, so we've now got our own school-based induction policy . . . And this has been now taken on across the borough.

(Brian, head teacher, Hawthorn High School,
secondary)

Thus the school and the NCSL benefited, not just by a particular idea, but by many different opportunities and ideas that could result.

Although we discovered that networking by electronic means, for professional development purposes, was little used in LHTL project schools at the time of our study (see Carmichael and Procter, 2006, for a full account), there were instances of the use of electronic tools as gateways or portals to information elsewhere (Castells, 2000, layer 2). There was also evidence that future possibilities were being explored. For example, one local authority co-ordinator (in an NLC) explained how her local authority was trying to stimulate the actor layer by adding a photograph and some biographical information to the list of names and telephone numbers on its website.

Differing conceptions of *brokers* and *brokerage* (bridging, mediating and gate-keeping) give us a way of representing roles and activity in school networks. Our analyses of such representations reveal categories of broker that are often neglected in the literature on schools. For example, in contrast to writers who attribute this kind of activity only to local authority personnel (for example, Fielding *et al.*, 2005), we are able to show that individuals within schools, such as head teachers, can act as brokers. We have also been able to show that individuals who have a role in relation to work outside the school, such as the school's LHTL project co-ordinator (or indeed the co-ordinator for an NLC), can create a range of links. Such links come from what network theorists call *intensional networks* because, although they reflect personal and social networks, they are set up deliberately and managed purposefully. (The odd spelling is intended to indicate an element of tension in any such network.) These intensional networks contrast with those of most head teachers, which are also personal, but rely on embedded links that are built up informally (not intentionally) over many years of attending meetings, and other events, where they meet other school leaders.

We know from the literature on networks in other kinds of organisations and sectors that these different kinds of links, networks and network roles are important in knowledge creation and sharing. If schools are to create and share new teaching practices, and knowledge about such practices, they also need to know about, and cultivate, networks and networking of the kinds described here. Head teachers could usefully reflect on how they can give *all* teachers opportunities to network, so they can create the intensional networks that will supplement their own embedded links, and those of the senior management team. (This would be a reflection of the networking factor, identified in analysis of the staff questionnaire, discussed in Chapter 4.)

Mapping networks

An important step to becoming aware of, and perhaps developing, links and networks is to represent them in some tangible form. We asked head teachers, school co-ordinators and local authority co-ordinators who were part of the project to draw their networks (Figures 5.1 and 5.2 are examples). We asked them to do the following:

• Show how you visualise the networks your school/local authority/ virtual education action zone is involved in.
• Show with whom all communications involving the organisation are made, and how they are made.

We provided prompts to help our respondents make the drawings as complete as possible and to ensure they indicated how the communications were made. This left the form of the visualisation open, which stimulated a wide variety of what we called 'network maps'. For some respondents this activity proved difficult, but everyone was able to draw a map. Some of our respondents indicated that they found the exercise useful and they looked favourably on the possibility of using it in their schools. (See Fox *et al.*, 2007, for an account of the design and use of this mapping technique. The tool is available for schools to use in James, M. *et al.*, 2006b.)

One head teacher saw the potential to use knowledge of informal links for the benefit of the school:

> Now our staff connect with a huge number of other schools informally. Their partners work there, or their kids go there, or

their best mate used to work here but now he's moved on and he teaches somewhere else . . . I guess we've received a significant amount of informal information in schools as a result.

> (Nick, head teacher, Beech School, secondary)

Asking staff to reveal these informal networks might of course not be in the best interests of individual teachers, so it is important to be clear about issues of confidentiality and privacy. Our respondents were mindful of the ethical implications and said they would need to be very clear about the professional purposes, which they would discuss with all the staff likely to be affected. If agreements can be secured, such an activity might be worth exploring because asking staff to produce a network map is one way of obtaining information about links and knowledge sharing that could be useful to the school.

Using resources

In the last analysis, the value of networks and networking rests on what 'flows' along the links. We have drawn attention to material resources but, in many cases, it is ideas or reported practices that flow. Our investigations revealed that it was mainly these orally communicated 'objects' that were exchanged. We found few examples of physical resources being shared. Local authority co-ordinators told us of electronic mechanisms they were setting up for the creation and exchange of such physical resources, but we found no evidence of this in schools. Nor was there much evidence of schools sharing resources directly, although this was beginning to take place towards the end of the project. Perhaps the following is characteristic of schools:

Head teacher: I don't document it, no. I don't write anything . . . oh, I suppose I should . . . No, just pick up ideas, and I come back. We worked really hard to develop the curriculum co-ordinator, curriculum leaders, and that all came through the collaboration with [name of another school co-ordinator] up the road, because it so happened that through talking, we were both working in the same direction at the same time, and you think, well, why are we both doing this separately when we could work together . . .

Researcher: So what's happened as a result of that?

Head teacher: Well, we've now worked together, we've got almost a
                joint action plan, we've got a joint development day
                organised next term between the two staff, run by
                someone who's going to work on subject leadership.
                (Dave, head teacher, Goldenrain Junior School)

Such observations reinforce the finding we mentioned earlier about
the predominance of face-to-face communication. There may be little
trading of materials or documents, but trading ideas developed in
schools was much more widespread.

Despite our efforts (we created an area of the project's website for
sharing 'practice knowledge'), and the efforts of local authority co-
ordinators, there was little evidence of interest or capacity to produce
accounts of practice, other than through members of the research team
'capturing' these as data. One local authority person, responsible for a
web presence, expressed our collective hope:

> Well, I'm sure your research project will show that . . . I know the
> bits that I'm involved in certainly will, because that's particularly
> what we're interested in. So we're going to go into our schools
> and look at pieces of practice, identified by people who want to
> share that practice and then we're going to look at ways in which
> we can make that shareable.
>   (James Noon, webmaster, Redbridge local authority)

Creating networks

As we indicated at the beginning of this chapter, initiatives designed
to create networks, for instance, those promoted by agencies such as the
NCSL, the DfES Innovation Unit, and the Specialist Schools and
Academies Trust, often presume that electronic resources will play a
prominent role in facilitating professional knowledge creation and
sharing. However, our investigations of electronic networking practices involving schools in one VEAZ and NLCs, indicate that schools
make little use of ICT as part of the collaborative work of teachers
(although they may use these resources for other purposes). This is not
to say that NLCs are unsuccessful; in other respects they make a large
impact, most notably by helping schools to work together productively.
In a competitive policy climate where there are few incentives for
schools to collaborate, this is a significant achievement. Whether this
collaborative activity will be sustained, after the end of funding, remains
to be seen.

In at least one of the NLCs we studied, the head teachers deliberately created common activities and shared staff (e.g. an ICT technician was shared by all the schools, which was especially important for the primary schools). They also used funds to provide a networking infrastructure, of which the administrator for school visits, noted earlier, was part. So this NLC might be expected to have a commitment to continue, although, as we indicated earlier, it will not be easy to afford a large-scale school visiting programme. This notwithstanding, there will surely remain a need to develop 'organised' networks in the ways discussed in this chapter.

Networking as part of continuing professional development

We suggested earlier that networking, and the value of networks, should be promoted as part of the professional development of all teachers. We discussed the identification of the strength of links and, indeed, the importance of weak links to assist the creation of new knowledge and practice in schools. Subsequently we considered the importance of informal links and informal networks, and brokers and brokerage, and argued that these too can be added to the agenda for professional development in relation to networking. Our evidence suggests that building on network links and encouraging networking will help schools create new knowledge and practice in ways, discussed in Chapter 2, which will help tackle the problem of scaling up and spreading innovation.

Will electronic tools and processes ever be part of this? Elsewhere we have argued that there is much to be done (Carmichael and Procter, 2006), although we found some positive indications of potential. The LHTL project developed a sophisticated website for multiple purposes: to provide a public interface; to facilitate the storage of, and controlled access to, data generated in a large, physically dispersed team; to enable communications between researchers and participants and to disseminate development materials and research outputs (see http://www.learntolearn.ac.uk). A strong motivation for investing in this web presence was the hope that it would stimulate interest in web-based means of creating and sharing practice knowledge. Of course, use of a particular resource cannot be mandated; getting across the point that such resources can be helpful for development purposes is more important. Moreover, direct links to other schools, rather than mediated by universities, or other such agencies, can have the greatest credibility with teachers:

> We actually recently found another school, [name] Primary School
> . . . and I have looked up their website and they have got a fantastic
> link on there for Learning to Learn and it mentions all about
> Learning to Learn and what it looks like in their school. And the
> school sounds just like this school.
>
> (Daphne, co-ordinator, Oak Infants School)

This co-ordinator recognised the potential of a school website to inform
others (including governors) about the work of their school, and clearly
saw it as way forward. Others see the same for electronic conferencing,
where teachers can hold discussions:

> That's now been launched so internally we now have a FirstClass
> [a propriety form of software for conferencing] email system –
> now it works . . . and so now staff here are now tuned in to
> *FirstClass* email . . . what we're not yet doing I think is *FirstClass*
> conferencing . . . I don't see much of that going on.
>
> (Nick, head teacher, Beech School, secondary)

A condition for successful creation and spread of AfL and LHTL ideas
and practice must be that learning how to network becomes a goal of
professional development. In the world of the twenty-first century, the
use of electronic resources should be part of this. However, there is still
work to do to convince school leaders of this.

Conclusion

An agenda for developing teachers' capacity to create and share
new LHTL ideas and practices, through networks and networking,
needs to recognise the various strengths and the value of links that
teachers make. Awareness and development of informal links
are particularly important, although this needs to extend beyond
the embedded links familiar to head teachers. Of considerable significance are *intensional networks*, based on personal and social
networks, but developed in a deliberate way, by staff who have been
given a specific role that permits external networking. With suitable
protection for individual privacy, schools could benefit from
mapping these networks and using the information gleaned in a
purposeful way.

Finally, we express optimism that, despite the current reluctance of teachers to use electronic networking, this could become part of continuous professional development as society in general becomes more ICT networked. However, the particular barriers that confront teachers – they spend most of their days working with classes, rather than sitting at computers – need to be recognised and strategies found to deal with these circumstances.

Chapter 6

Case studies of LHTL from primary schools

This chapter illustrates how key themes and issues, which were identified across our sample of schools, emerge and are interconnected
in individual infants and primary schools. (Chapter 7 does the same
for secondary schools.) We found many schools endorsing the central
importance of promoting autonomous or independent learning
but grappling with the challenge of finding the best relationship
between beliefs and practices, principles and procedures, when trying
to move things forward in the classroom. They also struggle with
the dilemmas and tensions that arise when teachers attempt to
innovate in what is often perceived as a constraining performance-
orientated environment. Teacher learning is recognised as crucial
so professional development is a key role for leadership teams.
Encouraging collaborative teacher inquiry focused in classrooms, and
finding strategies to facilitate 'double-loop learning' at school level,
is challenging and demands the development of cultures and
structures of support. Again, whether the creation of structures should
come before the development of cultures, or whether they develop
iteratively, is a source of variation in school management ideals and
practices. Building organisational capital, both intellectual and social,
is a key to embedding and spreading innovation, and the need
to understand, develop and exploit formal and informal network
links, within and beyond the school, is part of this. These insights and
puzzles stimulate schools to rethink the roles and tasks of leadership.

These themes from the different levels of our research – in classrooms, at school level, and from the study of networks (explored in
Chapters 3, 4 and 5) – come together in the experience of individual

* Authored by Mary-Jane Drummond, Mary James and David Pedder

schools. Our case studies explore some of the ways in which these themes interrelate. For this reason, they are case studies of themes or issues from schools, rather than 'complete' case studies of schools. The lack of space, in this book, to provide a comprehensive account of development in each school also led to this decision to focus on themes. These accounts have been 'validated' by the research team and we believe that the different content, structures and 'voice' of these studies give them authenticity, variety and interest.

The three case studies in this chapter are therefore very different. The first is essentially the story of one teacher's trajectory of development over the course of her engagement with the project. It tells of struggle and doubt but great capacity for critical reflection in search of principled practice to benefit children's learning. The second case study illustrates how long it may take to develop the organisational structures and a culture for embedding learning how to learn practices and expectations in the thinking and behaviour of both pupils and teachers throughout a school. And the third case study, of a 'successful school' according to performance measures, explores the various influences that may have contributed to that success and concludes that there is likely to be no single 'cause', although the effect of increased networking for sharing ideas and spreading practice is particularly marked.

Janice's story: the possibility of change

This is a story that illustrates how some teachers can negotiate and begin to break free of what we (following Ball, 2003) have described as the performativity culture in which they practise. A teacher of particular interest is also the project co-ordinator in her school, and her case is worth considering at some length. Janice, the deputy head of Aspen School, a one-class entry infants school, teaching children of 5 and 6 years old, is almost painfully aware of the difficulties she faced in learning to be a LHTL teacher. Her story tells of the constraints and compromises she had to negotiate, the compromises that seemed to be forced upon her, and the questions that participation in the project threw up.

In an early interview, Janice articulates some of her firmly held beliefs about learning, including the centrality of 'learning by doing', the key concept of 'meaningful purpose' and the working principle 'thinking is more important than knowing'. She describes the 5- and 6-year olds in her class as 'natural learners', who have been learning since they were babies; she argues that much of their earlier learning in the Foundation Stage was characterised by choice, control and self-motivation. She emphasises the value of child-initiated activities.

As she discusses the transition from the Foundation Stage to Key Stage 1, she expresses some of her doubts and uncertainties:

> Does it actually help them learn if they are sitting how you want them to sit?

> I don't know how whether they are learning about learning or they're learning what I'm telling them.

> Looking at the children and thinking whatever we're doing isn't working and thinking this is not right for them . . . I think we feel in a rush . . . and there's not enough time to talk to the children or to think about how they are going to learn best; it's all been about what I'm going to teach them.

She goes on to distinguish between two different kinds of learning. The first is the learning for which outcomes or intentions can, and should, be clearly stated in advance: 'I have to be very specific about knowing what they are going to learn.' But she also describes the learning that goes on in an investigation: 'where we don't know what the learning outcome is going to be'. This distinction is clearly rooted in her classroom experience and her knowledge of children, but it sits unhappily alongside the structures of target-setting and specific learning intentions that uncomfortably shape her teaching and assessment practices.

In a later interview she makes another distinction. On the one hand, she describes children's self-motivated learning: 'they will try over and over again to do something that they have set their mind on doing'. On the other hand, there is the learning that the teacher initiates – 'that may not have that same intrinsic value' – when children are 'expected to learn the things that the teacher decides'. To support this latter kind of learning, Janice and her colleagues do their utmost to make their learning objectives clear and explicit, using the acronyms WALT (We Are Learning To . . .) and WILF (What I'm Looking For). These acronyms derive from the work of Shirley Clarke (1998, 2001) in promoting formative assessment in primary schools. They feature frequently in the practice or conversation of teachers in LHTL primary schools – all three of the case studies in this chapter make some reference to them – although the project team did not explicitly introduce these specific ideas. Indeed, we were somewhat concerned about their potentially prescriptive interpretation; see also Janice's comment below. However, the fact that teachers make links between LHTL project ideas and others is interesting because it shows how teachers attempt to make connections between the various initiatives to which they are exposed.

The videotapes of two of Janice's lessons show her use of these techniques and the post-lesson interviews with the children show that this is a familiar routine: the children remember the learning targets that have been set for them, and make realistic assessments of their progress in meeting them. But Janice is by no means satisfied with this procedure, even though it is clearly congruent with what we have called the 'letter' of AfL:

> I think the whole process of giving an objective and saying to the children if you do this, you will learn it, it is too simplistic . . . it's like a child said today, 'Well, I'm sad because I haven't hit the target.' And you almost feel that you're letting that child down, because you're saying this is the objective, if you do this, this is what I'm looking for, you will achieve it. And learning isn't like that.

Janice's dissatisfaction, her nagging doubts about the effectiveness of her chosen strategies, led, in time, to a change in her practice. The objectives she specified at the start of a lesson gradually changed from focusing on content/knowledge (capital letters and full stops, for example, in literacy learning), to objectives relating to thinking, creativity, developing ideas. At the end of the calendar year in which her lessons were observed, she moved to a headship in another school and marked the occasion by writing a reflective account of her experience of the LHTL project, coolly appraising her own learning as well as the impact on her pupils:

> The advantage of sharing specific objectives is that it helps children become more aware of what teachers are trying to teach them or the kind of learning that is required. The disadvantage is that learning does not happen in this simplistic way.

She explicitly connects this problem with her recognition of what she calls the difference between shallow learning and deep or profound learning: an issue she has been worrying about for some time. For example, in one post-lesson interview she ruminated on 'the difference between being taught something and actually learning it'. But Janice is an indomitable spirit, a dedicated learner, and the following account, given in her end-of-year review, shows her facing up to some important questions. She is beginning to formulate answers to some of these to her own satisfaction:

> How can teachers meet the demands of the National Curriculum while still focusing on the needs of children as learners? How do you teach children who do not necessarily want to learn the things you want to teach them at the time you need it? The LHTL project has helped me work through these questions. Sharing the 'big picture' with the children, involving them through the use of mind maps to clarify what they already know and what they might like to learn, making the learning explicit *but also* recognising that it can also be diverse and unexpected, helping children talk about the language of learning, and to recognise what kind of thinking is required for different activities . . . enabling children to pose questions so they can make sense of the world in which they live.

A few months later, however, Janice watched, for the first time, the videotape of the lesson that had, certainly, demonstrated many assessment for learning (AfL) techniques or procedures. She was shocked. But, generously, she recorded her reactions in writing, in a moving passage of stark self-criticism and trenchant analysis. She concludes: 'this lesson was a prime example of how specific learning objectives can hinder learning'. Along the way to this conclusion she identifies a number of aspects of the lesson that, she ruefully remarks, 'made uncomfortable viewing':

- the unequal ratio of 'teacher talk' to 'time for children to think';
- the tightness of her control: one track, one intention;
- how specificity drove out flexibility;
- how the push to 'improve' stifled versatility and improvisation;
- starting at the wrong end of learning, pre-empting the outcome, rather than offering the broad experience and articulating the variety of outcomes at the end of the session.

This short piece of critical reflection, which cannot have been easy to write, shows Janice moving on in her thinking. She seems to be making connections between the underpinning principles of her pedagogy and the ways in which they are (or in this case, are not) translated into practice, in terms of the tasks and activities she offers children. She is committed to the LHTL principle of making learning explicit, but is coming to realise that some kinds of specificity are the wrong kind. The value of making learning explicit depends on what kind of learning is required by the task. Some tasks make little personal sense to the students; some tasks have no meaningful purpose; some tasks close down on divergence and individual interpretation. Most significantly, some tasks make the wrong demands on learners – remember, repeat and apply by the book – rather than: interpret, understand and apply for yourself.

Janice is equally committed to the principle of creating learner autonomy, but is coming to realise that this principle requires the teacher to design tasks that treat children as trustworthy agents in their learning: capable of selecting resources and strategies; capable of making their own meanings and interpretations. The wrong kind of tasks align with the factor identified in analysis of the LHTL staff questionnaire (see Chapter 4) as 'performance orientation': they stimulate the display of the desired behaviours (objectives, targets, and so on), but preclude the need to ask or explain why these behaviours are desirable. Furthermore, some tasks prioritise meeting the success criteria over understanding, over individual interpretations, or personal acts of meaning-making that promise divergence and variation.

In another fascinating text, written in August 2004 (i.e. two and a half years after her involvement in LHTL began), Janice looks back on her experiences as LHTL co-ordinator, classroom teacher and now head teacher:

> All the reading and learning from the project has helped me to recognise what is happening to me during the learning process . . . has helped me to think about what it is like to be a learner . . . I think this is why the Ofsted model and QCA [Qualifications and Curriculum Authority lesson schemes] are not enough. To simplify learning into 'this is what it looks like and have you achieved it?' denies the human element.

She continues to brood about the human, emotional dimension of her own learning, and the difficulty, even pain, of working outside the comfort zone: trying to do things differently. She is moving towards what she calls a more holistic approach to learning: 'Learning connects my mind, body and soul to understanding . . . as teachers we search for wider understanding of the whole person.' She contrasts her present understanding with the WALT/WILF approach: 'knowing what something should look like or what you should do does not mean you can do it'. She is close to rejecting explicitly the practices associated with the performance orientation factor: 'Are the models which we try and help children aspire to becoming too simplistic, based on skills and techniques?'

This last question brings us back to a central dilemma: there is no 'quick fix' to be added to existing practice, to create a LHTL classroom overnight, as it were; but equally, there is no future in presenting teachers with general principles without also offering ways of translating them into everyday practice. Which comes first? A change in mind-set, beliefs and values? Or a change in practice, new skills and techniques? For Janice, the problem of putting principles into practice seems to have been worked out within both spirit and the letter. And now, two and a half years down the line, Janice is realising that there is still thinking work to be done in bringing letter and spirit, practice and principle, closer together. She is, however, by no means despondent; her thoughtfulness is resolute, her voice cautiously optimistic. She has not lost 'the love of looking at children's learning', which she says was generated by her involvement in LHTL. She is steadfast in her aspirations: 'my agenda is the children's learning,' both for herself, and for the whole school community: 'I want to make a learning community here.'

Janice's account of her development is evidence of the difficulty of finding that delicate balance between adopting techniques that will affect practice and engaging with the principles which underpin them. But it seems clear, as argued in Chapter 3, that simply to present teachers with a list of strategies is insufficient to bring about the kind of change promised by AfL. Beneath the surface of techniques, such as peer assessment or sharing the criteria with learners, lie deeper principles. Unless these are engaged with, teachers are limited both in how they develop their practice and how they adjust that practice if the techniques do not appear to bear fruit. The experience of Janice seems to indicate that negotiating between the underlying principles of AfL and its procedures is an iterative process, more chicken and egg than a clearly defined sequence.

Promoting LHTL at Hazel Primary School: a longer process than anticipated

Hazel Primary School caters for over 300 boys and girls aged between 4 and 11. There are eleven classes: five in Key Stage 1 and six in Key Stage 2. Few pupils have minority ethnic backgrounds and there are fewer still with English as an Additional Language. Betty Jane Miller, the head teacher, and LHTL school co-ordinator, is an experienced head teacher. At the time of the project there were eleven teachers and nine learning support staff at the school.

Attainment patterns, over the course of the project, were below the school's expectations. As Table 6.1 shows, raw performance scores, aggregated across English, maths and science, show Hazel School ahead of the local authority (LA) and national average in each year of the project. Indeed, there was a marked increase between 2003 and 2004 and again in 2005. However, value-added scores, reveal a rather different picture. (These contextual value-added scores take account of pupils' prior attainment, and a range of pupil and school contextual indicators, and are calculated by comparison with all maintained primary schools nationally.) These scores were lower than expected across the duration of the project. In value-added terms Hazel School achieved a percentile rank of 73 for English, 50 for maths, and 61 for science.

Promoting learning how to learn at Hazel School turned out to be a longer journey than expected. Although it was a journey taken together by staff, there were different starting points; not everyone moved at the same pace, or necessarily in the same direction. Progress was patchy and there were no easy solutions. This is a brief story of struggle and challenge. We start with the question of what learning how to learn meant to staff and pupils.

Table 6.1 Hazel Primary School: year-by-year comparisons of aggregated Key Stage 2 Level 4+ percentages in English, maths and science

	Hazel School	LA	England
2002	251	237	234
2003	254	239	234
2004	261	237	237
2005	267	244	240

Note: The aggregate is defined as percentages achieving the expected level (Level 4) on each of the three core subjects (English, maths and science) giving a maximum percentage of 300.

Making sense of learning how to learn: viewpoints of the head teacher, teachers and pupils

From Betty Jane's point of view, LHTL entailed fostering independent learning among pupils with learning as the focus of reflection and discussion among pupils and between pupils and teachers. She spoke in terms of 'talking about and reflecting on learning and finding ways for children to articulate what they know and what they need to learn next in their learning and it's that creation of space to allow that to happen'.

LHTL was also about,

> [T]aking charge of your learning. It's about being in control of it and taking responsibility for it and it's about changing that view, that Mary James started off with at the beginning of the project about pouring in [knowledge to children's minds as if they are empty vessels to be filled]. It's about changing that, and helping learners, whoever they are within the school community, not just pupils, but principally I suppose it works through pupils, to have a view of where they're going. There was that wonderful quote at the beginning [from the initial Inset, see James *et al.*, 2006b, p. 15] about being on the ship and not being . . . you know, that children are in a sense only concerned with what's for dinner at the moment. They haven't got a view about where the ship is going and that's where we need to get them . . . It is moving from being done to, and being told, to sharing with someone who can facilitate for you, and moving on in your own learning. And it's about engendering that desire to learn.

These views were echoed in the interviews with a number of teachers and Year 6 pupils. For example, this pupil emphasises the focus on the 'how' of learning: 'it's about learning how you learn . . . And like how you think and like, um, how you know that you're learning.' For another pupil, it was about thinking what he could do, as well as what he found difficult: 'and when I think about what I can do, it improves my confidence'.

Most pupils focused on opportunities for sharing ideas about learning with their peers and developing a heightened awareness of their strengths and weaknesses as learners. Teachers, too, tended to speak about LHTL in terms of increased reflection on learning: 'It gives the children an opportunity to think about their own learning . . . they're more conscious about their learning.'

One teacher aimed to help pupils think more about both the purposes and processes of learning activities in class by 'making sure that they've understood the learning intention, making sure that they know what's expected of them during the lesson and that they can evaluate it and reflect on it at the end'.

From the head teacher's perspective, Betty Jane spoke about the challenges posed in a performance-oriented environment:

> But I think it's very, very hard with the constraints of the curriculum that you have now and knowing those end results with SATs [national tests] and so on, to actually keep that going. And the pressures that children have on them to attain and achieve in an area like this, where there is a lot of parental pressure but not necessarily parental support. There's a lot of pressure to achieve but not necessarily support in the kinds of ways that will enable it. So a lot rests with us.

Nevertheless, the focus on helping pupils become more 'articulate and aware of how their learning is taking place' was the reason why Betty Jane agreed to participate in the LHTL project. She said that:

> [the project] will give us an opportunity to focus on the feedback that children get and the ways in which children can be involved in their own learning . . . It will sharpen up assessment practice . . . It will help us by focusing on what more able children do well by talking a lot more, and reflecting on learning and finding ways for children to articulate what they know and what they need to learn next in their learning. And it's that creation of space to allow that to happen and I want it to enable us to find a kind of structure within lessons.

Leading: a journey taken together

At the beginning of the project, Betty Jane expressed principles of leadership that reflect a commitment to inclusive and collaborative approaches to decision-making and developing practice through team-work. She values the expertise and know-how of her staff at all levels and is ready to incorporate their insights and ideas in the development of policy. She is committed to a view of Hazel Primary as a learning school and is keen to develop a culture of experimentation and risk-taking in which teachers and pupils explore different ways of promoting

LHTL practices. Her approach grows out of a strong personal identification with norms and practices of co-operation and collegiality
underpinned by recognition of the need to have the right people on her
staff team:

> I view my role as a head teacher very much as a kind of facilitator,
> as a means of bringing people along together with me. I'm not a
> dictatorial kind of person. I'm very much a co-operative, collegiate
> kind of operator and I suppose this whole ethos has come through
> by sharing ideas with people and feeling that the staff I have
> with me – and I have appointed all my staff except one – are people
> who share my views and my vision. And there are times when you
> have to be very brave, if you like, in terms of recruitment and about
> what teachers we're prepared to have in school and being very
> brave about accepting that maybe we won't have them if we can't
> find the right sort of people.

Collaboration among teachers was promoted through three small teams
of teachers: a Key Stage 1 (Year 1 and 2) team together with a Year 3
and 4 team and a Year 5 and 6 team. Teachers plan, share and develop
teaching practices and ideas in these teams. It is through the sharing
of ideas and practices, questioning, struggling together to find the best
way to frame different problems, and then working together to find
solutions to them, that Betty Jane sees staff putting the principle of
teacher interdependent learning and relationship-building into practice.

> Hazel is a place where we're all here to learn, and we're all learning
> from each other, and we haven't all got it . . . It is very much about
> exploring and taking, in a sense, a journey together. And
> everybody's got things to learn from everybody else in a variety of
> ways.

At the heart of Betty Jane's account of Hazel as a learning school is a
careful balance between openness to change and consistency:

> [T]he school has to be open-minded, it has to have a certain amount
> of freedom but it has to have good underpinning structures that
> people can work with and understand. It has to have consistency
> and teamwork. And I think with those things it can deal with change
> and it can deal with implementing new ideas and changing things.
> But there has to be that underlying agreement about how things

are, about how teachers plan, how they teach, the kind of things that they are going to acknowledge and work with children on.

Whole staff meetings and the teams were the key structures for supporting capacity-building, staff development, and decision-making within this inclusive and collaborative culture.

LHTL at Hazel

Betty Jane talks about Hazel School in inclusive terms: 'valuing people within our team' and 'everybody feeling that they have an important part to play at Hazel'. Yet running alongside this was: 'a sort of uncomfortable feeling that people have about taking risks, about trying things out . . . I can detect times when people feel worried and feel frightened about taking things on board.'

Betty Jane's approach to leading and co-ordinating the development of LHTL throughout the school emphasised local starting points, with individual teachers, rather than a whole-school approach. This is characteristic of a leadership approach that aims to listen, and to be responsive to teachers, rather than telling and directing from the top down.

> It was very much an encouragement, but leaving it to individual teachers to choose their line of practice in relation to learning to learn . . . At Hazel, we try and take everybody from the point that they're at and travel onwards, and to open up debate and to allow all the views to be heard, so that we hope with everybody on board, at whatever point, they feel that they can do that . . . I felt that it was a really big step forward to be taking towards this understanding about how we learn and how learning to learn can benefit everybody. And then it was pointless assuming that everybody was just going to be automatically able to do things that actually I think require a lot of depth and understanding.

Betty Jane was keen to point out, at the end of the first year, that leading LHTL involved processes that were marked by ambiguity and uncertainty: developments that needed more time to work through into practice than initially expected:

> All of these things take a great deal longer than we'd anticipated. I think when we started out, and it's like the start of any project,

you kind of think, 'Well, here we are, we're launched on this, and somewhere along the line we will be able to see X, Y and Z.' And it's much more fuzzy than that. It's much more grey. There are certain things you can pinpoint, but it's not throughout the school. I suppose the journey, as it were, is not quite as straightforward as we might have thought it was from the outset.

The complexity she speaks of is linked to her approach of devolving the initiative to individual teachers:

And there are lots of reasons for that, not least of all the fact that we didn't actually start out by saying everybody will do whatever. It was very much about people wanting to explore certain areas. We started off with reviewing the marking policy because we wanted to look at feedback particularly. But from then on nobody was obliged to go down any specific route. So it really was a question of taking up ideas and thoughts that people have read about, obviously things that inspired. This is the work on assessment, particularly Shirley Clarke and Paul Black and Dylan Wiliam. All of those, but none of them specifically.

They used the project workshops, downloaded from the website, as a way of exploring strategies for promoting LHTL. Progress in developing practices in the classroom during the first year was slower than expected with different teachers taking LHTL forward at different speeds and at different levels of confidence:

And we've learnt that it isn't done very easily and that it takes time. And I think that, although not all staff have actively been involved in trying out some of the strategies and ideas that we initially talked about, the feedback from those that have has influenced those who have been more tentative.

Whole-school perspectives

At the start of the project the research team administered the LHTL staff questionnaire (see Chapter 4). These survey data allow us to compare staff perceptions of practice with their values and provide a useful whole-school perspective for understanding conditions considered important for promoting LHTL at Hazel School. They also allow us to compare Hazel's scores with the average scores for the other schools in the project. These comparisons help us to identify similarities and differences between levels of practice and values at Hazel and at other project schools. These scores are summarised in Table 6.2.

In broad terms, the responses of staff at Hazel are consistent with the perspectives expressed by the head teacher and show a staff and head teacher in touch with one another. The tension Betty Jane had discussed in relation to fostering greater independence and depth of learning, while at the same time ensuring curriculum coverage and examination preparation, is reflected in the large negative value-practice gap score of −17.6 for 'performance orientation'. This shows that levels of practice for 'performance orientation' were perceived by staff to be a long way ahead of their values. Thus, one thing appeared clear at the outset of the project: there was a marked inconsistency between perceptions of classroom practice and professional values at Hazel.

Staff viewed the promotion of LHTL in the classroom as a tough challenge. This is also reflected in the values-practice gaps for 'making learning explicit' (8.3) and, more markedly, for 'promoting learning autonomy' (19.0). Here reported practice lagged behind what they thought was important. Systems of support and encouragement among staff were expressed in warm collegial relations outside the classroom. However, low practice and value scores for the 'inquiry' group of professional learning practices support the view that there was little collaborative learning and experimentation in classroom lessons.

In fact, Betty Jane commented:

> We've got to create not only time for discussion, but time for observation . . . It can only be through time investment and with people working together, coaching if necessary, people learning from each other. So people who feel confident about it working with people who don't feel confident.

At the end of the first year, she was still wrestling with the problem of a lack of collaboration among teachers in classrooms:

> What we could perhaps have done – again, there's a money implication which I think we couldn't probably have dealt with – was to provide opportunities for people who have not felt that they could take any of these ideas on board yet . . . to go and see how it works with teachers, like Lily and Sarah, who have really incorporated it into their teaching approaches. And I think rather than just hearing about what people are doing, those that are not quite so confident, not quite so happy about trying things out, they need the opportunity to go and see.

Table 6.2 Hazel Primary School: staff responses to 11 LHTL factors illustrating practice and values scores and the gap between them (N =21)

HAZEL PRIMARY	Factor	Practice/ Value Scores	2002	All schools (average)	Value-Practice Gap: Hazel	Value-Practice Gap: all schools (average)
Classroom Assessment	Making Learning Explicit	Practice	76.0	80.9		
		Values	84.3	84.7	8.3	3.8
	Promoting Learning Autonomy	Practice	45.2	58.2		
		Values	64.2	69.6	19.0	11.4
	Performance Orientation	Practice	68.3	69.6		
		Values	50.7	53.5	−17.6	− 16.1
Professional Learning	Inquiry	Practice	56.5	58.7		
		Values	59.7	66.6	3.2	7.9
	Building Social Capital	Practice	76.4	79.9		
		Values	78.2	81.0	1.8	1.1

Dimension					
Critical and Responsive Learning	Practice	73.4	77.0	0.3	3.3
	Values	73.7	80.3		
Valuing Learning	Practice	96.5	90.1	−3.0	1.7
	Values	93.5	91.8		
Systems					
Deciding and Acting Together	Practice	66.6	57.6	13.2	22.3
	Values	79.8	79.9		
Developing a Sense of Where We are Going	Practice	75.5	69.6	7.8	12.5
	Values	83.3	82.1		
Supporting Professional Development	Practice	66.9	59.9	14.8	21.5
	Values	81.7	81.4		
Auditing Expertise and Supporting Networking	Practice	45.9	45.5	20.0	23.5
	Values	65.9	69.0		

Note: Practice and values scores were calculated on a scale 0–100. By the term 'values' we mean the importance that teachers attach to different practices for creating opportunities for pupils to learn. Practice scores were subtracted from values scores to give a values-practice gap score. Negative gap scores in the table mean that values are behind practices; there would need to be a reduction in levels of practice in order to bring such practices into line with teachers' values. Positive gap scores mean that values are ahead of practices; there would need to be an increase in levels of practice in order to bring such practices into line with teachers' values.

Returning to the questionnaire data, practice scores for the 'deciding and acting together' group of practices were a long way below levels of values, but clearly ahead of the levels of practice typically recorded by staff at other project schools. In common with most other project schools, perceptions of school management practices were behind values in all four areas listed in the bottom third of Table 6.2. Encouragingly though, levels of practice were ahead of average levels recorded for other project schools for 'developing a sense of where we are going' and 'supporting professional development'.

Wrestling with the challenges of taking collaboration into the classroom and developing practice across the school

Throughout the first year the focus in promoting LHTL had been on opportunities for both pupils and teachers to reflect:

> In the course of the first year I think at Hazel we have come to reflect a great deal more about children's learning. And we've done it on two levels. We've tried to enable children to reflect more, but we ourselves have tried to be more reflective. We've tried to understand, or to help children to understand what it is they need now in order to improve and to get better at whatever they're doing. And we have thought quite hard about how that can best be done.

However, there was little in-class collaboration between teachers as a way of developing the thinking into practice. During the second year of the project the promotion of LHTL remained patchy and inconsistent across the school. Betty Jane admitted:

> I'm conscious that the way we've done this could leave us with inconsistency. You have some teachers who've really taken off, and others who, you know, need structure or need support to take it on board.

Opportunities for pupils to develop LHTL practices depend very much on who the teacher is:

> I mean, certainly children who've been working with teachers who've been working more on the feedback issues are much more confident in talking about their work. And also, in talking about

what has helped them to learn those new things, or to achieve those things. But again that doesn't necessarily go throughout the school. It's still quite patchy at the moment.

However towards the end of the project there were encouraging signs that 'out of class' kinds of support among teachers were being augmented by increased lesson observations. Betty Jane claimed:

> We now have a lot of staff involved in observing each other, and we've shifted the focus now to looking at what children are learning . . . It has a much higher profile . . . And I think that's coming through the discussion, the development of people's understandings about learning.

At the end of the project, LHTL appeared to be changing behaviour and expectations of pupils in some classes at Hazel School. The challenge for the school continued to be how to develop systems and a culture for embedding LHTL more widely in the practices and expectations of both teachers and pupils throughout the school.

Eucalyptus Junior School: alternative explanations of success

This story is not a comfortable one for the research team but it allows us to analyse the conditions that enable innovation to flourish in a school, with only minimal support from a project, but with valued informal links with other schools. It also provides a basis for considering the role of different initiatives in overall school improvement, and the possibility of competing alternative explanations for a school's success. It illustrates the complexity of educational change and the dangers of attributing particular effects to single causes.

School context

Eucalyptus Junior School occupies a cluster of one-storey buildings on a site with a feeder infants school next door. The classrooms are light and brightly decorated, somewhat in contrast to its surroundings which, though not particularly deprived, feature a wide road, an open space with grass and trees, and uninspiring housing, a small shopping precinct and play area.

The school is three-form entry and caters for 7–11-year-olds, almost entirely White British, of which 24.3 per cent in 2004 had special educational needs. The school roll during the LHTL project was around 300 but steadily rising. In 2004, the school made a net gain of 18 pupils. This had not always been the case. In 1993, when the head teacher, Peter, was first appointed to the school, he discovered that the school was losing seven children from the feeder infants school next door to another nearby junior school. He recounted:

> The school over the way was three form infant, four form junior. Now the headteacher had not perfected cloning at that stage so it was obvious he was taking children from other schools. I was told by the senior accountant of [the local authority], 'I've looked at your numbers, you're going to have to lose a teacher next year.' And I said, 'Great that's a really nice thing to say to me. Just got the job and you're telling me that I haven't got a budget.' 'I am.' And I said, 'OK, watch this space mate. I haven't been appointed here to sit back and watch it decline.'

The competitive environment is an inescapable feature of context. There are 53 potentially competing primary and junior schools, from two adjoining local authorities, within a five-mile radius of the school. Parents watch the fortunes of the school in league tables carefully, not least because a selective secondary school system is retained in the area and about 50 per cent of parents opt to enter their children for the 11 + selection test.

In 1998, five years after Peter's appointment, the Ofsted inspection found standards 'to be average and progress satisfactory, with the need for some improvement'. Peter was disappointed by his apparent lack of impact and was galvanised into further action – with better results. In terms of raw performance scores, aggregated across the three core subjects, the school was ahead of the local authority and national average in 2002, 2003 and 2004. Value-added scores were also significantly higher than expected in every year 2002 to 2004, and across the three years combined, giving a three-year combined percentile rank of 11. The same was true for separate subjects, with the exception of English which rose to the top quartile in 2004. Ofsted inspectors, returning in 2003, found 'a very good school with some excellent features'. In these performance terms, Eucalyptus Junior School was the most successful primary school in our sample (see Table A2 in the Appendix).

The school participated in the LHTL project from 2002 to 2004, so it would be good to claim that this had contributed directly to the school's success. However, causality cannot automatically be inferred from simple association. We needed to be more sceptical and ask what role, if any, the project played in the improvement of this school. Was it crucial, or was it just part of the armour that the school put on in its fight to increase its success in a very competitive context?

The LHTL project in the school

The first recorded contact with the project team was in July 2002 when the school co-ordinator, Sophie, attended a meeting for school and local authority (LA) co-ordinators in London. Sophie was a young teacher with only five years experience. However, Peter was committed to the career development of young teachers and gave her a responsibility point to manage the project by liaising with the school's critical friend from the project team, attending meetings, feeding back to the school, getting people involved and sharing ideas.

The London meeting was intended to explain the nature of the project and the roles of the university-based critical friends who would support development in the schools, the LA co-ordinators/advisers who would provide local support, and the full-time researchers who would collect the data. The resources on the new project website were also demonstrated.

The next contact involved the researcher arranging to interview the head teacher and administer baseline questionnaires in November. Four months had elapsed since the meeting in London and Peter was increasingly concerned that the initial Inset day for his staff had not yet been scheduled. All staff training days had been planned for the remainder of the academic year so fitting this in was going to prove difficult.

Part of the difficulty had arisen from the fact that the critical friend (CF1) initially allocated to the school was prevented from joining the project because of other pressures. A second academic (CF2) agreed to work with the school but he hoped the web resources would play a significant role. He had many other commitments too and it was not until February 2003 that he found the space to deliver the whole-school Inset during an after-school 'twilight' session, shared with another local school. Given the pressure of time, he concentrated on explaining the research base. According to Sophie:

We got the theoretical side of things but we didn't get many of the practical suggestions at all. We got lots of research explained to us, which is interesting, but we're classroom practitioners, you know. What we wanted someone to say is, 'There are all these ideas in learning how to learn. Some of these ideas may help children to learn – may help children to be more aware of when they're learning' – and we wanted someone to say 'Well, you could try this. You could try this.' That didn't happen.

Meanwhile the researcher continued to work in the school during the 2003 spring and summer terms, especially with Janet, the enthusiastic and receptive Year 5 'focal' teacher whose lessons were observed. This enabled the researcher to establish a productive working relationship with the school.

Sophie attended another school co-ordinators' meeting in June 2003, to hear about progress and share ideas:

I was really enthused by that, although, a lot of the [LA] schools were frustrated, the same as we were because of circumstances. To hear the other schools and to hear what they'd been doing . . . was good. We got some ideas from them and that was motivating. So, you know, that sort of networking element . . . I've made contact now with Fir Tree Primary [in the same LA but not in the same catchment area]. I've sent them an e-mail and hopefully we will be able to work together on this and, whatever approach they're doing, we'll share and maybe share the workshop sessions.

Sophie had looked at the workshop materials on the website and wanted to use them but felt she needed a critical friend to lead them, for reassurance and credibility. It seemed that this was not to be. The LA co-ordinator decided to convene a meeting in July to see what could be done, however, no-one from Eucalyptus could attend because the school was about to be inspected by Ofsted. Everything stopped for Ofsted, as Sophie explained:

We came to the meeting in June in London and I was really enthusiastic again. Then we got the Ofsted envelope and I just felt that I couldn't say anything to anyone. It was the last thing on people's minds, to be quite honest. So it all went quiet again. So I was just waiting until September really so that we could get it all sorted out and get started again.

Feedback of the results of the staff questionnaire, administered the previous November, was also awaited. This was arranged for July but was also postponed. When CF2 left the project in August to take up a new post, the future of the project in the school looked dismal. Its first year had generated little more than guilt – all round. Then at the beginning of the new academic year things began to change.

A third critical friend (CF3) stepped in and fed back the results of the questionnaire data analysis to the school in September. Sophie wanted to follow up the possibility of working with Fir Tree Primary so CF3 offered to provide some money for cover so that teachers could meet. Two weeks later CF3 received an upbeat email:

> Hi!
>
> Just thought I'd let you know that Peter and I had a very productive LHTL meeting this afternoon. I gave him my analysis of our questionnaire feedback and we have identified some interesting issues. I am putting my analysis into a presentation to deliver in a staff meeting on 5th November.
>
> I also gave him my proposal for 'LHTL@EJ' this year and he was really pleased with it. This will also be presented to staff in the same meeting and will be put into practice immediately after that. I have attached my 'LHTL@EJ' file for your information.
>
> Just a point about the feedback – we felt that the 'Don't know' and 'Bad practice' responses would be better separated. This would enable us to determine whether we had an issue which could be dealt with by educating (don't know responses), or whether we would need to change ingrained perceptions (bad practice responses).
>
> By the way, I posted my 'Smile/straight face/frown' idea on the website this morning!

So Sophie, with the help of Peter, had decided to seize the initiative and set up a rolling programme of strategies for year groups to try out on a half-termly basis, accompanied by questionnaire evaluations and discussion in staff meetings. 'Traffic lights' was the strategy to be tried out for self-assessment; WALT (we are learning to) and WILF (what I am looking for) for sharing learning objectives and success criteria; 'two stars and a wish' for feedback; and 'no hands up' for questioning. This was proposed and illustrated on two sides of A4 which included the schedule in Figure 6.1.

Year	Autumn Term 2	Spring Term 1	Spring Term 2	Summer Term 1
3	Self-Assessment Traffic Lights	Sharing Criteria WALT & WILF	Feedback Two stars & a wish	Questioning No hands up
4	Sharing Criteria WALT & WILF	Feedback Two stars & a wish	Questioning No hands up	Self-Assessment Traffic Lights
5	Feedback Two stars & a wish	Questioning No hands up	Self-Assessment Traffic Lights	Sharing Criteria WALT & WILF
6	Questioning No hands up	Self-Assessment Traffic Lights	Sharing Criteria WALT & WILF	Feedback Two stars & a wish

Figure 6.1 LHTL strategy schedule at Eucalyptus Junior School

Some of these ideas can be traced to project material but others originated elsewhere. WALT and WILF, also mentioned by Janice in the first case study, are associated with the work on formative assessment of Shirley Clarke who had worked with primary schools in the locality, although not directly with Eucalyptus. These ideas had been gleaned from other schools, especially through networking at school co-ordinators' meetings.

Sophie's interim evaluation, at the end of the Spring Term 2004, reported:

- The four strategies are all becoming part of normal classroom practice to varying degrees.
- Different teachers are adopting the strategies in different ways – some are using all four, some are only comfortable using one.
- All of the strategies are suitable for all years in Key Stage 2, although some need adapting for younger or older children.
- All abilities are able to use the strategies to varying degrees.
- Although some strategies lend themselves more easily to specific subjects, other curriculum areas can benefit from all four of the strategies.
- It has been very hard to quantify results, in terms of whether or not children are more aware of their learning, however, the children's awareness of objectives has definitely increased, along with their desire to work towards the success criteria.
- Teachers have also stated that children are more focused when using certain strategies.
- At times, teachers have used creativity and professional judgement to adapt strategies to make them easier to use in their own class-rooms with their own children.

During the 2003/2004 school year, Eucalyptus also began collaborating with Fir Tree Primary. Facilitated by a new LA co-ordinator (the previous one left in the summer of 2003), the head teachers and project co-ordinators in the two schools met to talk and compare what they were doing. Teachers from Fir Tree then visited Eucalyptus to observe strategies in practice in Years 3 and 4, and a return visit enabled Sophie and Janet to observe in Fir Tree. Sophie commented on the different ways in which strategies were used e.g. 'traffic lights', and emphasised how important it was to see things in practice:

> When they came to us for a day to look around, we sat in the library and spoke and they talked about all these things they used, but then once Janet and I actually went there and saw them using them it actually brings it alive.

Opportunities to network and share practice were the most highly valued aspect of the project experience for the school. As Sophie put it:

> That's probably been the most useful to be honest, with the, you know, exchanging of information in co-ordinators' meetings and setting up this relationship with Fir Tree. That's been really useful – just to have someone to talk to and to bounce ideas off of each other.

In late June 2004, the LA co-ordinator convened a meeting at Eucalyptus to discuss progress across all the participating schools in the authority. The benefits of peer observation, between schools, was a focus of discussion, especially how this kind of activity might be supported after the end of the project. It was agreed that discussion of this would be useful at the next meeting of project school co-ordinators arranged for July 2004. There Sophie, and the co-ordinator at Fir Tree, made a PowerPoint presentation on their partnership work. Their concluding slides (see Figure 6.2) reported what the schools and children had gained from the project.

Progress in the second year of the project was therefore very different from the first with much greater engagement, though little more involvement from the project team. What was it, then, that prevented the school from giving up and opting out in the first year?

What have the schools gained from the project?

– Provided the opportunity to forge links between schools, which would not normally have been possible.
– Allowed us to discuss and exchange information and observe other schools in action.
– Realisation that there are many successful interpretations of any learning strategy.

What have our children gained from the project?

– Due to changes in teaching styles, the children are more aware of their own learning.
– An increased awareness of what is expected of them as learners, due to the widespread sharing of learning intentions and success criteria.
– Confidence and enthusiasm has developed as a result of the children becoming more independent as learners.
– The children are now equipped with a range of portable learning strategies for use throughout their academic career.

Figure 6.2 Slides from the presentation on partnership work between Eucalyptus and Fir Tree schools

Agents of change

Undoubtedly the school co-ordinator, Sophie, and the Year 5 teacher, Janet, were keen and enthusiastic and did not want to see the initiative fail. The responsibility point awarded to Sophie also created a sense of obligation. However, this would probably have been insufficient to overcome the negative circumstances encountered in the first year. In her efforts to get the project moving in the school Sophie spoke of regularly running her ideas past Peter. The leadership of the school was therefore important.

The motivation to do better in the league tables in order for the school to thrive was tangible. However, the strategies to achieve these ends came from the head teacher's vision. Peter's prior experience as a head of science in a secondary school, and then part of a local authority advisory team with responsibility for a 'bridging group' i.e. across sectors, had taught him the importance of a problem-solving approach and team building. A former colleague, a workaholic head teacher who produced a bulletin every day to spread ideas among his staff, had also been a 'guru'.

Influenced by these experiences, the management strategies he pursued were designed to create a climate founded on a number of principles:

- *Confident, independent learners and whole-child development*: in the classroom and through 'vital' residential visits.
- *Targets for all.* But, 'The one thing I wanted to avoid was tick boxes . . . So we're looking specifically at major movements rather than minuscule movements in terms of children's progress, because those are the key issues.'
- *Open climate, parental involvement*: involvement of parents in developing teaching and learning policy; an open-door policy to parents, in the morning until 9.30 p.m., if necessary.
- *Team spirit to create an open friendly ethos*: staff who are reluctant to change are 'not encouraged to stay'; like-minded staff are appointed.
- *Support for younger, newer teachers to develop and spread innovation*: recent work of the literacy co-ordinator, and Sophie as LHTL co-ordinator, are examples.
- *Career development for staff*: revolving job descriptions e.g. for the deputy head, and for Sophie who moved on to being modern foreign languages co-ordinator at the end of the LHTL project.
- *Involvement of support staff*: learning support assistants (LSAs) and classroom assistants are involved in staff meetings to talk about teaching and learning because they often 'get to know the children best'; also dedicated meetings with LSAs every two weeks with copies of minutes to the senior management team.
- *Focus on classroom inquiry*: 'encouraging people to talk about successes and about failures in classrooms' and using self-evaluation instruments.
- *Spreading ideas.* As an advisory teacher for science, Peter 'wanted to share everything that I'd picked up and was picking up'.

This, of course, was Peter's perspective and we might ask how far his view and vision were shared by the rest of the staff. The evidence from the LHTL staff questionnaire administered in 2002 and again in 2004 sheds some light on this (see Table 6.3). There were 12 teachers in the school and around seven LSAs. In 2002, 20 staff responded, and 17 in 2004.

Table 6.3 confirms some of the claims and aspirations of the head teacher. In terms of management practice, 'deciding and acting together'

Table 6.3 Eucalyptus Junior School: reported practices and values in 2002 and 2004 in relation to 11 factors (N =20 in 2002; N = 17 in 2004)

	Factor	Practice/Value	2002 Mean factor scores (whole project sample means in brackets)		2004 Mean factor scores (whole project sample means in brackets)	
Classroom Assessment	Making Learning Explicit	Practice	81.2	(80.91)	82.00	(82.53)
		Values	83.3		82.5	
	Promoting Learning Autonomy	Practice	50.2	(58.23)	48.6	(62.16)
		Values	60.1		60.8	
	Performance Orientation	Practice	77.5	(69.57)	61.4	(63.58)
		Values	62.4		50.6	
Professional Learning	Inquiry	Practice	62.4	(58.67)	62.4	(65.40)
		Values	65.8		69.4	
	Building Social Capital	Practice	79.3	(79.94)	87.4	(81.34)
		Values	78.2		77.1	
	Critical and Responsive Learning	Practice	76	(77.03)	76.5	(79.97)
		Values	79.4		75.1	
	Valuing Learning	Practice	94.7	(90.14)	94.8	(90.41)
		Values	89.7		87.5	
Systems	Deciding and Acting Together	Practice	72.7	(57.60)	76.7	(62.49)
		Values	82.7		83.1	
	Developing a Sense of Where We are Going	Practice	71.9	(69.57)	75	(71.54)
		Values	82.7		82.5	
	Supporting Professional Development	Practice	50.3	(59.92)	60.5	(65.00)
		Values	79.7		77.9	
	Auditing Expertise and Supporting Networking	Practice	36.4	(45.54)	57.2	(53.22)
		Values	69.3		66.2	

is higher than the project sample as a whole, and rising. Much the same is recorded for 'developing a sense of where we are going'. 'Supporting professional development' lagged behind the whole-sample mean in 2002, but a sizeable 10 per cent increase in this factor score was recorded for the school in 2004. 'Auditing expertise and supporting networking', a key feature of Peter's strategy, lagged behind the whole-sample mean in 2002 but had overtaken it by 2004.

Professional learning practices were broadly comparable with whole sample means although 'valuing learning' featured more highly in both years, and 'building social capital' had accelerated more quickly than the sample as a whole from 2002 to 2004.

In the classroom, 'making learning explicit' remained much in line with whole-sample means. 'Promoting learning autonomy', however, lagged behind and decreased slightly between the two administrations, in contrast to other schools. This might be a source of concern to the school, given its desire to create independent learners. Performance-oriented practices, although higher than the average at the beginning of the project, reduced very significantly to below average in 2004. This was not reflected in a decline in results in tests; quite the reverse, in fact, which must be a source of satisfaction.

Alternative explanations for outcomes

By the end of 2004, when the project's work with the school formally ended, there was evidence of both change in school practices and increasing success in children's attainments as measured by national test results. Had the project contributed to this? It is tempting to claim a causal link but, as social scientists, we have to remain sceptical about this. Too many things were happening at the same time and it is difficult, in this authentic, real-world setting, to disentangle their separate influences.

When interviewed at the beginning of the project, Peter said:

> We've gone to our highest National Curriculum achievements ever this year, so you could then turn back and say, 'Is that because of better teaching and better learning or is it because you're getting used to the tests and you're able to prepare the children better?' I'd say yes to both because I'm a realist and I'm honest.

After her last visit to the school, in June 2004, the school's critical friend recorded on the web-log:

There was much debate about the possible effects of the performance culture and staff had different views on the value or
otherwise of league tables. The head teacher, whilst not happy with
the pressures to achieve numerical targets, said (for the third time
in my presence) that he has felt forced to introduce revision lessons
in Year 6 in order to stay in the game . . . The head was inclined to
attribute raised test scores to revision lessons rather than LHTL.

But perhaps it is neither the project, as such, nor the revision lessons
that moved the school forward. What is most striking, in both the quantitative and qualitative data, is the increased level of networking,
involving both strong and weak links. Building the social capital, which
enables intellectual capital to be exchanged, is also prominent. Social
relationships were formed, trust was established and practice knowledge was shared at meetings, in school visits and through peer
observation in classrooms. All that the project provided to this school
was light critical friend support, opportunities to meet other school co-
ordinators, and a small amount of money for cover two school visits
by two teachers on each occasion. Perhaps this is sufficient if the
organisational conditions of the school – culture, structures, processes
and leadership – are robust enough to take advantage of these minimal
resources.

The irony of this case study is that, although the networking element
comes over so strongly, we did not anticipate this. The school was not
part of the VEAZ, nor a networked learning community, therefore we
did not collect data here through our network mapping exercise. Fir
Tree school, with which Eucalyptus linked, was some considerable
distance away, but the fact that it did not compete with the school for
the same children made networking between the two schools relatively
non-threatening.

Conclusion

The three case studies in this chapter are written to illuminate some
of the different themes, and interrelationship among themes,
discussed in previous chapters. However, it is worth summarising
some of the common issues that arise because they are knotty.

First, all three studies are about challenge and struggle and show
just how difficult innovation can be in complex organisations, such

as schools, working in constraining, high-stakes policy contexts. The idea that new ideas can simply be 'disseminated', and have effect, seriously underestimates what is involved in implementing and sustaining change, something that Fullan (2001) emphasises. The introduction of new ideas, from a project or other initiative, is only the start of a process of change that depends fundamentally on the quality of a school's internal expertise, relationships and processes.

Furthermore, change involves risk-taking, critical reflection, learning from failure, building new relationships, finding the motivation and energy to try something new – all those things that make psychological and social demands on individuals and groups – as well as finding and mobilising financial and material resources. For Janice, the challenge is to move forward while developing principles and practice together: not losing sight of the former under pressure to change the latter. A question for Hazel Primary School is how to transform teachers' well-developed practices of mutual support *out of class* into collaboration and joint inquiry *in class*, as a strategy to enhance the quality of pupils' learning. And in Eucalyptus Junior School, there is the struggle to maintain a balance between supporting experimentation while not jeopardising too much the school's fragile position in a competitive environment. In all three cases, the key players share a gritty resolve to triumph, although they realise that this will happen incrementally, by small steps, which inevitably takes time.

These concerns focus mainly on teachers and schools, rather than directly on pupils, but their struggles are all directed towards providing the best conditions in which pupils can learn how to learn and therefore become autonomous learners – the justification for the LHTL project.

Chapter 7*

Case studies of LHTL from secondary schools

This chapter illustrates how some of the key themes and issues, identified in earlier chapters, feature in the way individual secondary schools engaged with the LHTL project. It is therefore a companion to Chapter 6 which contains case studies from primary schools. By clustering case studies in these two chapters according to sector, the different preoccupations and issues for primary and secondary schools become clear. For example, in the four case studies in this chapter, issues of leadership, internal communication and the challenges of spreading practice across a large organisation are especially prominent.

As in the previous chapter, each case study has a single author who has selected, in discussion with the project team, a range of issues to focus upon while attempting to provide a flavour of the school as a whole, and the experiences of LHTL within the school. The first is a study of strong leadership in a highly successful school with a commitment to assessment for learning at the heart of its teaching and learning policy. It nevertheless raises issues about how to achieve an appropriate balance between a drive for consistency and scope for informed dissent that might be important for creative development. The second case study focuses upon how the project was set up in a school, the false starts and changes of tack, as the school's management team sought to align LHTL with other initiatives to ensure embedding of ideas and practice. The third case study analyses why familiarity with assessment for learning, since the late 1990s, failed to transform practice beyond a small group of teachers, and how the school co-ordinator sought more deep-seated and

* Authored by John MacBeath, Bethan Marshall and Sue Swaffield

wide-spread change based on an understanding of principles of learning. The final case study returns to the theme of leadership, in another successful school, although here the approach is somewhat different, which illustrates that there may be several routes to similar goals.

Leadership without compromise at Hawthorn High School

Hawthorn High School sits in the very heart of its community. The surrounding streets are wide and the houses are typically large and set back from the pavements. Terraces of Victorian houses are interspersed with more modern terraces of less imposing, 1930s vintage. Housing patterns present a patchwork of styles: some well kept, some recently renovated while others appear as if they have been untouched since they were put there a century ago. The variety of cars which line the residential streets, parked where front gardens once were, also represent a mix – from the modest family saloon to the most recent showcase models, attesting to a community with a degree of affluence and ambition.

Close by the school, the small parade of shops contains an eclectic mix of grocery shops, newsagent and take-away establishments. A group of homeless men sit on a bench near the train station, swigging beer from cans held tight in gloved hands, a stark contrast with the 'suits' heading west to Central London. This commuter station and proximity of the Underground make the area and its well-regarded secondary school attractive to upwardly mobile families.

This is a community with aspirations for its children and young people. In an interview in 2002, Brian Turner, the head teacher explained: 'Parents are very pro-education; they're very aspirational. I mean it's partly the make-up of the kids that we get.' This is truly a multi-ethnic school with the largest single group of children being from Indian background (about 40 per cent of the school population). The parental commitment and support for young people's education contribute significantly to the LHTL school co-ordinator's claim that Hawthorn is a 'very, very good school'. It is a view endorsed by Ofsted who reported in 2002 that the school was providing its pupils 'with an excellent education'.

Enlisting the school in the LHTL project, the head teacher did not concur with the Ofsted judgement that there were 'no significant areas for improvement'. He saw involvement in this project as an opportunity to take the school to a new level: 'I would be appalled if anybody thought that we were satisfied . . . This school, I like to think, operates on the basis that you're only as good as your next set of results.'

Of almost 1,300 pupils in the school, 75 are in the sixth form; their A level achievements a key factor in the school's high profile and reputation. Its statistical profile is testament to its pursuit of high standards. Attendance has run, consistently over the last few years, at around 94 per cent. While more or less on the national average for free school meals (about a quarter of the school population) at the time of the 2002 Ofsted inspection, 81 per cent of the pupil body were attaining five A*–C grades in the GCSE examinations, a 12 per cent rise on the previous year, and commended by Ofsted for being within the top 5 per cent of schools nationally. By 2004, the proportion of five A*–C grades had risen to 84 per cent and, in November 2004, David Miliband, then Minister for School Standards, attributed this to the school's embrace of assessment for learning. This progress has continued and, in 2006, 92 per cent of Year 11 pupils achieved five A*–Cs.

The story of improvement is one that has to be told over two decades. When Brian Turner joined the school as head teacher, the school results did not reflect the aspirational nature of the parent body, which he put down to a disparity of quality among departments, low expectations and lack of whole-school policies.

Recruitment and retention

Recruitment and retention of high quality staff have been a central plank in the school's improvement strategy: head-hunting combined with incentives for good staff to stay and disincentives for underachieving staff, to encourage them to move on. 'Playing to the winners' is an essential part of the strategy – an avowedly '100 per cent self-centred' policy within a competitive environment in which this school takes pride of place. The key ingredients in making this 'a very, very good school' are seen as:

- hand-picking and nurturing staff;
- a focus on self-evaluation;
- the alignment of individual teacher, departmental, and school practices;

- constant emphasis on standards with an eye to national policy;
- visionary and directive leadership.

Leading from the front

As a new head, Brian Turner's first step in improvement was to confront the current ethos of the school. Words such a 'battles', 'major rows', 'tough', 'brutal', figure large in his discourse. He portrays himself as a head not afraid of conflict or friction, with a personal challenge to 'rewrite' the school in respect of policies, expectations and outcomes. 'It was quite brutal, it was quite tough, it was me, you know, where one's effectively saying, "This has got to change or there will be mega consequences." That's a bit blunt!'

'The buzz of being in the job', Brian confesses, 'is the change element', driven by a passion for young people whom he sees as having been discriminated against by too easy an acceptance of the status quo. If the head doesn't take the lead, set and chart the course, who else will? he asks. This leads him to insist on classroom learning being firmly teacher-directed – literally from the front with forward-facing desks – enshrined in the school's teaching and learning policy. Intolerance of 'facing the wrong way' is a metaphor writ large in conviction-led leadership, which wants what is best for the school and best for young people, two goals conceived as synonymous.

The embedding of assessment for learning (AfL) and learning how to learn (LHTL) is set within this context: applying what Brian describes as 'a mini Ofsted', realised through intensive monitoring, structured lesson observations, as well as spontaneous 'nipping into lessons'. The monitoring of nine practice elements of AfL (including 'no hands up', increased 'wait time', and 'phone a friend') produces an at-a-glance matrix, department by department, under four rubrics: embedded; often; sometimes; not in place. Using the same four rubrics, a pupil survey provides a further source of evidence, contesting some of the judgements made by staff. From time to time pupils are 'quizzed' about the feedback they receive from teachers, while senior leaders and heads of departments scrutinise children's work to ensure that there are 'no marks' and 'high quality formative comment'.

The embrace of assessment for learning is with total conviction, leaving no room for dissent, as the LHTL school co-ordinator, Sally, describes it:

> In terms of assessment for learning, we've got a policy which is very, very directive. You must carry out peer or self-assessment

once a term. You must not use grades. You must, you know, it's very, very prescriptive.

Sally speaks of an 'unanswerable case', by intellectual conviction and by institutional authority, which pre-empt debate. Beneath what might be caricatured as the iron fist in the iron glove, is a both a passion and an anger. Some might call it 'tough love'. The passion is for the welfare and achievement of young people and the anger is directed at what is seen as the betrayal of their futures.

Brian admits to the nature of the struggle to let go, to create more space for teacher initiative, but he is frustrated by his inability to stand by and witness bad practice. 'I have had considerable inhibitions about interfering too much with teachers', he says, but he cannot resist intervention when he sees 'stupid things'. At the same time, he has pursued a more collective approach to policy development, setting up a succession of working parties and sub-groups to 'rationalise' whole-school issues, with teaching and learning and assessment to the fore, including a school improvement group to function as a 'think tank' with its membership rotating on a six-monthly basis.

Hawthorn is also a member of a networked learning community (NLC) which includes 14 primary schools. It pursues a programme of observations, and a programme of Inset sessions. Teachers are paid to go on courses and feed back at the project leaders' meetings. Supply time and cover money allow teachers to work on the projects in their school.

Changing values, changing practice?

People's attitudes have changed enormously in a very short period of time, says Sally, the LHTL co-ordinator, a view confirmed by evidence from the staff questionnaire administered in 2002, and again in 2004 (see Table 7.1). Within that relatively short time frame, nine of the eleven factors showed a significant positive change, most markedly in relation to 'supporting professional development' and 'auditing expertise and supporting networking'. Equally significant was the reported decrease in teacher-centred 'performance orientation', interpreted by the research team as a positive move away from a preoccupation with curriculum coverage and teaching to the test. The largest gap between practices and values is in relation to 'deciding and acting together', a gap that decreased only marginally between 2002 and 2004.

Table 7.1 Hawthorn School: staff reported practices and values in 2002
and 2004 in relation to 11 factors (N = 69 in 2002;
N = 72 in 2004)

	Factor	Practice/ Value	2002 (mean)	2004 (mean)
Assessment	Making Learning Explicit	Practice	79.3	85.4
		Values	88.6	89.3
	Promoting Learning Autonomy	Practice	63.6	72.6
		Values	81.5	80.4
	Performance Orientation	Practice	70.6	58.4
		Values	52.1	54.6
Professional Learning	Inquiry	Practice	56.4	65.2
		Values	72.8	69.7
	Building Social Capital	Practice	74.3	80.6
		Values	83.7	84.8
	Critical and Responsive Learning	Practice	71.5	79.2
		Values	83.2	83.7
	Valuing Learning	Practice	90.4	90.9
		Values	95.0	92.1
Systems	Deciding and Acting Together	Practice	47.3	54.2
		Values	81.7	82.6
	Developing a Sense of Where We are Going	Practice	76.3	73.7
		Values	85.5	84.2
	Supporting Professional Development	Practice	51.4	62.9
		Values	85.9	84.2
	Auditing Expertise and Supporting Networking	Practice	44.7	62.1
		Values	76.4	74.6

Diagnostic and formative uses of performance data

Evidence of improvement is also evident in the attainment data provided
by the school. Table 7.2 compares Hawthorn with local authority and
national averages with reference to 'non-moving' pupils, that is, those
who entered Key Stage 3 at Level 4 and who are still at Level 4 at the

Table 7.2 Hawthorn School: pupils who enter KS3 at Level 4 and who are still at Level 4 at the end of KS3

2000–2003	National		Local authority		Hawthorn	
English	21%	(46,000)	14.7%	(203)	0.5%	(1)
Maths	13%	(29,000)	9.3%	(121)	0.00%	(0)
Science	31%	(83,000)	30.00%	(365)	5.8%	(11)

Table 7.3 Hawthorn School: pupils who entered KS3 at Level 3 and progressed to Level 5

2000–2003	National		Local authority		Hawthorn	
English	26%	(26,679)	34.1%	(158)	60%	(15)
Maths	27%	(34,211)	34.6%	(207)	41%	(15)
Science	10%	(6,238)	15.1%	(49)	63%	(6)

end of KS3. In contrast, Table 7.3 shows KS3 pupils who entered at Level 3 and progressed to Level 5; these percentages are also compared with local authority and national statistics.

In Hawthorn School, such data are seen as serving a formative as well as a summative purpose. At individual pupil level they are used to identify different categories of progress. The following typology emerged:

- Disengaged, lacking motivation.
- Feeling unnoticed; completes work but are invisible, or others' behaviour disturbs them.
- Work stalls and declines and they don't know how to get help.
- Start to drop through sets.
- Daunted by the shift to abstract and conceptual work that is a requirement of Level 5 work – they often can 'do' the work needed for Level 4 but find Level 5 work too conceptual.
- Skilled in avoidance and miss crucial bits of learning and don't catch up; KS3 is not coherent for them – it is disconnected learning. They are clear about what primary learning was about, and understand GCSEs, but KS3 is seen as a 'waiting room'.

- Lack formal language.
- Don't feel prepared for the demands of KS3 tests.

From this diagnostic approach a number of strategies that motivate and engage pupils were identified:

- motivated by particular subjects and enthusiastic teachers;
- respond to interactive and hands-on teaching;
- want to be given independence, not to be spoon-fed;
- want to see relevance and purpose in their work;
- respond to good classroom management;
- crave attention and respond to mentoring, targets and monitoring.

These strategies might not, it was agreed, hold true for all pupils so other approaches adopted were setting targets and tracking progress, identifying high-risk pupils, allocating high-engagement teachers, explaining the purpose and relevance of work, providing mentors wherever possible, using a robust grouping policy (sets), and using an active rewards and sanctions policy.

A residue of honest doubt

While applauding 'the most fantastic outcomes', Brian still expresses unease about spoon-feeding and is concerned as to whether these young people are being taught to think, 'rather than the mechanics of getting an A grade at Chemistry'. This worry is shared by a teacher who said, in interview: 'We get brilliant results and they have a nice experience in the school but they're not lifelong learners.' She quotes former pupils who return to the school and recount their university experience.

> Our drop-out rate from university is too high . . . I say to them, 'Did we prepare you for university?' and they say 'No. You didn't. You did in terms of work ethic, to make us work hard but independent learning? Forget it.'

It would be too easy to interpret leadership in Hawthorn as un-ashamedly dictatorial. In fact, Brian Turner admits to worrying about getting the balance right: struggling with the tensions and paradoxes between empowerment and deskilling of staff. Nowhere is the paradox more clearly expressed than in the following:

> I'm actually more sensitive than people think I am to deskilling
> teachers. I think teachers have got to feel that they're making
> decisions but what, I suppose, I'm forcing them to do is making
> those decisions.

What is clear is that this head teacher, with a passion for his school and
for the welfare of young people, is uncompromising in his belief that AfL
is the right way. Yet, in spite of a concerted effort to create a like-minded
community of practice, the LHTL co-ordinator is frank about the depth
of commitment across the school:

> People on the outside think that AfL is totally 100 per cent here
> and it's not. We've got to make sure that we kind of keep it going
> and push it in areas where it needs to be more consistent. It's
> pockets you know . . . So it's getting that consistency and making
> sure people don't do a bit of peer assessment in the autumn term
> and then forget about it because it's done.

However, if the following pupil's statement speaks for his school mates,
the evidence is encouraging: 'I now know it's about thinking and skills
and learning, when before I thought it was about stuff.'

Elm County High School: finding the best way forward

This is a case study of the way a large secondary school managed its
engagement with LHTL and, particularly, how it attempted to work out
the relationships between various initiatives taking place at the same
time. The story can be interpreted in at least two ways. On the one hand,
it can be seen as a school where senior leaders took six months to begin
to get to grips with the project, changing their mind about which groups
to align it with, and then spent another year involving only a small
proportion of the staff. On the other hand, it can be viewed as a school
where reflective senior leaders were determined that LHTL should
complement, and be integrated with, other initiatives; that it should
have a solid base, and that whole-school development would be led by
pioneering practitioners working together.

School context

Elm County High School is a 11–18 mixed comprehensive school that gained arts college status in 2001. In 2002, over 1,600 pupils were accommodated in its sprawling brick buildings. There had been considerable staff change in 2001, reflecting the increasing size of the school and recruitment difficulties in the area, with 25 new teachers appointed, including, according to the head teacher, 'quite an exceptional group of NQTs [newly qualified teachers] . . . to really invigorate the school'.

The Ofsted inspection in October 2002, at the beginning of the LHTL project, described the school as good and improving, with very good leadership and management and providing good quality education. The proportion of pupils on the special educational needs register was about average, and fewer than 3 per cent had backgrounds other than White British. The proportion of pupils eligible for free school meals was broadly in line with the national average. Standards of attainment were close to the national average at age 14 but often below average at age 19; however, Ofsted reported that this represented satisfactory or good achievement for all groups of pupils. The inspectors judged much of the teaching and learning as very good, and some excellent, although they observed varied practice and identified issues with pupil independence and teaching style. They said there was room for improvement in a number of departments throughout the school.

School and departmental self-evaluation was well established, and the head teacher reported that the school improvement plan drove professional development, but its objectives were rather generalised (for example, to develop independent learning and study skills) without specifying the concrete steps needed to alter practice.

At the beginning of the LHTL project in 2002, Elm School was grappling with implementing the Key Stage 3 (KS3) national strategy with a particular focus on the core subjects, and the 14–19 curriculum. The head teacher felt that the foundation departments and subjects in KS3 were lacking attention. The KS3 strategy was being implemented in pockets, but there was inconsistency across the school. Along with a teaching and learning group that had been established in 2000, there was also a KS3 group and a 14–19 group.

The head teacher was willing to get involved with LHTL as long as it fitted in with other initiatives rather than becoming an 'extra'. He saw the project as a means of bringing in external expertise and the opportunities to revise, evaluate and research school practice. In 2002, the head teacher expected LHTL to involve some departments at first, taking longer to go across the school, but said he would be delighted if it moved more quickly to the whole school.

January–July 2002: who should lead LHTL developments?

During this period the critical friend contacted and met a number of people in the school as the Elm leadership decided who should be the school co-ordinator, which member of the senior leadership team (SLT) should have oversight, and which groups within the school should take the project forward. Initially LHTL was aligned with the existing teaching and learning group, although this group had very little engagement with the project in the longer term. Entries in the log by the critical friend during this period testify to a school trying to attach LHTL to different existing initiatives (for example, Cognitive Acceleration in Science Education (CASE), Cognitive Acceleration in Mathematics Education (CAME), Gifted and Talented). The critical friend emphasised the centrality of assessment for learning and the importance of planning for whole-school development, and drew attention to the difficulties of communicating with the appropriate person either through email or telephone.

In the summer term, the school's senior vice-principal, Liam, was made LHTL co-ordinator – a decision that afforded status to the project within the school. LHTL was linked to the 14–19 group, on the grounds that the structures were in place, and that the KS3 group already had the national strategy as a focus. However, it soon became clear, at least to Liam, that LHTL needed to be a whole-school development.

> What I found was, within the first real session that we had, that we're looking at something that there's no way we could just link to Key Stage 4, because we were using the same ideas right across all of our teaching.

Baseline interviews by the researcher, with both the head teacher and the new co-ordinator in late June, seemed to assist their understanding of the project and encouraged them to focus on how to take it forward. These interviews provided the opportunity for two senior leaders to give more concentrated attention to the project than they had done previously. In July, Liam attended a project meeting in London for all the schools, and productive discussions with the critical friend indicated that there would be a late but promising start to the school's real engagement with the project at the beginning of the next academic year.

September 2002–July 2003: a small group get involved

The new academic year began with part of a professional day for the whole staff devoted to LHTL – the baseline questionnaire, initial presentation, and a meeting of a staff group focusing on LHTL. However, the head teacher had just received notification of a forthcoming Ofsted inspection, and the staff were informed at the start of the professional day. Despite the news, the teachers engaged with the presentation and responded favourably, but undoubtedly much of the energy and focus at Elm school for the first half-term was directed towards the Ofsted inspection scheduled for the end of October.

The original 14–19 group was reformed as the LHTL working group, comprising two teachers from each of eight departments. It was conceived as a professional development group and a discussion forum, whose members would try things out in their classrooms, discuss practice, and possibly inform the revision of school policy. The group met twice each term and used workshop materials from the LHTL website.

Despite the availability of these support materials, Liam, the co-ordinator, felt that he wanted more input, and supported the setting up of a group of other project schools in the authority run by the local authority adviser. She visited the school during the year and arranged group meetings, but the summer term meeting, which was to have focused on questioning, was cancelled – much to the disappointment of Elm's co-ordinator.

In the spring term the critical friend fed back the data from the questionnaire to the head teacher and co-ordinator, and these data were in turn discussed by the LHTL working group. This, together with the findings of the Ofsted inspection in the previous term, influenced the focus and direction of the group's work towards comment only marking, questioning, and dialogue between pupils and teachers. The project's focal teachers were members of the group and worked hard to develop their classroom practices in these areas. An outcome of the group's work was the rewriting of the school's marking policy, concentrating upon comments and targets, for implementation from September 2003.

It had been a deliberate policy to involve pairs of teachers from the same department in the LHTL working group so that they could share and discuss practice and support each other in their trialing of new approaches. However, as Liam, the co-ordinator, observed:

> We've got sixteen members of staff who now have been fully immersed in a number of ideas related to learning how to learn, but we've got a staff of a hundred. And how can we therefore impact on the rest of those who haven't spent the year working in the same way?

Lesson observations and comments in other meetings reinforced the necessity of spreading LHTL practice. The challenge then for 2003–2004 was to engage the whole staff.

September 2003–July 2004: engaging the whole staff

At the start of the year, Kelvin, an assistant head teacher, who had been a member of the LHTL working group, took over the co-ordination of the project. Nevertheless, Liam, the school's senior vice-principal, retained a strategic oversight and was pivotal in directing the path of development.

A series of teaching and learning workshops was devised as a way of pulling together all the disparate developments that were growing under the auspices of LHTL, KS3 strategy, 14–19 developments, and responses to inspection and evaluations. There were nine sets of workshops, two of which particularly focused upon LHTL – questioning and modelling, and peer and self-assessment. The workshops were led by teachers who had been members of the LHTL working group the previous year, and who therefore had a bank of materials and experiences upon which to draw. As Kelvin explained:

> Those people were used to talking about learning, and they were used to evaluating our learning, used to sharing ideas, used to teasing out good practice, and therefore they had the skills to then be able to help others to do the same thing, to consider what they were doing.

Kelvin invited the critical friend to meet with the workshop leaders in advance to discuss their plans for running the workshops, and to suggest additional materials.

Each set of three sessions was planned to be repeated each term, following the pattern of an initial brief look at the principles and research that underpins the work, then a consideration of existing good practice, sharing of ideas, and an undertaking to try things out in order to report back to the group in the following session. Once again it was policy that no one would attend a workshop as the single representative of a subject department – there were always at least two teachers from the same department in any workshop, thus enabling development work within as well as across departments. Through the workshops teachers devised materials to be used in classrooms (for example, videos to assist peer and self-assessment), and incorporated developments into the schemes of work. Every teacher had one performance management target relating to teaching and learning, and these individual targets were incorporated into departmental action plans. The opportunity to work in departments was considered so valuable that in the summer term the planned workshops were dropped in favour of time for consolidation and for whole departments to work together.

September 2004 onwards: continued learning how to learn?

In July 2004, an interview with Kelvin, the school co-ordinator, looked ahead to the following academic year. The teaching and learning workshops were planned to continue, particularly bearing in mind the need to involve staff new to the school. LHTL featured on the school improvement plan, and was expected to remain there for the following year. Kelvin said he would like to see the school become better at self-evaluation, and to link it with pupil self evaluation, and for teacher peer observation to become more of the norm and less threatening. He expected to see increased transformation in the classroom, with teachers realising that they have even more to learn, and are capable of doing so.

Whatever happened to KMOFAP at Willow School? The challenge of spreading innovation

Before it became an LHTL project school, Willow was involved with the King's, Medway, Oxfordshire, Formative Assessment Project (KMOFAP) (see Black et al., 2003, and Chapter 1). A chief motivation for recruiting the school to the LHTL project was to build on the experience of teachers who were expected to be 'ahead of the game' with respect to AfL, and to see how their expertise had spread, or could be helped to do so.

However, each time the head of Willow School mentions KMOFAP, he does so in the context of other initiatives that the school has been involved in over the years. Even when he refers to the 'King's Project', which is not often, it is unclear whether he is speaking of KMOFAP or LHTL. The two projects seem to blur and he portrays them as general undertakings rather than anything with a very specific content. This is interesting in the light of the school's 2003 Ofsted report which commends the leadership of Willow for attracting 'significant additional resources through national and local initiatives'. Yet, despite involvement with KMOFAP from 1999 to 2001, and with LHTL from 2002, the report observes, 'Assessment information is not used as effectively as it could be to analyse and improve performance at either whole school or departmental level.'

The juxtaposition of these two statements is indicative of a school that is keen to take on board new initiatives for the benefit of 'educational provision' but illustrative of the difficulties of sustaining the impact of such initiatives. Judy, the deputy head and school co-ordinator on the LHTL project, states why she feels this might be: 'KMOFAP . . . is a project which some people were doing rather than a set of ideas. I think that was a shame.' Implicit in her critique is the sense that the adoption of a project does little to effect change unless it spreads beyond a few individuals, and the principles that under-gird that project are understood by all those involved. Judy felt neither of these happened in KMOFAP and she regretted that this should be so. This latter issue reflects, at school level, the distinction between implementing the 'letter' of AfL, and capturing the 'spirit', which was a dominant theme in Chapter 3. This case study provides an opportunity to revisit a KMOFAP school and explore the manner in which Judy, especially, searches for ways of doing things differently with LHTL – by making the spirit of AfL more explicit.

School context

Willow School is in a picturesque corner of England. The nearest small town has a 'chocolate box' pretty centre with golden stone buildings on narrow, meandering streets. The surrounding countryside undulates gently, luring city dwellers away from the metropolis with the promise of a less hectic life and the benefits of small community living. The nearby motorway makes the practicalities of commuting to London a real, if somewhat exhausting, possibility.

Émigrés from London, as well as those from the area, look to the local school to provide a safer environment than they believe might be found in a city comprehensive. The spacious, slightly rolling, green site of Willow offers such reassurance. Set in the grounds of a long-gone stately home it retains many of the features of a more easeful past. The coach house and stables, built in the same stone as the town, remain but now contain classrooms.

But the very attractions of the area are changing it. Beyond the quaint centre of the town sprawls new housing, built from the 1960s onwards. The demographics of place are shifting as the community grows. The school reflects this also. The site is scattered with new buildings and huts to accommodate the size of the intake. At almost 1,400 pupils, it is a large school. Pupils come from a wide catchment area, including some who have chosen to opt out of the neighbouring authority's selective system. A fleet of coaches arrive at the beginning and end of every school day. Lateness to lessons is a real problem as pupils walk between blocks. Communication between departments is difficult to achieve. Go to the staffroom at any time of day and it is hard to get a sense of how large the staff is, or how hard they are working after the school day has finished.

Though the area is undoubtedly changing, and with it Willow's intake, the school's profile still shows a relatively, and unusually, homogeneous pupil population. The number of children who have English as an additional language, for example, is less than 1 per cent – well below the national average. The number on free school meals, at 7 per cent, is also very low, as are the number of pupils who have a statement of special educational needs – 1 per cent (although the 18 per cent who have some kind of special need is average). More pupils arrive with Key Stage 2 national test scores of level 4, and above, than is found nationally. It is, according to Ofsted, in 2003, 'an effective school' but one that does no more or better than schools of a similar kind. Performance results for 2002, 2003 and 2004 suggest that this judgement was generous: five A*–C grades were 55 per cent, 53 per cent and 52 per cent, respectively, giving a three years combined percentile rank of 92, when adjusted for prior attainment and school context.

KMOFAP at Willow School

Willow's involvement with KMOFAP started in 1999 with maths and science and a year later included English. The three focal teachers on the LHTL project – those who were interviewed and whose lessons were observed – also came from these departments. Their comments corroborate Judy's perspective. Neither the head of maths or science were directly involved in KMOFAP: the head of science, because he sent other members of his department to join the project: the head of maths, because she joined the school after the project had finished. Only the English teacher had actually participated in KMOFAP.

The comments each of these three teachers make about KMOFAP, explain, to an extent, why the principles of AfL at Willow failed to take hold. They confirm Judy's perceptions about the way they related to KMOFAP as a set of procedures, rather than deeper principles of learning, which AfL procedures support. Thus little sense of ownership of the project was engendered. According to Tom, the head of science, the two things are related. Like Judy, Tom believes that Willow, 'Didn't get back from it what we should have done.' He compares this response to that of a neighbouring school, which 'really took it on board, I think'. Despite being head of department at the time, with presumably some control over events, he attributes this perceived failure, 'To those who went, I think, and the dynamic' within the department. But more deep-rooted causes may have played their part, not least his beliefs about the applicability of AfL to science.

Tom acknowledges that his department only really uses summative assessment, in the form of end of unit modular tests, to assess pupils' progress. While he is aware that this is not a wholly effective approach, his rationale betrays some of his misgivings about AfL:

> One of the problems I have always had with formative assessment . . . formative assessment to me is excellent in a skills-based curriculum because you've got generic things going on in this topic and the next topic and the one after. One of the problems we have with assessment in science often is, so you're talking about electricity, in a week's time you're doing cells, and responding in a formative way to something about circuits is a very short-term thing. By the time you look at it, it may have gone. And certainly, you're not going to meet that bit of content for another two years by which time any formative sort of assessment about that topic is way gone. To be useful, it has to be so immediate.

For Tom, formative assessment is something of a problem. Latching on to a particular procedure as effective – traffic lights – he can only see the short-term benefits within a given topic. It is harder for him to see how this relates to learning *science*. He adds:

We tend to be content-driven people, scientists, you know. We go from topic to topic to topic to topic, being concerned about whether we've covered everything and not being concerned enough about whether we've actually taught the skills . . . I think [this] makes it harder for me to see formative assessment being so successful in science.

Maths, he feels has it easier because, for Tom, it is a skills-based curriculum.

Techniques rather than principles of learning

Anthea, the head of the mathematics department, found traffic lights a useful technique. She immediately saw sense in the system:

I never really saw the usefulness of all these numbers that I had in my mark book anyway so, you know, I was very interested in it because I'd not been involved obviously in the [KMOFAP] project and, you know, it was all very interesting and the whole idea. I mean, I started straight away to record just the traffic lights in my mark book because I saw absolutely no point in having all these numbers.

The system is also adopted by pupils:

Marking assessing homework, we don't do any marks for homework . . . and the kids do the green, amber, red assessment of, you know, the traffic lights system . . . a lot of my Year 11 top set will write, you know, a little dialogue for me about, you know, this was amber because, and these are the mistakes I made and I now understand.

Like the head of science, these comments come right at the end of an interview. The usefulness of the procedure is not in question, not least as an aid to help pupils learn, but they come more as an addendum instead of arising out of a core, organising principle of learning.

Even for Gabriella, the English teacher who was directly involved in KMOFAP, and whose discussion of it is far more central to her interview, it is the easily applicable techniques that tend to dominate her comments:

I just came away at the end feeling really motivated. You know, we were told the sort of theories and the methodology and then in practice how things worked and how it, you know, would affect pupils. And they were just all very simple things that were very easy to take on board within my teaching, just very quickly and very directly . . . I think there are always things that you are going to need to tinker with, a little bit, to fit to what you are doing and what your lesson is. I mean, particularly to do with . . . peer and self-assessment. For example, it's going to be perhaps specific to the piece of work that they are doing and then sometimes it's about – they will swap over work and read and make comments about specific things you have asked them to. Or other times you might have asked them to choose a section to re-write in a certain way. You know, there's lots of different sub-strands of things that you can do from that. But they are – a lot of them are in traffic lighting. You know, it's something like that, it's something that you can just do.

Only at the end of this section of the interview does she mention, 'I just think really getting them to reflect on each piece of work as they move on has been really useful.' As with Tom and Anthea, consideration of pupil learning, while significant, is subordinate to the technique that produces it.

Seeking change

The focus on the techniques of teaching, rather than the principles of learning, is what Judy seeks to change at Willow. For her, procedures and structures are there to support a central aim. Willow needs to become 'a school where learning is absolutely central'. She is also very clear about what this means:

> The learner in a bit more control, or a lot more control really, of where they are . . . I also think it's particularly about generating thinking in the classrooms, and classrooms where real thinking takes place rather than activities take place . . . where there's more kind of intellectual ownership, if you like, of what's being learned so that learners have a sense they can shape things, learn things, move, manage their own learning much more.

It is this clarity of vision, throughout both the interviews with Judy, which make their tone very different from the interviews with the focal teachers. But it is also the consistency of her view of learning that creates a tension in her role as a manager. For, on the one hand, she is convinced that these principles need to be adopted consistently across the school in order for pupils to learn effectively, and yet, on the other hand, but for the same reason, she believes teachers need to internalise the principles for themselves if they are to work: 'First of all they need to believe in it.'

Resolving this tension dominates Judy's reflections in her second interview, in 2004. KMOFAP was, for her, part of the first phase in bringing about change in the school. Perhaps because it failed fully to deliver on its promise, it raised questions about how such a shift might occur: 'I think we need to know more about the conditions in which everybody learns together. For me as a manager, that's quite an issue.' For Judy 'the conditions' mean creating what she calls a 'culture' or 'ethos' within the school. This culture or ethos has very distinctive attributes, which she qualifies and refines as she reflects. She describes what she calls:

> A listening ethos, a mutual listening ethos, and teachers who are going to succeed in these practices need to have the ability to listen to what is happening, to look in more reflective ways at what their pupils are saying.

In such classrooms, there is 'mutual trust, between pupil and teacher'. Listening and trust are words she uses frequently. 'Relationships' is also an important part of Judy's vocabulary. These values are set in opposition to a variety of metaphors, all of which refer to superficial techniques: 'It's not a paint it by numbers approach to teaching at all'; nor is it a, 'Jump through hoop sort of exercise' or a 'ticked box and move on'. She does not simply want to hand out a 'blueprint'.

She is aware that to create the culture she desires, teachers who are not currently working in the way she believes they should, who do not share her values, need to change.

Balancing structure and culture

Two years into the LHTL project, she has begun to think that impetus has to come from the top. This marks, what Judy calls a 'development point' in her understanding of her role as a senior manager.

> I think we have moved on now, a year ago or so, I suppose to a more whole-school approach where there's been kind of leadership from the front which I've taken on as a kind of personal interest.

Otherwise, as with KMOFAP, the necessary cultural shift across the school will not occur and,

> You will end up with a few enthusiasts, who will do a very good job, but the impact on some pupils will be very little because it won't happen without a whole-school expectation, which is reinforced and modelled.

The question she is left with is, 'How can I get the balance right between shared values leading to shared practice and a top-down approach?'

> I want teachers to be creative individuals who make classrooms their own but I also need to feel that they're part of a team. [A framework] will help them get that balance right between being a creative individual in the classroom and having a clarity of structure and a team approach, sort of shared approach.

This tension arising out of a search for equilibrium recurs throughout the interview. At times her attempts to come to terms with the difficulties lead her into the almost paradoxical:

> What I did there was I avoided a prescriptive approach except the prescription if you like that learning should be explicit . . . I had to get the balance right because I'm not prepared to go down the totally prescriptive route and yet I feel, for example, that everybody should be making the learning explicit in their classroom.

And it is through the concept of making learning explicit that she attempts to resolve the tension between insisting on certain practices to achieve 'consistency' and enabling teachers to internalise what is being asked of them. Making learning explicit is her main vehicle, focus and priority for AfL in the classroom. More significantly, this concept makes clearest the synergy between how she believes she can bring about changes, in her role as a deputy head, for both pupil and teacher learning. For Judy, making the values she expects of her staff explicit, through 'expectation, which is reinforced and modelled', is the equivalent of making learning explicit in the classroom.

As with pupils, this requires clarity of purpose and direction in order that they come to learn and understand how to become effective AfL teachers. The two are also linked because:

If I as a teacher know what learning I want to take place, then I know what thinking needs to take place. So [making it] explicit to myself, and then making it explicit to the pupils again will give them an opportunity to engage in this dialogue. I think that's what it's all about.

What she wants in the classroom informs her philosophy of leadership. These connections are reinforced in a later comment: 'Classrooms are activity-based places, not necessarily learning-based places, and if we talk about learning, we may have better access to improve our own learning.'

But even making learning explicit is insufficient if this simply becomes 'formulaic' as Judy puts it. 'I think one of the questions in my mind is to what extent making learning explicit can put a lid on learning?'

What she wishes to avoid,

is the business of making . . . an instrumental, direct link. I say, 'You are learning subordinate clauses, I've taught you this, you've done those exercises, you've got them all right, you've learned subordinate clauses.' In fact, you haven't really engaged and thought about it.

She views this type of procedure as 'a sort of game', rather than learning, because for Judy learning is always dynamic.

There is a danger that with making learning explicit that it becomes a limiting strategy as opposed to a generative opening up strategy. I think you have to pair it up with this ethos of, 'We are thinking together.'

Any procedure or structure has to be continuously assessed against the principle it is intended to enshrine. In this way, Judy's implementation of organisational learning is based on the same 'high organisation based on ideas' mentioned by Dewey (see Chapter 3). Her discussion of the culture or ethos she wishes to create echoes the spirit of AfL. And perhaps, most importantly, her view of learning means that she sees nothing as fixed for either teachers or pupils.

There is a sense that if they are led in the right way they will buy into the optimistic view of schools and pupils' learning. So there has to be a degree of optimism in the leadership and there's no place for any kind of despair or negativity about pupils and learning. There has to be a refusal to tolerate that attitude.

All else can change, can be negotiated except the principle that learning can transform and this is the basis of her optimism, another of her favourite words, along with 'positive'. In this way, Judy brings Dweck's (2000) view of incremental intelligence to an organisation. Her job is to review constantly and refine the structures she has in place in order to enable the staff to learn for the benefit of the pupils. For Judy, this is about an interdependent culture which,

> needs to be optimistic about young people. It needs to have faith it can work and happen because in secondary schools there are challenges to optimism so without that you don't even want the outcome. Without a degree of optimism about young people and learning that's an absolute prerequisite. Without it you forget it. So it needs optimism. It needs to be a listening environment, listening to each other and to pupils. It needs to be an environment where there is mutual respect.

Towards the end of the LHTL project, Judy was appointed head teacher of Willow School.

Leadership as teamwork at Mulberry School: a positive and confident place

It is not easy to find Mulberry, hidden as it is behind the neat row of detached and semi-detached houses which line the main road into the town. Overshoot the school and you arrive in the busy centre of this market town, its pleasant façade belying the inhibitions and lack of self-belief that surface in the day-to-day life of Mulberry School.

The sprawl of buildings that are Mulberry tell the story of a process of accretion, reflecting in microcosm the changing demographics of the county: a period of growth then decline as the school became progressively undersubscribed and was later merged with its nearest secondary neighbour, another school feeling, even more acutely, the pinch of falling rolls. The 1960s vintage buildings were complemented in the late 1990s by new build to accommodate the merger between the two schools. New wings were added piece by piece over the following two years. The school now houses 1,100 pupils, 15 per cent from minority ethnic groups.

Mulberry was inspected for the first time in 2001. The highly positive Ofsted report commended the school in respect of its value-added performance in GSCE, its range of provision, its approach to inclusion, relationships with parents, and 'excellent leadership and management' achieved in challenging circumstances. Since then, the school has witnessed a steady rise in GCSE results: in 2004, 57 per cent of pupils gained five A*–C grades at GCSE, rising to 74 per cent in 2006.

As a visitor to the school, the immediate impression is of a very welcoming and highly ordered environment. Systems are in place, protocols are observed and you are left in little doubt that this is a very well-managed school.

The leadership challenge

When the new school opened in 1997 the leadership challenge was less a matter of how to make the most of the physical constraints of inadequate buildings than how to build a cohesive culture among two sets of staff. Many of them brought anger, frustration, the hurt of being made redundant, and disappointment at seeing the closure of their schools despite strenuous opposition from teachers, parents and pupils.

Anna, the new head teacher, was appointed a year before the opening of the new school. Her remit was to forge a new alliance and build a collaborative culture from the ground up. Six months before the closure of the two schools she circulated a questionnaire to every teacher and every pupil in both establishments, asking them what they valued in their current schools that could be retained, enhanced and built into the culture of the new school, and what they would like to be different in the future. Using data from these surveys a professional development day was held in a local hotel, giving staff the opportunity to explore the findings, and to brainstorm how the issues raised could be meaningfully addressed in a school development plan.

If there was to be a cultural rebuilding, it implied a concerted move from a teaching-centred view to a learning-centred view, something that would not be achieved by executive mandate but by a gradual transformation of thinking and classroom practice. As Anna described it, the investment in re-culturing was 'massive', requiring an immense commitment of time and energy from members of the senior leadership team (SLT). For the SLT, the developmental priorities were clear, echoing the in-flight instruction: 'put the oxygen mask on your own face before putting it on the child's face'. For the SLT the project presented the opportunity to take learning further by developing a process of reflection on the very process of learning itself – in other words, learning how to learn.

Fertile ground

From the research team's point of view the commitment to learning and reflection on learning offered fertile ground. The most talented teachers were already providing Inset sessions for their colleagues, complemented by departmental reviews, lesson observations, self-evaluation interviews with staff about lessons observed, interviews with young people who had taken part in that lesson, and completing questionnaires about their learning in that subject.

The LHTL baseline staff questionnaire provided insights into the how staff viewed the issues facing the school in 2002. Table 7.4 shows staff views of current practice on 11 factors compared with their values or aspiration for the school. In each case a 'gap index' between the two is provided. Comparisons with all project schools are also shown to illustrate areas in which reported practice was similar to, or different from, other schools (the comparative data include primary schools).

These data provided an agenda for an extended discussion between the project critical friend and the senior leadership team, with a focus in particular on the gaps between practice and aspiration. A salient theme was the pressure to maintain and improve the school's standing in national performance tables, the continuing pressure of government targets and an overloaded curriculum, evidenced in the gap between perceived practice and staff values on the factor labelled 'performance orientation'.

Another striking feature is the data related to system factors. The gap measure among Mulberry staff is significantly less than other schools, most markedly in relation to 'developing a sense of where we are going' and 'auditing expertise and supporting networking'. This is testimony to the efforts of the leadership team to create a sense of direction, ownership and collegiality among staff.

A story of improvement

The embrace of the LHTL project was seen by the SLT as 'putting learners in the driving seat' with peer and self-assessment a key strategy in bringing learning closer to the learner. Setting learning objectives and understanding criteria were viewed as an essential perquisite for promoting learning autonomy, which, as the survey evidence showed,

Table 7.4 Mulberry School: staff responses to 11 factors illustrating practices and values and the gaps between them (N = 66)

Factor		Practice/Value	2002 (mean)	All schools (mean)	Gap Mulberry	Gap all schools
Assessment	Making Learning Explicit	Practice	82.9	80.9	6.6	3.8
		Values	89.5	84.7		
	Promoting Learning Autonomy	Practice	61.5	58.2	13.7	11.4
		Values	75.2	69.6		
	Performance Orientation	Practice	70.5	69.6	-17.8	-16.1
		Values	52.7	53.5		
Professional Learning	Inquiry	Practice	69.3	58.7	3.9	7.9
		Values	73.7	66.6		
	Building Social Capital	Practice	85.8	79.9	0.5	1.1
		Values	86.3	81.0		
	Critical and Responsive Learning	Practice	88.4	77.0	-1.5	3.3
		Values	86.9	80.3		
	Valuing Learning	Practice	96.5	90.1	-2.3	1.7
		Values	94.2	91.8		
Systems	Deciding and Acting Together	Practice	66.6	57.6	3.5	22.3
		Values	80.1	79.9		
	Developing a Sense of Where We are Going	Practice	84.5	69.6	1.8	12.5
		Values	86.3	82.1		
	Supporting Professional Development	Practice	76.1	59.9	11.2	21.5
		Values	87.3	81.4		
	Auditing Expertise and Supporting Networking	Practice	67.2	45.5	9.5	23.5
		Values	76.7	69.0		

left ample room for the gap to be closed and aspirational values to be raised further.

Learning how to learn was made explicit through school policy, occasional leaflets, newsletters and continuous reinforcement. Different members of the leadership team said that creating a 'learning how to learn' mindset was dependent on teacher feedback, clearly focused on helping pupils to develop their understanding, to think more critically about their learning, and to self-evaluate. Guidelines to staff emphasised that for feedback to be effective it had to do the following:

- Encourage pupils to think
- Stimulate and scaffold improvement
- Help to create alternative solutions
- Inform planning and next steps
- Be seen as a shared two-way activity
- Tell pupils exactly why they have done well
- Involve both oral and written dialogue.

All staff are observed every year, by more than one person, as part of the performance review, while teaching and learning are a pre-eminent focus of staff development. Annually, every member of staff is given a form on which they can put down what they want by way of support; courses and consultancy are designed to address these felt needs.

The use of 'portfolio notes' is a system open to everyone to comment on a good lesson they have seen, given, or enjoyed. 'Anyone can give one', says the LHTL school co-ordinator, 'it might be that I've seen a fantastic lesson as I've been walking the school or observing a formal lesson. I'd give a feedback, say fantastic start, what a brilliant preliminary session, or what an ingenious way of approaching a subject.'

In addition to the formal observation by middle and senior leaders, teachers have opportunities for a more collegial and formative sharing of practice. A teacher of English emphasised the importance of clear focus and structure for observation and the value of immediate feedback: 'You get quick feedback, it's supported, it's practical, it gives you . . . helpful advice and opportunities also to progress forward.'

The focus on good practice is complemented by ongoing evaluation by pupils through an interactive pupil questionnaire on the school intranet. Examples of questions are: Does your teacher try to find out what you already know before you're starting a new topic? Does your teacher summarise what you should have learned at the end of the last lesson? Does your teacher give the class an opportunity to make choice and decisions about the work you're doing?

The school has also instituted 'research lessons' in which two teachers co-operate on planning a lesson with a specific focus on learning. Three pupils are chosen, across a range of ability or learning styles, and the learning taking place for these three pupils is observed. Audio or video recording may be used, but, whatever the process, within 24 hours after the lesson the two teachers make a commitment to sit down to talk through what went well and what could be refined. At a later date the lesson is carried out with another group to evaluate whether processes and strategies can be transferred to another context, another time, another subject. 'I want the whole place to be learning about learning and the craft of teaching', says Anna.

In search of excellence

Persistently and systematically over the years the senior leadership team has tried to squeeze the last drop from the resources budget, and then look elsewhere for more, to maintain and improve a high standard of achievement. To this end the school pursued Specialist Science status, the Artsmark Silver award for outstanding Arts provision, Leading Edge status and the launch of the Networked Learning Community, the latter involving a collaboration with local infants and primary schools. Other indicators of success have been recognition as Investors in Excellence, DfES Training School status, and The Schools Curriculum Award.

The tension between advancing on numerous fronts and the single-minded pursuit of LHTL is acknowledged by Ben, the school co-ordinator who admits, in respect of LHTL, to 'taking the eye off the ball'. Asked to match his perception of progress in the school with one of six 'levels of engagement' models he chose the graph with a high level start, followed by a dip (or in his terms 'the blip') before regaining momentum. Recognising the implementation dip, the SLT then made a concerted push to embed learning how to learn in the range of school programmes and initiatives – 'cascading rather than meandering' as the school co-ordinator put it. LHTL was subsequently embedded in training of NQTs and in the school's Initial Teacher Training, Graduate Teacher Programme.

Privileging pupil voice

In Mulberry School pupils have, from the very outset, been taken seriously. They are consulted formally on the whole range of aspects of policy and have an ongoing input to the evaluation of teaching and learning. The school website gives links to a pupil wiki which can be accessed with the appropriate pupil code – a forum for exchanging views, 'run by pupils for pupils'.

Involving pupils in appointment of new staff, although now increasingly common, was a pioneering and potentially risky venture in Mulberry half a decade ago. The senior leadership team, however, testify to being consistently impressed by the perceptiveness, honesty and fairness of young people. Although 'risk-taking', these initiatives always appear well calculated, resting on a conviction that young people can be trusted not to stray beyond the bounds of propriety. It is indicative, say members of the SLT, of 'a culture of risk', in which teachers and pupils are allowed and encouraged to learn from mistakes.

When risk is discussed, it is accompanied by reference to a comprehensive safety net. There appear to be few unwelcome surprises in Mulberry School. The senior leadership team meet for three hours every Tuesday night to review what's happening in the school and to keep tabs on all major initiatives. Three times a year, middle and senior leaders hold monitoring interviews with pupils and regularly scrutinise their work. Once every four weeks there is review group which keeps middle managers aware of what is happening in the school, and gets feedback from them. Research and development groups meet on a Monday night to examine topics ranging across issues such as language, thinking and understanding, and a 'learning how to learn' agenda. There is a standing commitment every week to a staff development hour at which issues of assessment and learning are addressed. A weekend residential Inset is held once a year for all staff; and heads of year have their own conference each term to evaluate and disseminate practice, 'feeding up' emerging issues to the SLT.

The vision of the senior leadership is to enable staff to rise above constraining demands and ritual 'delivery' of the curriculum, in order to grasp the possibilities that lie even within the bounds of the traditional classroom. For Anna, the goal is truly to become a learning organisation:

> A learning organisation would be open to change and develop what it was doing, enthusiastic about reflecting on what it's actually doing and learning about what other people are doing. It would be outward-looking to both . . . academic research and also actual practice in other schools and want to impart [to] the whole educational community. A positive and confident place.

Asked whether this truly described Mulberry, she replied: 'I'd say we're well on the way.'

Conclusion

The remarks that conclude Chapter 6 could well be reiterated here. Again the case studies tell of struggle to implement change by confronting the dilemmas, tensions, constraints and contradictions that inevitably arise when introducing new ideas and practices that disturb the status quo. Again, the difficulties of spreading innovation from a few committed individuals to the whole school are particularly evident, especially in secondary schools with strong departmental structures and many staff members. The challenge is to build the social capital, cultures and structures that will find, release and build the intellectual capital within schools, drawing appropriately on expertise from outside, such as a project like ours. This puts the idea of project dissemination in an entirely different light: viewing implementation from the point of view of the receiving schools, rather than from the perspective of the project team.

A key question for school leaders is to find the right balance between being prescriptive, to ensure consistency, and allowing a degree of freedom to foster creativity. A number of these case studies reveal school leaders worrying away at this issue, and especially about dividing lines between things that are non-negotiable, such as principles of learning and children's rights to a good education, and details of practice that should be open to debate and experimentation. Sometimes they take different positions. What is clear is that, in the schools sampled to provide the LHTL project with a range of school types, there are highly committed and intelligent professionals who are constantly seeking the best ways to promote learning, and learning how to learn, by both teachers and pupils. Indeed, the number of times parallels are drawn between the learning of pupils and the learning of teachers is remarkable. Organisational learning and teacher learning are, then, seen as key conditions for pupil learning.

Chapter 8

Differences between and within schools

Classroom assessment practices and values

In earlier chapters we viewed our data through a wide-angled lens as we reported research findings from whole sample analyses on learning how to learn in classrooms (Chapter 3), schools (Chapter 4) and networks (Chapter 5). In Chapters 6 and 7 we swapped our wide angle for a zoom lens in order to take a closer look at individual schools. In those chapters we explored how the emerging themes and issues were reflected in practices and approaches developed at particular schools. The case studies point towards differences in practical approaches to promoting LHTL and underlying values and beliefs between individuals, groups and schools. They showed how a complex combination of issues were involved, which were particular to individual schools.

In this chapter, and the next, we return to a wider perspective, but this time we examine evidence of some systematic differences between sectors, schools, and groups of staff and pupils within schools, drawing on our quantitative data. Here we take another cut through the rich data provided by the LHTL staff questionnaire in relation to teachers' classroom practices and values. In Chapter 9, we look at data derived from questionnaires to teachers and to pupils on their general beliefs about learning. In both cases, there are implications for implementing, embedding and sustaining LHTL.

A central part of the development and research work reported in this book involved working with schools in order to understand how they support teachers in combining different assessment practices as a strategy for promoting learning how to learn in their classrooms. We

* Authored by David Pedder and Mary James

thought it unlikely that all the schools we were working with would face the same kinds of challenge in providing appropriate kinds of support to their teachers. It seemed much more likely that schools would face different challenges in promoting LHTL not least because of the different 'mix' of approaches to classroom assessment among members of staff at our different schools. In order to understand the mix of approaches, profiles were developed based on the assessment practices and values that teachers reported in their responses to the LHTL staff questionnaire (see Pedder, forthcoming, for more detail of this aspect of the work).

Developing such profiles provides a way of characterising the mix of practices and values among staff at different schools and comparing them. We did not limit ourselves to an interest in differences *between* schools. We thought it likely that differences in the promotion of LHTL between teachers *within* schools would also be important. Teachers might differ in terms of their years of teaching experience, the subjects they taught or the kind of managerial responsibility they had (we distinguished between senior and middle managers, teachers with little or no managerial responsibility, and learning support staff). Furthermore, primary school teachers might differ from secondary school teachers in the assessment values and practices underpinning their promotion of LHTL in classrooms. Our evidence suggests that, in relation to LHTL, teachers differ most in terms of the subjects they teach (secondary school staff only), the kind of managerial responsibility they hold, and whether they teach in primary or secondary schools. Our evidence also suggests that the assessment practices and values of different groups of teachers changed over the course of the project.

Profiling teachers in terms of their assessment values and practices

As noted in Chapter 4, 1,212 members of staff in 32 schools completed the first administration of the LHTL staff questionnaire in 2002. Analysis of our sample of responses led to the identification of distinctive groupings of teachers with quite different profiles of assessment practice.

How teachers' profiles were developed

Two main stages in the analysis of the questionnaire data lay the foundation for identifying distinctive groupings of teachers in our sample. As explained in Chapter 4, we used factor analysis to group together similar responses to the original 30 items in the questionnaire and develop a smaller, more manageable, set of underlying dimensions as a basis for comparing teachers' approaches to assessment. We thus identified three underlying dimensions or groupings of teachers' classroom assessment practice which we described as:

1. Making learning explicit (MLE)
3. Promoting learning autonomy (PLA)
4. Performance orientation (PO).

We interpreted the first two of these dimensions as referring to groups of assessment practices most closely related to the classroom promotion of LHTL.

The second stage of the analysis, not described earlier, was to group together individual members of staff to find out if they clustered in different groups that each shared distinctive characteristics in terms of our three dimensions of assessment practice. To identify these distinctive clusters or groupings of staff we used a statistical technique called cluster analysis (Box 8.1). Through cluster analysis we identified five different clusters of teachers, each cluster having a distinctive assessment profile in terms of the three dimensions of assessment identified through factor analysis.

Box 8.1   Cluster analysis

This is a statistical procedure for determining whether individuals are similar enough to fall into groups or clusters. People are divided up into groups with the intention of ensuring that members of any one cluster share more in common with each other than they do with members of other clusters. These are based on calculation of statistically significant differences. Cluster analysis is a common procedure used in market research, for example, in identifying brands or products that attract similar consumers. Different brands or products can be clustered into distinctive groups based on consumer characteristics. It then becomes possible to 'segment' consumers into different groups which may need to be targeted in different ways. This relates very closely to the purposes of the research reported in this chapter: identifying clusters of teachers based on their classroom assessment practices. Once clusters have been identified, the challenge is to identify different needs among different teacher clusters and develop appropriate and perhaps different kinds of support in response to these needs.

Comparing the cluster profiles

Figure 8.1 provides graphical representations of the profiles of the five teacher clusters in relation to their practice and values scores for each of the three assessment factors: MLE, PLA, and PO. These charts help you to see not only the levels of practice and values but also the gaps between the practices and values for each cluster.

There are one or two interesting and important conclusions that can be drawn from this analysis of teachers' profiles.

1. Teachers differ in their assessment practices. Members of staff in clusters 4 and 5 appear to promote LHTL more successfully than teachers with other cluster profiles. Their success is seen in their above average levels of practices for MLE and PLA. In contrast, teachers in clusters 1 and 2 report levels of practice below average on these same two factors. (The numbering of the clusters has no significance; they do not represent a hierarchy. It just happened that clusters 4 and 5 gave us profiles of practices that came closest to our understanding of what LHTL would look like in classrooms.)
2. The charts show that, not only are teachers in clusters 4 and 5 using high levels of MLE and PLA, their practices are also in very close alignment to their values. However, teachers in cluster 4 appear to sustain levels of PO well beyond their values and, on this dimension of assessment practice, they are similar to teachers in cluster 2. The difference is that teachers in cluster 4 are also able to sustain high levels of practice for MLE and PLA which suggests a very high level of expertise and flexibility indeed. Cluster 2 teachers do not sustain such high levels of practice, especially for PLA.

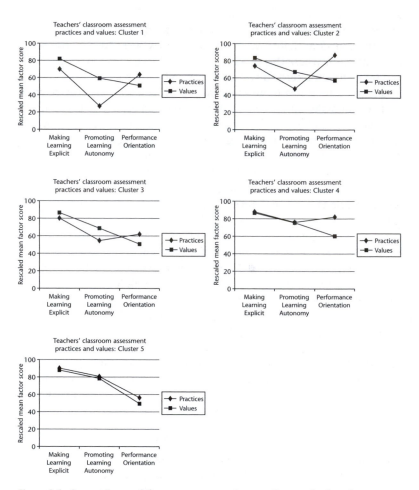

Figure 8.1 Comparisons of the average scores for practices and values for
members of each of the five clusters

3.   Figure 8.1 also shows that teachers in clusters 1 and 2 appear to
     struggle most in developing assessment practices in line with their
     values. Typically these teachers' levels of practice are ahead of
     the value they place on PO indicating that something external to
     them is 'requiring' this practice, and this is particularly marked for
     teachers in cluster 2. In contrast, their levels of practice for PLA are
     clearly below the value they place on such practices for improving
     the quality of classroom learning.

4. Cluster 3 teachers also appear to struggle with PLA with levels of practice behind their values, but this gap is less than for cluster 1 and 2 teachers. If clusters 4 and 5 represent successful teachers confidently using assessment practices and values to promote LHTL, then we can portray teachers in clusters 1 and 2, and, to a lesser degree, teachers in cluster 3, as struggling to bring their practices into closer alignment with their values in relation to PLA and PO. To do this they would need to raise their levels of practice for PLA and reduce levels of practice for PO.

We turn now to consider the characteristics of the staff members in each of these five clusters. Here, we consider the extent to which there are differences between groups of staff (for example, according to the subject they teach, their level of managerial responsibility, or whether they teach in a primary or a secondary school) in terms of their assessment practice profiles (their cluster membership). We then move on to consider the extent to which there are differences between schools in terms of the range and mix of profiles among members of staff.

Differences between primary and secondary school staff

Our analysis reveals statistically significant differences between primary school and secondary school staff in relation to their assessment profiles (cluster membership).

The first column in Table 8.1 lists the five clusters we identified. The second column, marked 'All', shows that teachers were quite evenly distributed across clusters 1, 2, 4 and 5. Cluster 3, which was close to the average on all dimensions of assessment practice, had the largest percentage of teachers, accounting for 26 per cent of the entire sample.

The columns show that there were equal percentages (19 per cent) of primary and secondary teachers in the successful and confident group of teachers in cluster 5, those most likely to capture the 'spirit' of AfL. Cluster 4 teachers, with high levels of PLA, MLE and PO, accounted for nearly a quarter of secondary teachers but only 14 per cent of primary teachers. Cluster 2, with an emphasis on PO, accounted for 21 per cent of secondary teachers but only 11 per cent of primary teachers. Clusters 1 and 3 accounted for over half (55 per cent) the primary teachers in our sample but only 37 per cent of the secondary teachers.

These percentages show quite different patterns of cluster membership for primary compared to secondary staff except for cluster 5. The

Table 8.1 Incidence of cluster types broken down by school type

Cluster	All (%)	Primary (%)	Secondary (%)
1. Low levels of MLE and PLA. Average PO.	17	23	14
2. Marked emphasis on PO	18	11	21
3. Close to average for all three dimensions	26	32	23
4. High levels of MLE and PLA but also high levels of PO	21	14	23
5. High levels of MLE and PLA with low PO	19	19	19
Total (% of staff)	101	99	100

Note:
χ^2 test indicates there is significant association between cluster membership and job type
($\chi^2=41.668$, $p<0.001$).

high levels of PO in clusters 2 and 4, combined with the evidence that there was a markedly higher percentage of secondary teachers who were members of these clusters than primary teachers, might suggest that teachers in secondary schools tend to develop a more performance-orientated approach than their primary colleagues. Given the pressure of public examinations in the secondary sector this might not be surprising. However, the higher percentage of secondary teachers in cluster 4 compared to the percentage of primary teachers also suggests that secondary teachers are more likely than primary teachers to sustain high levels of PLA and MLE alongside PO. This might indicate that teachers in this cluster are able to resolve some of the 'internal conflicts' that PO must inevitably create. Nevertheless there was a core of nearly one-fifth (19 per cent) of secondary and primary staff who, as members of cluster 5, reported high levels of PLA and MLE and low levels of PO. You will recall that in Chapter 3, about 20 per cent of the lessons observed were described as capturing the 'spirit' of AfL. This almost exactly coincides with the percentage of members of cluster 5, taken from this larger sample. Following our argument in Chapter 3, this might suggest that this group of teachers accept their own responsibility for what happens in their classrooms and, with a strong sense of their own agency, believe that their pupils can learn and achieve without succumbing to perceived external pressures for rushed curriculum coverage and teaching to the test.

Differences between senior and middle managers, teachers and support staff

Staff members differ not only according to whether they teach in primary or secondary school, there are also statistically significant differences in the assessment profiles of teachers according to the kind of job they have. We distinguished between senior and middle managers, teachers and learning support staff.

Figure 8.2 shows that for clusters 4 and 5 there is a preponderance of senior managers (white bars) and middle managers (black bars) over teachers (light grey bars) and support staff (dark grey bars). There is a similar, though less marked, pattern for cluster 2, with its emphasis on high PO. In contrast, clusters 1 and 3 are dominated by teachers with little or no managerial responsibility, and support staff. Managers have much smaller representation in clusters 1 and 3. You will recall that staff in cluster 1 have the lowest levels of practice for PLA, and both clusters record levels of practice for PO that are well ahead of their values.

% of staff in each cluster for each job type

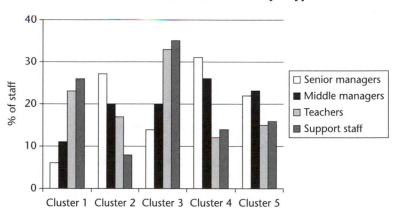

Figure 8.2 Primary and secondary school profiles by job type

Note:
χ^2 test indicates there is significant association between cluster membership and job type (χ^2=105.970, p<0.001).

We need to exercise caution in interpreting these results. We asked teachers to report their own practice, whereas we asked managers to report more broadly on practice across the school (on the basis that some would not be classroom teachers). Thus their responses are not so strictly comparable. What these answers may indicate is what managers *perceived* to be the case rather than what was actually practised in colleagues' classrooms. As such, it may provide another indicator of their aspirations, or how they want their school to be seen. What is most interesting may be the differences among managers, some of whom focus on PO, others who focus on MLE and PLA, and a third group who emphasise all three. Our case studies in Chapters 6 and 7 provide some illustrations of such differences in the orientations of head teachers.

Differences between secondary school teachers according to the subject taught

Table 8.2 reports the incidence of the five clusters across the sample of secondary school staff according to the subject they teach. These data help us investigate whether staff adopt distinctive approaches to classroom assessment according to these subject categories.

Table 8.2 contains plenty of percentages. For ease of reference we highlight the percentages of interest in this discussion. Those in bold type with a larger font size indicate high incidence in clusters 4 and 5. A larger font size but underlined indicate high incidence in clusters 1 and 2. Reading across the table, from left to right, we see the percentage of each subject group that were members of each cluster. Reading down each column of the table, we see the distribution of teachers in each subject group across the five clusters. It is worth remembering that members of clusters 4 and 5 report assessment practices that we think facilitate the promotion of LHTL best. Our data indicate that there is a statistically significant association between the assessment profile (cluster membership) and the subject taught by secondary school teachers.

Cluster 5 accounted for over 30 per cent of teachers in each of English, creative arts and physical education. Clusters 4 and 5 together accounted for 75 per cent of PE staff, 62 per cent of creative arts staff and for 50 per cent or more of English and modern foreign languages staff. This might suggest that there is something in the nature of these subjects (or the way such subjects are construed by teachers) that is particularly conducive to the promotion of LHTL through the use of classroom assessment practices. In contrast, clusters 4 and 5 together

Table 8.2 Incidence of the five clusters across different subjects at secondary school

Cluster	Maths (%)	English (%)	Science (%)	Humanities (%)	MFL (%)	Creative Arts (%)	PE (%)	DT+ICT (%)
1. Low levels of MLE and PLA. Average PO	22	6	21	21	11	6	3	18
2. Marked emphasis on PO	30	13	38	24	18	11	15	27
3. Close to average for all three dimensions	23	31	19	15	20	21	6	18
4. High levels of MLE and PLA but also high levels of PO	15	19	19	**24**	**34**	**26**	**39**	22
5. High levels of MLE and PLA with low PO	10	**31**	3	17	16	**36**	**36**	15
Total (% of staff)	100	100	100	101	99	100	99	100
Total (no. of staff)	60	48	78	72	44	70	33	55

Notes:
(i) Percentages in bold type with a larger font size indicate high incidence in clusters 4 and 5. A larger font size but underlined indicate high incidence in clusters 1 and 2.
(ii) χ^2 test indicates there is significant association between cluster membership and secondary subject taught (χ^2=95.206, p<0.001).

accounted for the smallest proportions of science (22 per cent) and mathematics teachers (25 per cent). Clusters 4 and 5 accounted for 37 per cent or more of staff in other subjects. This suggests that the content of science and mathematics (or the way such subjects are construed by teachers) appears to constrain the promotion of LHTL in classrooms.

In a comparison of two subjects, mathematics and English, Hodgen and Marshall (2005) examine the extent to which there is indeed a subject specificness of formative assessment (represented in our analysis by MLE and PLA). They indicate that, although formative assessment has generic ideas (e.g. the value of questioning, feedback, sharing criteria, and peer and self-assessment), they are manifest differently in different subjects. These differences reflect the guild differences that students are being introduced to in each subject. For example, criteria for assessing work in English reflects English as a subject discipline, which values analysis of individual response, debate about what constitutes quality, alternative perspectives, and so on. In contrast, school mathematics tends to be taught as formal and abstract concepts. Hodgen and Marshall (ibid., p. 172) conclude: 'Despite, or perhaps because of, the differences in the nature of the disciplines, we feel that the two subjects have much to learn from each other.' Our analysis of cluster patterns supports this conclusion.

We also found that the practices of mathematics and science teachers are characterised by a particularly strong PO. Cluster 2, with its marked emphasis on PO, accounted for 38 per cent of science staff and 30 per cent of mathematics staff. Close behind their maths colleagues were the design technology and ICT staff with 27 per cent of their staff in cluster 2. An important characteristic of members of cluster 2 is not simply the high levels of PO but also the large gap between practice and values. Cluster 2 teachers find it difficult to balance their approach to assessment in line with their values. This is reflected in practice levels of PO ahead of values, and in practice levels of PLA behind values. Subjects with the lowest proportions of staff in cluster 2 were creative arts (11 per cent), English (13 per cent) and PE (15 per cent). We are inclined to interpret these findings as manifestations of subject cultures that either prioritise or minimise the importance of tests and examinations in shaping teaching and learning in classrooms. Frequent internal tests are familiar in science and mathematics classrooms, which may account for 'formative use of summative tests' being added to the repertoire of AfL strategies in the KMOFA Project (Black et al. 2003) which worked with a majority of science and mathematics teachers.

In addition, mathematics (22 per cent) and science (21 per cent) together with humanities (21 per cent) have the highest proportion of cluster 1 teachers. Cluster 1 has the lowest levels of practice for PLA of all the cluster groups. This pattern appears to reinforce the argument that science and mathematics staff face particular challenges in promoting LHTL through MLE and PLA. In contrast, cluster 1 accounts for the smallest percentage of PE (3 per cent), English (6 per cent), and creative arts (6 per cent) staff.

In the next section we consider our data in relation to whether, and how, particular schools differed in the assessment practices and values of their staff.

Differences between schools in the mix of assessment profiles of their staff members

We analysed our 2002 data to look at school differences. We knew we would also need to exercise caution in interpreting some of the results because, for the smaller primary schools in our sample, they are based on rather small numbers of staff. Nevertheless, different schools appeared to have a quite different mix of teachers in terms of their profiles of assessment practices and values (their cluster membership). Table 8.3 shows differences in the incidence of the five clusters across different schools, with reference to 'upper quartiles', 'lower quartiles' and 'medians' (the meanings of which are explained in Box 8.2).

Box 8.2 Schools at upper and lower quartiles and medians

Schools were arranged in descending order of the percentage of staff in each cluster to provide five separate cluster rankings of schools. For any given cluster ranking, the school at the top of the ranking had the highest percentage of staff members in that cluster. The school at the bottom of the ranking had the lowest percentage of staff members in that cluster.

Schools in this rank order were then divided into four equal parts. The upper quartile is the part containing the top 25 per cent of schools and the lower quartile is the part containing the lowest 25 per cent of schools. A school described as being 'at the upper quartile' is at the cut-off point where 25 per cent of schools have a

---

continued

higher percentage of staff in the given cluster and where 75 per cent of schools have a lower percentage of staff in the given cluster. A school 'at the lower quartile' is a school at the cut-off point where 75 per cent of schools have a higher percentage of staff in the cluster and where 25 per cent of schools have a lower percentage of staff in the given cluster. A school described as 'at the median' is in the middle of the ranking where 50 per cent of schools have a higher percentage of teachers in the cluster and 50 per cent of schools have a lower percentage of staff in the cluster. (All these descriptions are used in Table 8.3.)

Comparing the schools at the upper and lower quartiles gives us an indication of the differences between schools in terms of the mix of assessment profiles among their members of staff.

If we look at the cluster 5 row in Table 8.3a, the percentage of cluster 5 teachers appears to vary considerably across all schools in the sample. Schools at the upper (3rd column) and lower (5th column) quartiles, for example, differ by around 16 per cent. This is to say that 29 per cent of teachers at the upper quartile school were cluster 5 teachers while only 13 per cent of teachers at the lower quartile school were cluster 5 teachers. The difference between these percentages is 16 per cent. At the other end of the spectrum we find cluster 1 teachers who were struggling with very low levels of PLA. Schools at the upper and lower quartiles differed by 17 per cent in the percentage of staff in cluster 1. Similar differences between schools can be seen for the percentage of staff in clusters 2, 3 and 4 as well. These differences suggest considerable variation across our schools.

Tables 8.3b and 8.3c report the incidence of clusters across secondary and primary schools respectively. These allow us to compare secondary and primary schools at the upper and lower quartiles for each cluster and this gives an indication of how much primary and secondary schools vary in their mix of teachers for each cluster. It appears that primary schools vary more than secondary schools in the percentage of teachers in each of the five clusters, but, as we mentioned earlier, their size may exaggerate these differences because a very few teachers can represent a high percentage of staff in a small school.

The largest differences between primary schools at the upper and lower quartile were on the percentage of their staff in cluster 3 (a

Table 8.3 Incidence of the five clusters across schools

Cluster	Highest two schools (% of staff)	School at upper quartile (% of staff)	School at median (% of staff)	School at lower quartile (% of staff)	Lowest two schools (% of staff)
3a. Primary and secondary schools combined					
1. Low levels of MLE and PLA. Average PO	54, 38	27	17	10	4, 4
2. Marked emphasis on PO	33, 29	24	15	4	0, 0
3. Close to average for all three dimensions	61, 46	37	26	19	0. 0
4. High levels of MLE and PLA but also high levels of PO	37, 36	23	18	14	0, 0
5. High levels of MLE and PLA with low PO	67, 63	29	20	13	5, 5
3b. Primary schools only					
1. Low levels of MLE and PLA. Average PO	54, 38	29	20	13	10, 4
2. Marked emphasis on PO	33, 29	19	15	0	0, 0
3. Close to average for all three dimensions	61, 45	43	33	13	0, 0
4. High levels of MLE and PLA but also high levels of PO	30, 27	20	14	10	0, 0
5. High levels of MLE and PLA with low PO	67, 63	35	19	11	5, 5

continued

Table 8.3 continued

Cluster	Highest two schools (% of staff)	School at upper quartile (% of staff)	School at median (% of staff)	School at lower quartile (% of staff)	Lowest two schools (% of staff)
3c. Secondary schools only					
1. Low levels of MLE and PLA. Average PO	27, 24	17	11	9	4, 4
2. Marked emphasis on PO	28, 27	24	22	15	10, 5
3. Close to average for all three dimensions	46, 36	26	20	19	17, 16
4. High levels of MLE and PLA but also high levels of PO	37, 36	27	21	18	17, 15
5. High levels of MLE and PLA with low PO	31, 29	26	20	13	12, 11

difference of 30 per cent) and cluster 5 (a difference of 24 per cent). For secondary schools there was far less variation. The largest difference between upper and lower quartile secondary schools was 13 per cent for the percentage of staff in cluster 5.

In order to illustrate these between-school differences, we thought it would be interesting to look at the cluster patterns exhibited by the schools we have focused upon in our case studies in Chapters 6 and 7. Figure 8.3a shows the assessment practice profiles for the infants' primary and junior schools mentioned in Chapter 6; Figure 8.3b shows the assessment practice profiles for the four secondary schools mentioned in Chapter 7. However, we have also included the profile for all primary schools in our sample, in Figure 8.3a, and the profile for all secondary schools, in Figure 8.3b. (The profiles for all primary and all secondary schools are derived from the percentages given in Table 8.1.) These seven graphs illustrate some of the different challenges schools face in supporting teachers in their efforts to promote LHTL.

Figure 8.3a shows that Aspen Infants School had a lower than average percentage of cluster 1 and 2 staff but a markedly higher than average percentage of cluster 4 staff. Janice's account of her struggle to provide genuine learning experiences for her pupils, in a constraining performance-orientated context, illustrates the tensions embodied in these cluster patterns. In contrast, Hazel Primary School had markedly higher percentages of cluster 1 and 2 staff and low percentages of cluster 4 and 5 staff, which reflects the head teacher's worries that her staff were uncomfortable with taking risks, frightened about taking things on board, and that piecemeal development had led to inconsistency. Eucalyptus Junior School was somewhat similar, although the percentage of cluster 3 staff was markedly lower than the average for primary schools. The emphasis on PO when the baseline survey was conducted in 2002 would however accord with the tangible anxiety to raise test scores or risk losing pupils and teachers in a highly competitive environment. All three graphs in Figure 8.3 suggest, what the cases studies confirm, that promoting LHTL presented considerable challenges for these schools at the beginning of the project in 2002.

In Figure 8.3b, the assessment practice profile for Hawthorn High School had a markedly higher percentage of cluster 5 staff, than the average, at the start of our project, while Elm School had a much lower percentage. This connects with the stories told in Chapter 7 which show how, at the beginning of the project, Hawthorn quickly adopted a whole school approach, by incorporating AfL into its teaching and learning policy. The project was much slower to get off the ground in Elm, and

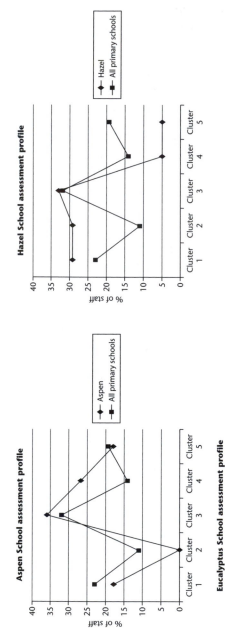

Aspen School assessment profile

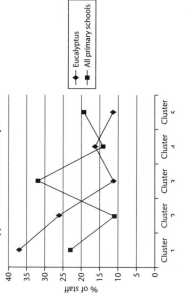

Eucalyptus School assessment profile

Hazel School assessment profile

Figure 8.3a Case study primary school assessment practice profiles

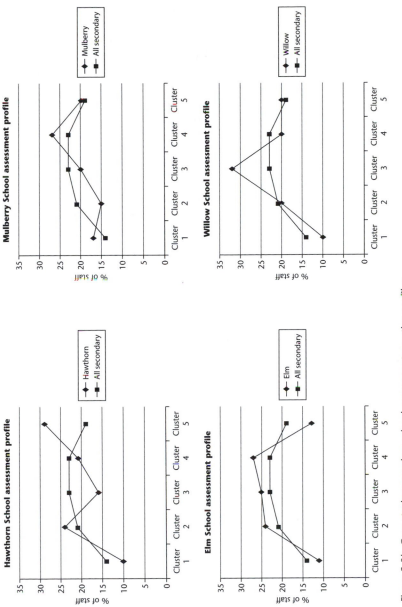

Figure 8.3b Case study secondary school assessment practice profiles

much less focused initially. Nevertheless the spread of cluster member-ship in both these schools illustrates the difficulty of getting all staff to 'sing from the same hymn sheet', even in a school like Hawthorn with very strong, directive leadership. Both Mulberry School and Elm School had a higher proportion of cluster 4 staff than average which suggests that both these groups of teachers were juggling commitment to LHTL practices with PO, although perhaps less so in Mulberry where the per-centage of cluster 2 staff was lower. This also resonates with the different characteristics of the two schools portrayed in the case studies.

These differences between schools in terms of their mix of assessment practice profiles provide quantified evidence, from all staff in each of the schools, to set alongside the rich qualitative evidence from the more limited samples of staff who were observed and interviewed. Taken together, they illustrate the different challenges individual schools face in their efforts to promote learning how to learn through AfL practices. The case studies in Chapters 6 and 7 describe some of the strategies and approaches developed by different schools for tackling these challenges.

Summary of key themes from the baseline data

Overall, our baseline survey data indicate that staff in secondary schools tended to develop different assessment practices from staff in primary schools. Secondary school staff appeared to be struggling more than primary school staff in reducing PO practices so they are more consistent with their professional values. We speculated earlier that the pressure of external examinations might contribute to this. However, primary school staff seemed to be struggling more than secondary school staff in PLA and increasing these practices in line with their values. This may have something to do with the age of children and whether teachers feel confident in handing them more responsibility for their learning.

In 2002, we also saw differences in the assessment profiles of staff according to whether or not they had managerial responsibility. Our data suggest that those with the major responsibility for classroom teaching – teachers and support staff – appeared to experience the greatest difficulties in developing strategies for PLA. They clearly need to be supported in meeting these challenges. As reported in Chapter 4, school support for classroom-based collaborative learning among teachers appears to be a key precondition for developing successful ways of promoting LHTL in classrooms.

In addition, our 2002 survey evidence indicates some quite striking differences in secondary schools between teachers of different subjects. It appears that teachers of more discursive or expressive subjects, such as English and creative arts, but also PE, appeared to be more likely to sustain high levels of PLA and MLE. At the beginning of the project, physical education and modern foreign languages teachers had the highest percentage of staff with high levels of PLA and MLE, alongside high levels of PO practice (cluster 4), of any subject group. The results for PE and modern foreign languages are difficult to explain and warrant further study. Black *et al.* (2003, p. 72) report that, 'we have found that modern foreign languages present the greatest challenges in embedding formative assessment in classroom practice', although why this should be so is a puzzle to them because they believe the subject creates many opportunities. Like PE there is usually a clear focus on improvement and mastery within the lesson rather than learning for some later test, although this may matter too (hence cluster 4 membership). Perhaps our evidence, from 44 modern foreign languages teachers and 33 PE teachers, shows that the KMOFAP evidence is anomalous and there is much potential in these subjects with teachers already attempting MLE and PLA. Mathematics and science teachers, in contrast, had the highest percentages of teachers in cluster 2 with a marked emphasis on PO, and cluster 1 with low levels of PLA and MLE. Humanities also had a higher percentage of teachers than most other subjects in cluster 1. What unifies these groups may be a perception that these school subjects are 'content heavy' with a 'correct' version to be acquired – a point made by Black *et al.* (2003, pp. 67–74). Like Black and his colleagues, we would argue that there is more scope for LHTL through AfL than might be imagined, although teachers of these subjects may need specially targeted help to develop their practice. The challenge for schools would seem to lie in achieving an appropriate balance between generic and subject-specific kinds of support for helping teachers develop strategies for promoting LHTL.

Finally, our evidence suggests that there are important differences between schools in terms of the range and mix of the assessment practice profiles (cluster membership) of their staff members. In a substantial minority of schools at the outset of the project, one or two clusters tended to dominate the profiles. Some schools appeared to have a majority of staff in clusters 1 and 2, characterised by an emphasis on PO and/or low levels of PLA. Some other schools appeared to have a majority of staff in clusters 4 and 5 with high levels of PLA and MLE. An important challenge here is to find ways of minimising unhelpful diversity on these dimensions so that different groups of staff develop a shared view on the direction they wish to take. They also need to be supported, according to their group needs, in putting their values into practice.

Leaders at all levels of the school organisation are called upon to optimise scope and support for different groups of staff to realise their values in practice in ways that explicitly relate to current school improvement priorities. Differences may still remain in the extent to which leaders at different schools aim for a shared vision across all staff groups or whether, instead, they embrace diversity of perspective as an invaluable resource for developing more differentiated approaches to promoting LHTL across the school. We saw a sophisticated approach to leadership in the Hawthorn secondary school case study that promoted, from the top, a very clear whole-school sense of direction. Within this framework, different groups of staff were 'permitted' to develop ways of realising their values in practice. Similar approaches were adopted at other secondary and primary schools. In contrast, the Hazel primary school case study exemplifies an approach that is more explicitly responsive to the preferences and starting points of different members of staff. This kind of leadership approach was also evident elsewhere.

Each of these strategic approaches to leadership, in school contexts where staff practices and values are diverse, requires a delicate balance to be struck. On the one hand, there is a need to ensure that whole school improvement priorities are realised in practice across the school, on the other, there is a need to listen and respond to the perspectives of different groups of staff

In our final section, we find out whether, during the course of the project, different groups of teachers managed to bring their assessment practices into line with their values as one way of promoting LHTL in their classrooms.

Patterns of change: 2002–2004

A common difficulty in carrying out school-based research with the same schools over a number of years is in sustaining the participation of school staff in the full range of data collection activities over the duration of the research. The LHTL project was undertaken at a time when schools were facing a steady stream of reform initiatives and these placed considerable demands on teachers' time. Nevertheless, over half the number of teachers who completed the 2002 questionnaire did so

in 2004 (1,212 teachers from 32 schools completed the 2002 questionnaire, and 698 teachers from 23 schools the 2004 one). Given the
differences in sample sizes, we need to exercise caution in reporting
patterns of change. However, the composition of the 2004 sample was
very similar to that of the 2002 sample in terms of gender, school sector,
managerial responsibility and years of teaching experience and, for
secondary school teachers, subjects taught (Pedder, forthcoming). Both
samples reflected almost identical proportions of staff according to
these categories. This increases our confidence that, despite the smaller
sample size in 2004, there is unlikely to be a systematic bias in the
sample that distorts the patterns of change we report here. For reasons
of space the summaries of change are brief and selective, based on the
following questions that arise from our discussion so far:

•   Were teachers and support staff able to increase levels of PLA in
    their classrooms?
•   Did primary school staff manage to increase levels of PLA in line
    with their values?
•   Did secondary staff manage to reduce levels of PO in line with their
    values?
•   How did teachers of different subjects change their practices
    between 2002 and 2004?

By 2004, teachers across the whole sample, but not support staff, had
managed significant increases in levels of PLA, thus bringing their
practices more closely into line with their values. Senior managers,
too, reported significant increases in levels of PLA, but not middle managers. One of the changes reported at the end of the project was an
increase in PLA practices among primary school staff; this brought
their practices more closely into line with their values. Furthermore,
the PLA practices reported by primary staff in 2004 were much more
consistent with levels of practice reported by their colleagues in secondary schools than had been the case in 2002. Secondary staff had
also managed to increase levels of PLA but the increase was not as large
as the increase reported by primary staff.

    As we can see in Figures 8.4 and 8.5 there are interesting differences
among secondary staff teaching different subjects. The asterisk against
some of the subject labels in both of the figures indicates that the
differences between the 2002 and the 2004 levels of practice are significant. This is to say that the differences we have observed among this
sample of secondary staff has not occurred by chance but is more than

95 per cent likely to be reflected in the wider population of secondary teachers from which they were drawn. Two patterns emerged. First, there are significant increases in PLA practices recorded by maths, English and science staff only. In contrast, the only subject not to record significant reductions in PO was maths. Staff teaching all other subjects reported significant reductions in levels of PO between 2002 and 2004. It seems from these data that staff became less reliant on performance orientated practices, such as teaching to the test, as a means of promoting learning and achievement, although mathematics staff remained resistant to change in this respect. However, as with science teachers, there was some progress in maths towards practices for promoting learning autonomy, although these groups started from a lower base than other subjects. English teachers continued to develop those practices that they seem to have favoured from the beginning. We do not want to portray English teachers as heroes and maths teachers as villains but clearly there are different professional development needs to be met.

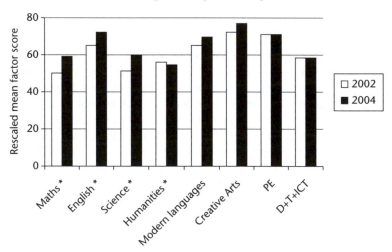

Figure 8.4 Promoting learning autonomy: changes in levels of practice according to subject taught at secondary school, 2002–2004

Note: The asterisk against some of the subject labels indicates that the differences between the 2002 and the 2004 practice scores are significant.

Performance orientation

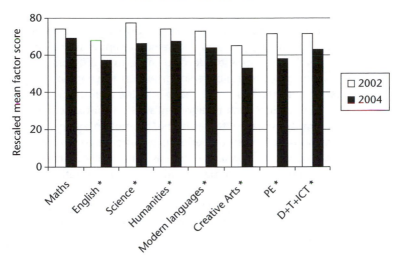

Figure 8.5 Performance orientation: changes in levels of practice according to subject taught at secondary school, 2002–2004

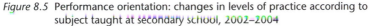

Note: The asterisk against some of the subject labels indicates that the differences between the 2002 and the 2004 practice scores are significant.

Overall, the trends are encouraging. The main changes that occurred appeared to relate to PLA and PO. High levels of practice and value recorded for MLE at the outset of the project were sustained by all groups of staff throughout the project. Little change was reported. The patterns of change reported in this chapter suggest increases in practices of PLA and decreases in practices of PO so that, in the main, practices were more consistent with values. The responses from secondary staff suggest that they managed to reduce levels of PO more than they managed to raise levels of PLA. Primary teachers had managed to record larger increases in PLA practices than their secondary school colleagues. However, it is as well to remember that, despite these systematic differences, it is changes that occur within particular schools that are responsible for these improvements, whatever the general conditions of different phases or subject orientation of teachers. The main challenge is for schools to find ways to support different groups of staff in sustaining increases in the promotion of learning autonomy as a key strategy for promoting LHTL.

Conclusion

What is clear from this chapter is that the diversity of classroom assessment practice profiles among different groups of staff under-pins the need for schools to develop more fully differentiated strategies aimed at helping different groups of teachers to bring their assessment practices more closely into line with their values. Our data suggest that such realignment would lead to increased levels of practice geared towards the promotion of learning autonomy and a decrease of performance orientated practices. During the course of our project, there was some significant change of this kind, although we remain cautious about attributing this solely to the impact of the project.

A key message of this chapter therefore is that realigning practice in line with values represents a different set of challenges for different groups of teachers. Effective systems of school support will develop strategies for taking account of such differences.

Chapter 9

Differences between and within schools

Pupils' and teachers' beliefs about learning

A dominant theme throughout this book has been the importance of developing both beliefs and practices in promoting learning how to learn. Quantitative evidence from our LHTL staff questionnaire (Chapters 4 and 8) and qualitative evidence from classroom observations and interviews (Chapter 3) suggest that introducing new practices without understanding or valuing the principles that underpin them can lead to superficial, even mechanical and ritualistic, implementation. And this can apply to both teachers and pupils. If change is to be become embedded and sustained, it needs a deeper commitment to some important underlying beliefs about learning and effective teaching. These provide frameworks for teachers and pupils to, according to Piaget's definition of intelligence, know what to do when they don't know what to do. They also offer potential for what Perrenoud (1998) describes as the regulation of learning processes (see Chapter 1) and for learning as knowledge creation i.e. beyond knowledge acquisition.

In this chapter, therefore, we look in more depth at the more general beliefs about, and attitudes towards, learning held by teachers and pupils in our project. These were investigated by designing and administering two questionnaires: one was given to Year 5 (aged 10) and Year 8 (aged 13) pupils in project schools; the other was given to teachers and assistants. Each was administered on two occasions, a year apart during the project's implementation. The results of these surveys are presented below, including analyses of some between-school and within-school differences.

* Authored by Paul Black with Joanna Swann and Dylan Wiliam

Pupils' beliefs about learning

Questions and factors

The questionnaire that we used with pupils was composed, and tested so that we could explore a wide range of pupils' beliefs. The results of our development were a questionnaire for primary pupils comprising 25 questions, and another for secondary pupils containing these same 25 questions, with a further 20 added. (These questionnaires are available, under 'self-evaluation resources' on the website – http://www. learntolearn.ac.uk – and may be downloaded for use by schools.)

Our first steps were to think about ideas about learning which pupils may hold, and to set these out as statements with which pupils may or may not agree. An example we used was:

I like doing things where I can use my own ideas.

In order to present pupils with a choice on any opinion, we then turned each suggestion into a pair of alternatives. Thus the example above led to the following:

Ex.1

I like to be told exactly   □ □ □ □ □ □   *I like doing things*
what to do   *where I can use my*
                                                      own ideas

The pupil was asked to express an opinion by choosing between the two. To record this choice, the six boxes were placed between the two, and pupils were asked to tick the box that best expressed their opinion, choosing the extreme left it they felt that the left-hand alternative was correct (and vice versa), and somewhere in-between if they did not completely agree with either alternative.

When we had collected responses from pupils, each would first be given a score: 1 for the left-hand box; 6 for the right hand; 3 or 4 for the central two, and so on. These could then be added to calculate an average over all the pupils. Thus, an average of, say, 4.8 would indicate that most pupils strongly agreed with the right-hand statements, while 3.5 would indicate that opinions were evenly split between the two.

The questionnaire was given on two occasions, in 2003 and 2004, with the same pupils so that we could investigate the change in their beliefs. The primary school version was completed by about 200 pupils in Year 5 of six schools, and the secondary version was completed by about 900 pupils in Year 8, and about 600 in Year 10, of seven schools (see Black *et al.*, 2006, and forthcoming (a), for full accounts, especially for results for Year 10 pupils, which we do not report in this chapter).

One feature that we looked for was the ways in which pupils' answers to any one question were related to their answers to others. An exploration of such relationships indicated that many of the questions fell into two factors, each of which was a group of inter-related questions.

There were nine questions that constituted one of the factors, the common focus of which was expressed in the label, 'School learning'. Three examples were:

Ex.1

I like to be told exactly   □ □ □ □ □ □   *I like doing things*
what to do   *where I can use my*
                                                    own ideas

Ex.2

I learn more when the   □ □ □ □ □ □   *I learn more when I*
teacher makes most of   *make most of the*
the decisions about   *decisions about*
learning   *my learning*

Ex.3

If you produce a lot of   □ □ □ □ □ □   *Just because you've*
pages of work it means   *produced a lot of*
that your work is good   *pages of work it*
                                                doesn't mean that
                                                your work is good

All nine questions in the factor were concerned with various features of the learning experience in school, rather than learning more generally. The mean score for the factor was 4.45 for both Year 5 and Year 8 pupils, showing that overall there was little difference between the older and younger pupils. Also, pupils were, on average, expressing positive attitudes – answers were mainly above 3.5. However, this overall average hides many detailed differences.

The second factor, labelled 'Involvement and initiative in learning', was composed of five questions which were about more general beliefs about learning, as the following examples illustrate:

Ex.4

I don't check my work   □ □ □ □ □ □   *I often check my*
unless I have to   *work so I can*
                                                            improve it

Ex.5

I like someone to tell   □ □ □ □ □ □   *I like to work things*
me what the answer is   *out for myself*

The overall mean for this factor, at about 4.2, showed generally positive responses.

Changes over time and differences between pupils of different ages and across schools

Over a period of a year, between the two administrations of the questionnaire, the mean scores on this factor showed no change for Year 8 pupils but an increase from 4.36 to 4.55 for those in Year 5 (by the time of the second administration the former were in Year 9 and the latter were in Year 6). There were many similarities in the patterns of differences and changes in responses to individual questions but, overall, there was no consistent pattern of changes.

However, the above changes were for averages calculated for all pupils from a given year group, irrespective of their schools. We also looked at the mean scores for the pupils in each school, which showed some striking differences. For example, the 'school learning' factor score in one primary school increased over the project year from 3.85 to 4.32, i.e. by 0.47. Figure 9.1 illustrates what this change represents in terms of the numbers of pupils with the different factor scores on the two occasions in this school. In another primary school, the change was negligible. Other primary schools showed increases in-between these two. The gains for the secondary schools were between 0.27 and –0.21 (i.e. a decrease in the latter case).

The second factor, 'Involvement and initiative in learning', showed little overall change between 2003 and 2004, and little difference

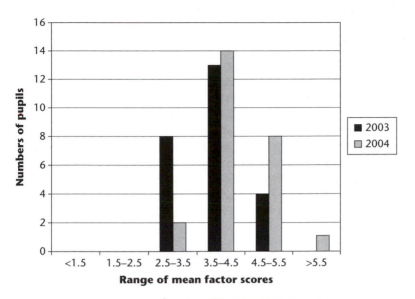

Figure 9.1 Pupils' beliefs about learning: change in responses of 26 pupils in one
school – 'School learning' factor

between the Year 5 and the Year 8 pupils. The issues explored by the
questions in this factor were less directly linked to the changes in classroom practice promoted in the LHTL project than those in the 'school
learning' factor, so less change might be expected. However, there were
still many differences in detail. There were more marked changes
when the means were calculated separately for each school. The mean
scores ranged from 4.66 to 3.97 over the seven secondary schools and
from 4.46 to 4.04 over the six primary schools.

In general, schools where pupils became more positive about 'involvement and initiative in learning' also showed the greatest gains in the
'school learning' questions.

In summary, there were increases in the score on the 'school learning'
factor for all the primary schools, but on the 'involvement and initiative
in learning' factor, half of them showed small gains and half showed
decreased scores. For the secondary Year 8 pupils, again changes were
generally twice as large for 'school learning' as for the other factor, but
there were both gains and losses in both.

Teachers' beliefs about learning

Questions and factors

The findings in this section are based on a 60-item questionnaire which was administered on two occasions – in the summer term in 2003 and a year later in 2004. Only 69 primary teachers in eight schools and 128 secondary teachers in four schools responded on both occasions. These responses could be aligned so that the changes discussed below were those recorded by the same teachers. The teachers recorded their views by selecting one of eight boxes, set between the alternatives as shown in the examples below; thus any mean score above 4.5 indicates a preference for the favourable alternative. (A full account of the results for the teacher questionnaire will be found in Black *et al.*, forthcoming (b).)

The first of four factors which emerged from analysis of the data is illustrated by two of its eight questions.

Ex.6

You don't have to   ☐ ☐ ☐ ☐ ☐ ☐ ☐ ☐   *You have to play*
play with ideas   *with ideas to*
to be a good learner   *be a good learner*

Ex.7

You don't need to   ☐ ☐ ☐ ☐ ☐ ☐ ☐ ☐   *To be a good*
know anything   *learner it is*
about learning to   *essential to*
be a good learner   *know about*
                                             learning

This group of questions is summarised by the factor label, 'Being a good learner'. While those questions made no explicit reference to schools, pupils, or teaching, the second factor did. This was labelled 'Learning principles for pupils' (see examples 8 and 9).

Ex.8

	□ □ □ □ □ □ □ □	
As a teacher, my principal aim is that pupils become able to able to recall specific information in the context in which it was taught		*As a teacher, my principal aim is that pupils become able to apply general principles to new contexts*

Ex.9

	□ □ □ □ □ □ □ □	
For some pupils, there's no point in them spending time in learning how to learn		*Time spent learning how to learn will enable all pupils to learn more in the longer term*

While all of the second factor's questions were general views about schooling rather than about classroom practices, those in the third factor, labelled 'Interaction and feedback in learning', expressed ideas which were more directly focused on specific kinds of classroom practice, as the next two examples illustrate.

Ex.10

	□ □ □ □ □ □ □ □	
It's better for pupils to give the right answer than to ask interesting questions		*It's better for pupils to ask interesting questions than to give the right answer*

Ex.11

	□ □ □ □ □ □ □ □	
In the classroom, good learners don't criticise ideas		*In the classroom, good learners criticise ideas*

The four questions in the fourth factor, labelled 'Collaboration in learning', dealt in turn with the subject contexts of English, mathematics and science, and with learning in general.

Ex.12

| In maths, pupils who collaborate learn less | □ □ □ □ □ □ □ □ | In maths pupils who collaborate learn more than those who learn individually |

Ex. 13

| In general, pupils learn very little from working with each other | □ □ □ □ □ □ □ □ | In general, pupils learn a great deal from working with each other |

Results for primary and secondary teachers

Figure 9.2 compares the mean scores of primary teachers with the mean scores for secondary teachers on the questions selected from the four factors.

Overall, the primary teachers' scores on three of the factors (F2: Learning principles for pupils; F3: Interaction and feedback in learning; and F4: Collaboration in learning) were higher than those of the secondary teachers. For the first factor (F1: Being a good learner)

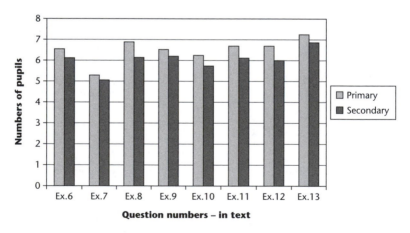

Figure 9.2 Teachers' beliefs about learning: mean scores of primary and secondary teachers for selected questions

however, and despite the difference shown by Examples 6 and 7, there was no such difference. These findings are interesting in the light of the finding in Chapter 8 (see Figure 8.2) that staff in secondary schools in 2002 tended to have a more performance-orientated approach to their classrooms, although their primary colleagues, at that time, struggled to promote learning autonomy. However, by 2004, there was an increase in practices aimed at promoting learning autonomy reported by primary staff. The results of the separate survey reported in this chapter, conducted in year two of the project, also seem to confirm a learning orientation.

Changes over time for teachers and differences between schools

We also analysed responses to the teachers' beliefs about learning questionnaire to explore the changes, from 2003 to 2004, in the mean scores for each of the four factors. This analysis provides evidence to support a few main conclusions:

- Overall, there are no very striking changes or differences, none, for example, larger than might be produced if all teachers changed their opinion by selecting, say, point 6 on the 8-point scale instead of point 7. The fact that the mean scores were high, many well above the 'break-even' points of 3.5 (pupils' scale) and 4.5 (teachers' scale) meant that it would be harder for increases to show up, e.g. with an initial score of 5.3 on a 6-point scale it is very unlikely that a significant improvement could be expected.
- However, there was large variability between schools. (Chapter 8 also noted marked school differences with respect to reported classroom assessment values and practices.) This emerged in analyses of both the 2003 responses and the 2004 responses, and in the analysis of change (gains) between 2003 and 2004. Figure 9.3, for example, shows the profiles of the changes for two primary and two secondary schools.
- It is difficult to interpret these changes in relation to the interventions of the project. It might be expected that any effects on teachers' views would show up directly in the factors concerned with beliefs about learning practices i.e. 'interaction and feedback in learning' and 'collaboration in learning'. Effects might be expected to be less direct on 'learning principles for pupils', and less directly again on 'being a good learner'. In fact, the only factor

which showed significant changes was 'learning principles for pupils'. However, this is important if, as we have argued throughout this book, principles of learning are important for the development of practice.

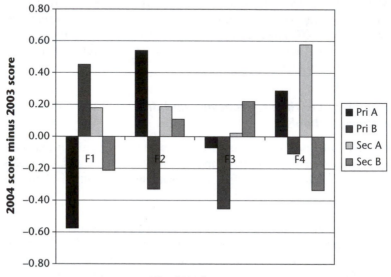

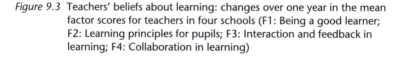

The four factors

Figure 9.3 Teachers' beliefs about learning: changes over one year in the mean factor scores for teachers in four schools (F1: Being a good learner; F2: Learning principles for pupils; F3: Interaction and feedback in learning; F4: Collaboration in learning)

The absence of any large overall changes, together with the diverse patterns of significant changes across the schools, suggests that different schools took the LHTL project's messages to heart in different ways and with varying effectiveness. These findings are entirely consistent with findings from the staff questionnaire (reported in Chapters 4 and 8) and our case studies (reported in Chapters 6 and 7), which also provide evidence that project innovations do not impact on schools in any direct, linear way. They are mediated, and integrated with other initiatives at the school site, and therefore the conditions within and between schools that facilitate uptake, implementation and embedding of project ideas are crucial – and justify the main focus of LHTL project.

Changes and differences for different staff groups

Teachers responding to the questionnaire were asked to identify their role in the school; almost half identified themselves in terms of the subjects which they taught. These were classified in subject groups which gave seven groups that were large enough (over 20 teachers in each) to justify analysis. The analysis yielded an overall rank order for Factors 1 and 4 ('being a good learner' and 'collaboration in learning') for the subjects, as shown in Figure 9.4. It is clear that the two factors follow the same trend.

It is interesting to compare these particular results with the evidence of subject differences in Table 8.2 (Chapter 8), which shows comparatively low levels of practice associated with learning how to learn reported by science, mathematics and humanities teachers in 2002, and high levels of performance-orientated practices from mathematics and science teachers, and technology teachers to a lesser extent. English teachers, in contrast, had high levels of reported practices associated with learning how to learn, which coincides with their positive beliefs about learning captured in the survey described in this chapter.

Another main finding is that there were marked differences between the responses of primary teachers and those of their classroom

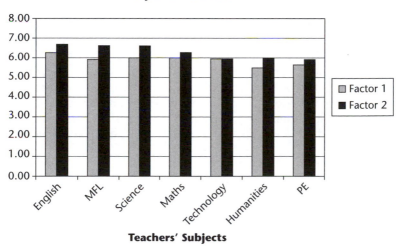

Figure 9.4 Teachers' beliefs about learning: subject differences on two factors: 'Being a good learner' (F1) and 'Collaboration in learning' (F4)

assistants, and between those of secondary teachers and of their classroom assistants. These again showed very wide variations between schools. In some schools, the responses of classroom assistants were very similar to those of their teacher colleagues; in other schools class-room assistants showed much lower scores. Qualitative data from case studies (yet to be reported) may shed some light on this and help to us to find out whether this is a staff category effect or a school effect. It could be the latter rather than the former because we know that some project schools included classroom assistants in school-based profes-sional development opportunities for teachers; others did not, which may have hindered their learning together.

Conclusion

One general finding from the analysis of these surveys of beliefs about learning is that the views of both pupils and their teachers in secondary schools are less likely to change than in primary schools, but that the changes differ markedly between different primary schools. At the same time there are also significant differences among staff within secondary schools.

While the questionnaire results were generally positive, they were designed mainly to reflect beliefs about learning, rather than to provide data about specific practices, so the results of these two questionnaires, if considered without reference to other evidence, leave open the question about whether the beliefs are consistent with classroom practice. But there are resonances with findings in other chapters, some of which have a strong orientation to practice. However, if as we have argued throughout, beliefs are important – as a foundation for practice (reasons to act), as inherent in practice (developed in action), and as an outcome of practice (and especially important for lifelong learning) – then it is important to pay attention to them.

Part III

What are the overall implications?

Chapter 10*

Unlocking transformative practice within and beyond the classroom

Messages for practice and policy

This chapter does two things. First, it draws together and summarises the key messages arising from the research findings reported in Part II.

Second, it discusses the implications of these findings for different groups of practitioners and policy-makers: teachers, school leaders, local advisers and school inspectors, teacher educators and policy-makers.

David Hargreaves (2003a) argues that the language of 'improvement' in education must give way to a language of 'transformation' because, at all levels in the system, there is growing recognition that top-down, centralist intervention in search of improved pupil performance has only limited success. As the upward curve of improvement on these measures falters, and begins to level out, pulling the same old levers ceases to work. What is needed, he says, is the creation of a learning system in which the creativity of professionals at all levels is released and shared. He quotes (ibid., p. 74) the words of Donald Schön, who over thirty-five years ago, wrote:

> We must . . . become adept at learning. We must become able not only to transform our institutions, in response to changing situations and requirement; we must invent and develop institutions which are 'learning systems', that is to say, systems capable of bringing about their own continuing transformation.
>
> (Schön, 1971, p. 30)

* Authored by Mary James

Hargreaves believes that,

> [such transformation] will demand a different kind of leadership from the centre; new, disciplined responsibilities from school leaders; and new roles and organisation from the 'middle tier', currently occupied by the Local Education Authorities . . . We must all acknowledge the limits of central interventions and capitalise rather on the power and commitment of the professionals and others with local knowledge to work the magic that makes a sustained and disciplined transformation.
>
> (Hargreaves, 2003a, p. 19)

This 'whole-system' view starts from a different point from our LHTL project but in some ways we come to similar conclusions. By looking first at learning in classrooms, we worked outwards to research the implications for teachers' own learning, within and beyond their schools, and for organisational learning. Learning at all these levels has implications for support systems and for policy frameworks that facilitate or constrain such learning, which implies that the 'middle tier' and central organisations need to learn too. 'Transformation requires everyone to learn' (ibid., p. 73).

In this chapter we examine these implications and propose some future directions for different groups of people. But first we summarise some of the key messages of the project from which the implications are drawn.

Key messages

These derive from our empirical research with schools, from our theoretical deliberations, and from the interaction between the two. We have attempted to draw out and explain our key findings throughout the book but a concise summary might be helpful. The following are our evidence-based propositions.

1. The ultimate goal of learning how to learn is to promote learning autonomy. This is not quite the same as 'independent learning' or 'personalised learning' which are often interpreted to mean that learners can learn in isolation from others. This is hardly ever the case and the concept of 'autonomous learning' should be seen as applying to groups as well as to individuals. The important point is that learners take responsibility for their learning (demonstrate

agency) and develop strategies that enable them to learn both on their own and inter-dependently.

2. Learning how to learn (LHTL) is concerned with the development of learning practices that enable learners to reflect upon and understand their own learning processes and develop ways of regulating them. It is not, in our view, a single entity such as a psychological ability or trait. Indeed, LHTL is closely linked with, and cannot easily be separated from, the actual content of what is being learned and therefore may look different in different subject contexts.

3. Assessment for learning practices provide important tools for learning how to learn and are a useful starting point, although other pedagogic tools may also serve the purpose. The crucial point is that the practices should serve underlying principles, such as making learning explicit and promoting learning autonomy. If practices fail to do this (as do some forms of 'traffic lighting' which have become proxy scoring systems), then they cease to be assessment for learning or learning how to learn.

4. Although teachers appreciate practical strategies for classroom implementation these can become ritualised and mechanistic if teachers are not stimulated to think about the principles of learning that underpin them. Thus the development of beliefs and practices are interrelated and need to be developed together or iteratively.

5. Those teachers (about 20 per cent) who had most success with implementing AfL and LHTL in their classrooms were those who demonstrated a capacity for strategic and reflective thinking and took responsibility for what happened in their classrooms. They were not inclined to blame external circumstances or pupil characteristics (such as innate ability or attitudes) but concentrated on the ways in which they could improve the learning experience for pupils. Most importantly, they applied learning principles to shape and help regulate the learning processes of pupils throughout the lesson, rather than just inject AfL techniques at various points.

6. Although most teachers held clear and positive educational values, the majority of teachers, at the time of our study, struggled to bring practice in line with their stated values. In particular, they did less promotion of learning autonomy than they would have liked, and more performance orientated practice than they thought important. These values–practice gaps closed somewhat over the course of the project but, as comments in interviews indicated, many teachers felt

constrained by a policy context that encouraged rushed curriculum coverage, teaching to the test and a tick-box culture.

7. Values, beliefs and practices are not uniform over all groups of teachers. Different groups of staff within schools have different configurations of practices, and, in secondary schools, there are differences in the beliefs and practices of teachers with different subject specialisms. In two different surveys we found that the highest percentage of teachers with classroom assessment practices consistent with our interpretation of LHTL, and the highest percentage with positive beliefs about learning, were teachers of English. In contrast, mathematics teachers, in particular, seemed to struggle with these ideas. In both surveys there were also differences between schools. All these differences indicate the level of the challenge for leadership and support, and particularly for development of differentiated strategies for professional development.

8. Classroom-based collaborative inquiry practices for teacher learning emerged as the key influence on teachers' capacity to promote learning autonomy with their pupils. These include learning from research and also working together to plan, try out and evaluate new ideas.

9. Such knowledge creation among teachers can extend beyond the classroom through networking across the school and with teachers in other schools. Despite hopes for an electronic revolution in schools, we saw little evidence that ICT is yet being used by teachers for the creation and exchange of professional knowledge, although the potential clearly exists. However, networking through face-to-face meetings of various kinds builds the social capital that supports the exchange of intellectual capital. We found that even weak links – a short exchange, an occasional meeting or the input of an influential speaker – can have a positive impact and lead to development.

10. Opportunities for teachers to learn in these ways, through classroom inquiry and networking, depend significantly on organisational structures, cultures and leadership. Particularly important is a school's knowledge of the expertise in its midst, or available to it, and its capacity to tap into this expertise, grow it and spread it through professional development activities and networking. And all of this needs to be done with a clear sense of purpose – a vision of where the school wants to go. The quality of leadership at every level is crucial to making this a reality.

11. The key challenge for leadership is to create the space and climate for school staff to reflect on and share aspects of their practice. This would include encouraging and stimulating dialogue, welcoming reasoned dissent, and informed risk taking. In this way, innovations can be tested, embedded and sustained. Without it they remain surface changes which decay and disappear when the next initiative comes along. In our case studies we have illustrations of both.

12. This 'double-loop learning' at organisational level, i.e. stepping back from the plan–do–review cycle to examine all its elements before stepping back in to try something new, reflects the collaborative, strategic and reflective thinking we found vital to teacher learning. This in turn corresponds with our definitions of learning how to learn by pupils. Thus pupil LHTL, teacher LHTL and organisational LHTL can be viewed as mirror reflections of one another.

Implications for practice and policy

In this section we take the messages summarised above and outline some of the implications for various groups of practitioners, advisers and policy-makers. We hope the discussion will have relevance to educators both within and beyond the bounds of the UK, and for times present and future. We begin in the classroom with teachers.

Teachers

If learning how to learn is about pupils taking responsibility for their own learning, then teachers need to provide learners with opportunities to exercise responsibility. This does not mean abandoning them to their own devices but it does mean planning activities with this in mind and developing the 'flow' of lessons to maximise these opportunities. Perrenoud's (1998) concept of 'regulation of the learning process' is helpful here because it shifts the emphasis from seeing the teacher's role as prescribing what tasks (stuff) pupils do, to seeing it as a kind of orchestration of the learning itself. This presents a considerable challenge because it asks teachers to reconceptualise their roles, and the familiar division of labour in the classroom, and move away from 'performing teaching' to 'supporting learning'.

Refocusing on the regulation of the learning process – being watchful, reflective and strategic so that teachers can help pupils to be watchful, reflective and strategic in their own learning – does not imply that the 'process' is all, and that what is being learned is of no account. On the contrary, it demands that teachers have what Shulman (1987) refers to as content matter knowledge, pedagogical knowledge and, perhaps most importantly, pedagogical content knowledge, i.e. the knowledge of how subject matter can be learned and taught most effectively. There is a sense in which teachers' thinking and regulating activity in the classroom needs to operate on at least two levels at the same time: moving between the learning itself and learning how to learn.

A group of researchers, working with Lee Shulman, has published a set of papers in a 2004 special issue of the *Journal of Curriculum Studies* (volume 36, number 2), in which they examine a pedagogy for fostering communities of learners (Brown, 1997). On the basis of their studies of learning in social studies, biology, English and mathematics, they argue that effective teaching and learning have to combine both generic and subject specific elements. This implies that teachers have to adapt generic strategies to fit the needs and requirements of subjects. This requires them to have subject knowledge as well as pedagogic knowledge and to be able to see how they inter-relate and, indeed, conflict. In turn, this means that teachers need to develop subject-specific practices from general principles about pedagogy. Further, they must also have a deep understanding of these principles to enable them to go beyond procedural superficiality (which we highlighted as a potential danger, in Chapter 3). This may look complicated but it is how expert teachers work. The challenge is to help more novice teachers to develop such expertise.

The practices associated with assessment for learning are helpful tools in this respect because they are ways of making space for explicit dialogue about learning and for sharing and transferring the responsibility for learning to the learners themselves. However, as our evidence illustrates, they can unwittingly be used (or even misappropriated) for other purposes if teachers are not clear about the principles that underpin them. This implies that even if novice teachers are encouraged to try out the practices first, before they fully understand their rationale, they will benefit from thinking more about their underpinnings as soon as they have developed some confidence in using them. They will then find ways of adapting them to new contexts, or using the principle to create new practices. The AfL practice of increasing 'wait time' between the teacher asking a question and taking an answer, is an example. When teachers realise that the principle is about creating space for pupils to think and reflect, a crucial aspect of learning, then teachers create other opportunities for pupils to think, individually or through group discussion.

Moreover, as teachers become aware of the principles underpinning AfL they blend such practices into the stream of lesson activity. They no longer feel the need, for instance, to write lesson objectives on the board but can internalise them and refer to them at any appropriate moment in classroom dialogue. Further, they involve pupils in discussion about the objectives and how they relate to pupils' personal objectives and learning. This avoids the danger of such practices becoming ritualised and ultimately ineffective.

The suggestion that relatively novice teachers need to develop the skills and understanding of those who are more expert, implies that, like apprentices, the former will benefit from learning from the latter. This is often difficult in schools where teachers do not have many opportunities to work alongside one another to develop their collective expertise in and through practice. However, our research produced powerful evidence that opportunities for all teachers to engage in collaborative classroom-focused inquiry was a key condition for developing practices associated with promoting learning autonomy. Such classroom-focused inquiry can take many forms. At its simplest it might involve teachers taking advantage of opportunities to visit one another's lessons and having structured discussions as to what is observed. A more formal approach is the format of 'research study lessons' pioneered in Japan and developed in England by Pete Dudley, a TLRP Research Fellow linked to the LHTL project (see http://www.tlrp.org/proj/phase111/rtfdudley.htm also http://www.ncsl.org.uk/networked/networked-publications.cfm)

Collaborative classroom-focused inquiry should help teachers to develop the support they need to deal with some of the dilemmas and tensions they face in trying to innovate in what is often perceived as a constraining policy context. Our interviews with teachers provided much evidence of the pressures they experience from the demands of a crowded curriculum, the deluge of central initiatives and a high stakes testing regime. Yet a minority were able to rise above this and, instead of blaming circumstances beyond their control, they reflected critically on their own role in pupil's learning and how they might improve things. This sense of responsibility and their own agency needs to be cultivated in all teachers. Opportunities to work collaboratively, in an atmosphere of trust and mutual respect, will help build the social capital needed for teachers to share, reflect upon, and develop their ideas and practices. These constitute the intellectual capital of schools.

But we also noted the challenge of scaling up worthwhile activity so that all teachers and all schools might benefit. On this issue, our evidence indicates that teachers benefit from developing networks with teachers in other schools. (Some of these network links may be of the weak type noted above.) It had been thought that the electronic tools would help with the spread of ideas, and hence assist 'going to scale'. Unfortunately, the supply of computers has not, according to our evidence, brought about much change in the ways that teachers communicate their professional knowledge. This is not to say that it will not happen. The tools exist and teachers are likely to benefit from using them, although more attention needs to be given to overcoming barriers, such as lack of time or space, inaccessible hardware and unreliable software. In contrast, we found that teachers made valued face-to-face informal links with teachers, and others, beyond their own schools. These can also be used and developed to provide an explicit channel for exchanging practice knowledge.

Of course, teachers need support to do these things, to which we turn next.

School leadership

The key responsibility for school leaders, indicated by our study, is to lead learning, including learning how to learn, in their schools. This means building the culture and creating structures that enable peda-gogical innovation to become embedded not only in day-to-day routines but as a way of thinking and being. While this may seem to be stating the obvious, in a climate where bureaucratic demands are heavy, school leaders are faced with considerable challenges in balancing external pressures against their aspiration to lead a dynamic knowledge-creating organisation. While, as our case studies attest, no single approach could be advocated as markedly more effective than another, a commitment to LHTL, and support for teaching staff, were critical elements. With that as given, there was a dividing line between those who believed in leading from the front in search of more rapid change and consistency of approach, and those who favoured team-building and distributed leadership, so as to release the creativity across the school. We took the view that structural and cultural approaches complement one another and that those in positions of leadership need to consider both.

According to our survey results, what is vital to promoting learning autonomy in both pupils and teachers is for school leaders to do the following:

• Develop a sense of where the school is going.

- Audit the expertise that exists within the school so that this intellectual capital can be mobilised, used and spread.
- Find out about the network links that staff in schools have developed in order to strengthen these and make them more purposeful.
- Support professional learning among teachers, individually and collectively.

Particularly important in this last respect is support for professional learning through collaborative classroom-focused inquiry.

All of this will demand the allocation of resources, which in times of pressure on budgets, may require some reprioritisation. However, our evidence suggests that even small amounts of money used to enable teachers to visit one another's classrooms, within the school or in other schools, can have very considerable benefits. The case study from Eucalyptus Junior School (Chapter 6) provides an illustration. Of course, if these small amounts of money are multiplied to cover all teachers in, say, a network of schools, then the funding needed is considerable.

But material resources are not all. Most important is the need to build a culture in the school which actively encourages teachers to take informed risks in developing practice and to develop critical reflection on the outcomes of their innovations in order to improve them. This might also entail critical reflection on those things that constrain them, including structural conditions that prevail in the school and impinge from outside. For those in positions of leadership, it implies an ability to view difference and 'dissent' as potentially fruitful, in turn requiring confidence, reflexivity and a capacity to mediate solutions. In other words, work by leaders to transform their schools into 'learning organisations', especially through double-loop learning, is an important condition in promoting learning to learn by teachers and their pupils.

These suggestions concern the broad conditions in schools. Our research also provides the basis for more specific guidance. For example, our analysis of the concept of LHTL leads us to the view that time-tabling separate lessons for learning how to learn would be counter-productive. LHTL can, we believe, only be developed in the context of the curriculum. An infusion approach is preferred because LHTL may look different in different subject contexts. This implies that, in whatever way AfL and LHTL practices are introduced, they will need to be evaluated and adapted for specific contexts, e.g. subjects and age ranges (James *et al.*, 2006b, offer suggestions for whole-school professional development activities). On the other hand, the fact that we found differences in practices and beliefs according to teachers' subject specialisms (see Chapters 8 and 9) also raises a question about a potential role for across-subject working groups within schools. Some project schools found these especially helpful in challenging teachers' taken-for-granted assumptions and in encouraging them to try practices found to be effective in other parts of the school. In secondary schools, where departmental structures can dominate, such opportunities for boundary crossing were found to be important, although as the case study from Elm County High School indicates (Chapter 7), there needs to be links between departmental and across subject groups.

School leaders can be helped to identify what needs to be done in their schools through the way they approach school self-evaluation. This is increasingly important in a policy climate in which schools are encouraged to follow prescriptive formulae. Just as assessment for learning may be associated with procedural techniques, so self-evaluation can be easily confused with audit and form filling, as a prelude to inspection. We believe the research instruments developed by the LHTL project may be helpful in fostering a more reflective process of self-evaluation, one more strongly embedded in the day-to-day life of school and classrooms. With a firmer grounding in AfL and LHTL principles, self-evaluation can feed creatively into school improvement policies, exemplifying the values of a 'learning how to learn' organisation.

These development tools can be downloaded as 'self-evaluation resources' from the project website (http://www.learntolearn.ac.uk).

Local advisers and school inspectors

In England, the role and function of the local authorities are constantly under review and subject to considerable local variation. Similarly the way Ofsted approaches its work is changing. So it is not sensible to make specific recommendations. However, the implications of the discussion in the previous sections are that consultants, advisers and inspectors need to understand the import, for their work, of what is being suggested.

In the case of advisers, they might be expected to provide support for these developments, for example, through their advice to school leaders, through their provision of local Inset courses and, and perhaps most importantly, for their support for networking. In the LHTL project, local advisers worked with us as local co-ordinators. They were geographically closer to the schools than university-based critical friends and, because they had an existing relationship with the project schools, were often able to respond more quickly and effectively to requests for specific help. By having better 'inside knowledge', they were also able to act as brokers between schools and better placed to set up networking opportunities. These could be at an informal level but they could also link teachers and schools into existing or new networks, such as the Networked Learning Communities, sponsored by the NCSL during the time of our project, or those more recently created by the Specialist Schools and Academies Trust and the DfES. All these things can be considered by local authorities interested in pursuing the ideas arising from our research.

In the case of inspectors, there is a need to develop monitoring instruments and reporting structures that are sensitive to innovations in LHTL. A tick-box approach to monitoring LHTL practices is unlikely to be appropriate because, as explained above, and in Chapter 3, it is the purposeful flow of activity in the classroom that is most important. Also, the focus needs to be less on the performance of the teacher than on the learning that arises from the activity of the pupils, and what the teacher does to support their learning. Observation of behaviours alone are unlikely to provide enough information about the learning that is taking place.

In the context of a New Relationship with Schools, inspection has shifted to provide shorter and more focused inspections, affording less time for classroom visits and reduced opportunities for dialogue with pupils and teachers. This is a consequence of the shift in emphasis to place the school's own self-evaluation centre stage. In so doing inspection teams have, themselves, to deepen their own understanding of the relationship between AfL, LHTL and self-evaluation and what inspection can do both to assess its quality and offer support for its further development.

This implies, however, a substantive change in perspective from an approach based on the demonstration of specified competences, to an approach that sees practices as infused with values, one open to adaptation according to a teacher's judgement of the best thing to do to enhance pupils' learning at a given moment.

Teacher educators

The discussion earlier about novice and expert teachers implies that there is a personal trajectory in the development of LHTL ideas and practice. An introduction to AfL practices is a starting point but needs to be developed and deepened through an understanding of the principles that underpin them. Teachers need to be encouraged to develop their own practice knowledge and to share and test that knowledge through collaborative classroom-based inquiry. This cannot all be accomplished in initial teacher training, although more might be done in relation to AfL and LHTL than is evident in England at the present time. For example, in association with our project, a group of secondary Postgraduate Certificate of Education trainees were provided with a semi-structured observational framework, derived from the analysis of the LHTL staff questionnaire (see Chapter 4), which they used to guide their observation of videos of classroom lessons. These semi-structured observations allowed them to identify effective practice, relate it to their own evolving craft knowledge, and discuss relationships and tensions between values and practices, in the teachers they observed, and in themselves (see Marshall *et al.*, 2005, for a full account).

Rarely do ITT courses find time to deal with assessment issues adequately, let alone assessment for learning, despite the fact that activities associated with assessment take up so much of practising teachers' time. A case can be made for AfL and LHTL to be given more prominence in training courses because they are centrally concerned with pedagogy. An unfortunate consequence of using the 'A' word in 'assessment for learning' has been to place treatment of it, as an ITT topic, at the ends of courses, on the assumption that assessment follows learning rather than being integral to it.

Realistically, however, it is in continuing professional development (PD) that most support for the development of AfL and LHTL ideas and practice might be expected. A role for school-based Inset, local authority-based professional development, and university and 'other provider' courses might be envisaged. The problem in England, at the present time, is that such CPD provision is fragmented and lacks rationale and structure. If the development of LHTL in schools requires teachers to grow their ideas and practices through trying them out on classrooms, and in reflective dialogue with colleagues, then one-off courses and ring-binders of materials are unlikely to serve the purpose, although, as we noted in Chapter 5, the occasional good speaker can make a lasting impression.

What may be needed is CPD, for the promotion of LHTL and other areas of pedagogical innovation, supported by an infrastructure for professional development that is truly 'continuing' and provides space and time for sustained reflection and developmental progression. This is likely to be mainly school-based, and need not be intensive, but it does need to keep development 'bubbling away', as teachers, quoted in Chapter 4, expressed it.

Policy-makers

As our evidence makes clear (see especially Chapter 3), the policy context can act as a powerful facilitator or barrier to innovation. Although at the present time in England a version of AfL has been incorporated into the National Strategies, it can be perceived as yet another initiative, adding to the burden of current central prescription, to be 'monitored' by Ofsted and evaluated as effective only if test and examination scores rise. This is not helpful. If learning how to learn is effective, it should not be judged, either by checklists or by school performance at the end of a Key Stage, but by the extent to which learners are equipped to thrive and flourish in their lives beyond the Key Stage and beyond the school. Finding appropriate indicators is difficult to do but not impossible. As mentioned in Chapter 1, an international group has been set up by the European Commission to develop a pilot indicator for Learning to Learn. Our project has contributed to discussions on this.

Innovation in LHTL, as in other areas, rarely proceeds by *diktat* and, however uncomfortable this may be for policy-makers who, for good reasons, want measures of the return on investment of tax-payers' money, the time has come to ease off prescription and 'initiativitis', and provide support in broader terms to develop the dispositions, skills, knowledge and cultures that will encourage transformation of schools into learning organisations. Alternative forms of accountability need to be found that add to this support rather than distort it. Despite Schön's plea of 35 years ago, we are not there yet, although schools such as Mulberry (see Chapter 7) show that the creation of a learning school is possible.

So, we are not looking for another central initiative on LHTL. What we would like to see, essentially, is a change in the discourse across all those agencies concerned with what goes on in schools. This would make strategic and reflective thinking about the processes of learning, by pupils, teachers and by schools as organisations, a priority, and it would value productive struggle to 'surface' and resolve dilemmas. Teaching and learning are human endeavours and they cannot, ultimately, be controlled in technicist ways.

Conclusion

Although we started our project with the development of assessment for learning practices as a way forward, we have, in a sense left them behind. They will continue to be important for those starting out on the path to learning how to learn with view to creating autonomous learners, be they pupils, teachers or schools as organisations. But they are simply tools to start to bring about more fundamental pedagogic change (hence the depiction of AfL as a Trojan horse). As we establish new educational purposes, e.g. promoting learning autonomy, to supersede old ones, e.g. raising standards based on narrow measures of performance, we would expect these tools to develop and change, and for new ones to be created. According to our research, teachers, schools and networks will have a crucial role in transformations of practice and need to be properly supported and encouraged.

Appendix*

How the research was carried out

'Learning How to Learn in classrooms, schools and networks' was a large and complex development and research project. Therefore it was necessary to say something about its design and methods in Chapter 1 and give brief summaries of particular techniques in subsequent chapters, in order to make the findings understandable. A detailed account of our research aims, design and analysis has been published in James *et al.* (2006a), and discussion of issues arising in James (2006b). Here, therefore, we provide just a short overview.

Antecedents

The project built on existing, highly regarded research that has shown through controlled trials that AfL practices improve learning and achievement. It also built on accumulated evidence of effective school improvement and professional development. These were areas of research in which members of the team had previously been engaged. The project team was also interested in knowledge sharing within and across networks of schools. This phenomenon is relatively un-charted territory in educational research so the team looked outside of education and drew on literature and research in other fields, particularly from the world of business, in order to develop concepts and methods to explore learning through networking. We brought all these fields together by developing a 'logic model' (see Figure 1.1, in Chapter 1) which we interrogated by studying how development based on existing theory was implemented in a sample of 40 schools in a range of contexts.

* Authored by Mary James

Sample

Some 43 schools (26 primary and 17 secondary) were initially recruited to the project although three withdrew early on. The criteria used for selection were:

1. A willingness of schools to be involved in the project for the four-year duration, and actively to contribute ideas.
2. Up to nine schools to be chosen from each of five LAs and one or two VEAZs with the proportion of one secondary school to two primary schools (preferably in cluster groups).
3. A range of contexts to be represented in the overall sample: urban/rural; small/large; mono-ethnic/multi-ethnic.
4. Schools' performance at one or two Key Stages to have been allocated an Ofsted PANDA 'C' benchmark grade, based on their results in 2000. This is a crude measure but indicated room for measured improvement.
5. Schools to be located within a reasonable travelling distance from the university bases of researchers and critical friends.

By working with 40 schools, the team estimated that the project would involve, at some level, approximately 1,500 teachers and 20,000 students. This estimation proved to be reasonably accurate.

In order to make data collection and analysis manageable, a decision was taken in 2003 to divide the 40 schools into a 'main' sample of 20 and a 'supplementary' sample of 20. Main sample schools were those where we were likely to collect the most complete data; they were not necessarily schools where we expected to find 'best practice'. As a result of this decision, more intensive fieldwork in classrooms was carried out in the main sample only.

Development work with schools and networks

The project was a development and research (D&R) project and the team stimulated activity through a limited number of 'interventions' at the school level of similar scale to the activities that a school might routinely carry out as part of its school improvement plan. There was no direct team involvement in the classroom; instead team members worked with teachers and school leaders using Inset activities of various kinds.

Most of this work was conducted with individual schools but opportunities for network development were also provided by regular meetings for school co-ordinators. What, and how much, activity schools engaged in was not prescribed; teachers and school leaders were encouraged to take responsibility for the pattern of development in their school. Variation was accepted and the research sought to examine the relative effectiveness of the different ways in which schools, and networks of schools, implemented ideas and developed practice.

Figure A1 provides a summary of development activities (on the left side of the figure) and research activities (on the right side of the figure).

	LOCUS OF DEVELOPMENT WORK	FOCUS OF DEVELOPMENT WORK	RESEARCH: QUANTITATIVE DATA	RESEARCH: QUALITATIVE DATA
CLASSROOM LEVEL		Initial inset, audit and action planning Workshops: • Questioning • Feedback • Sharing criteria • Peer and self-assessment • How people learn	Teacher and pupil learning: • Teachers' beliefs about learning (TBLQ) • Pupils' beliefs about learning (SBLQ) • Pupils' attainments (PAA: Key Stage test and GCSE data)	• Lesson observation sequences (LOS: recordings and interviews with teachers and pupils) • Lesson materials • Teachers' beliefs about learning (TBLI interviews incl. critical incidents)
SCHOOL LEVEL	LHTL Team provides inset and critical friend support to groups of teachers and schools	Feedback results of staff questionnaire Follow-up activities: • sch. cultures • force field • NQT/LSA view • leadership • working with parents/govs. • pupil voice • AfL policy dev. • Sch. meetings	Organisational learning: School climate/culture (Staff questionnaire – SQ): • classroom assessment (SQ:A) • professional learning (SQ:B) • management systems (SQ:C)	• Sch. co-ordinator perceptions (interviews and logs) • Headteacher perceptions (interviews) • Sch. policy (docs.) • LA/VEAZ adviser perceptions (interviews and logs) • Critical friend perceptions (interviews and logs)
NETWORK LEVEL		Network activity Opps, for sharing: • Sch. co-ord. mtgs • LA mtgs • Inter-school mtgs • Website resources	Network learning: • Staff questionnaire (L3Q or SQ:E) • School network audit • Records of network activity	• Co-ordinator network maps and logs • Headteacher interviews and maps • LA/VEAZ co-ordinator maps and logs • Knowledge creation and exchange (tracking transaction objects)

Figure A1   LHTL development and research activities

Data collection

The following (school and classroom level) instruments were used to collect quantitative and qualitative data (numbers of administrations and respondents are given in brackets):

- Head teacher interview and collection of school policy documents (once at the beginning of the project, N = 39).
- School co-ordinator interview (twice: once summer/autumn 2003, N = 32, and once summer 2004, N = 31).
- School logs of activity and comment entered into a confidential area of the project website by school co-ordinators, critical friends and LA co-ordinators (continuous access for data entry throughout the project, N = 40).
- Critical friend interviews and LA co-ordinators' interviews (once at end of project). These interviews covered the group of schools with which these individuals worked.
- Staff questionnaire (SQ) to all staff including managers, teachers and teaching assistants (twice: once before/at start of development work, N = 1,212, and again in summer 2004, N = 698).
- Teachers' beliefs about learning questionnaire (TBLQ) (twice: summer 2003, N = 576, and again in summer 2004, N = 190). These were completed both by teachers and by teaching assistants.
- Pupils' beliefs about learning questionnaire (SBLQ) to pupils in Y5/6, Y8/9 and Y10/11 (twice: summer 2003, N = 4,044, and the same pupils in spring/summer 2004, N = 1,811).
- Teachers' beliefs about learning extended interview (TBLI) with a sub-sample (focal teachers) selected from those who taught SBLQ cohorts and whose practice was observed (TBLI was carried out once, N = 37).
- Lesson Observation Sequence (LOS) (twice with each focal teacher, and four times with teachers in some case study schools). LOS included observation records, i.e. fieldnotes and video recordings (N = 27), plus post-lesson interviews with teachers and groups of 3 to 6 pupils. These involved two or three teachers in each 'main sample' secondary school and one teacher in each 'main sample' primary school. Teachers were chosen to achieve a spread of subjects, with a higher proportion of teachers of core subjects.
- School-level pupil performance data (PAA) for 2001/2, 2002/3, 2003/4 (N = 40 schools).

Network level data were also collected in nine of the 20 'main sample' schools. These nine schools were selected because they were known to be involved in specific network activity such as participation in Networked Learning Communities supported by the National College for School Leadership. Data derived from:

- ICT network audit, once in networked schools (N = 16).
- Staff questionnaire (N = 250).
- Co-ordinator and head teacher network maps and associated interviews (twice: summer 03, summer/autumn 04) in networked schools (N = 35).
- LA/VEAZ co-ordinator maps and logs (N=6).

In the 20 schools of the 'supplementary' sample, data collection was more limited. No focal teachers were identified and there was no classroom observation and associated interviews with teachers and pupils in these schools. Nor was there a second administration of questionnaires (SQ, TBLQ and SBLQ). However, sample norms were established on the basis of analysis of the first administration to both main and supplementary sample schools and these were used for comparison within and between schools, across the whole sample at baseline, and to measure change over time in main sample schools.

Timetable

The project was implemented in four phases:

1   *Phase 1 (January 2001–August 2002)*: Recruitment of research staff; setting up website; development and piloting of Inset activities; development, piloting and trialling of research instruments; recruitment of LAs and schools.
2   *Phase II (September 2002–August 2003)*: Main phase of development work based on critical friend and LA co-ordinator involvement, support and in-service training in schools; initial, including baseline, data collection; development of website.
3   *Phase III (September 2003–October 2004)*: Development work in schools continued but critical friends moved to a 'responsive' mode; LA co-ordinators, who had on-going local responsibilities, continued support; data collection was completed including 'exit' questionnaires and interviews; data analysis.

4   *Phase IV (September 2004–July 2005)*: Data analysis and beginning to write up; dissemination conferences for teachers and policy-makers; other forms of communication and impact work.

Data analysis

As a first stage in the analysis, each of the data sets listed above was analysed separately for patterns in the data. Our questionnaire data were analysed using standard quantitative procedures for item, factor and cluster analysis. Our interviews, and other qualitative data, were transcribed and coded using the *Atlas-ti* software package and standard procedures for qualitative data analysis, such as constant comparative method. We analysed video-recordings of lessons rather differently. Drawing on team expertise in media studies, we treated these as 'films' and subjected them to a collaborative form of 'practical criticism'. All these analyses produced important findings in themselves.

Once these initial analyses were completed, we directed our later analytical efforts towards investigating the conditions for learning in classrooms, schools and networks, by examining the links between variables. We did this statistically, where this was possible, using regression analyses. For instance, we used multiple regression analyses to examine the relationships between our data on classroom assessment practices, professional learning practices and school management practices, derived from the three sections of our staff questionnaire. In our case studies, however, we integrated insights from both qualitative and quantitative evidence in narrative ways. Our basic analytical strategy was to investigate associations between variables, mostly using simple correlational statistics, which could then be interpreted using qualitative evidence. Combining quantitative and qualitative analyses was a major feature of the plans for our analytical work.

Pupils' performance measures and project effects

Within the logic model (on the right-hand side of Figure 1.1, in Chapter 1), we record 'pupils' academic achievement' as an outcome variable and hypothesise links to classroom practices and beliefs about learning. We collected data on all of these variables, but we were unable, for reasons of practicality and confidentiality, to match attainment data for individual pupils to the data on their beliefs, their teachers' beliefs and their teachers' classroom practices. Therefore we were unable to conduct statistical analyses that would permit us to attribute outcomes for particular pupils to particular practices. Our data on pupil performance, although showing contextual value-added change over the three years of the project, are *school-level* data and we could only consider comparing these with school-level practices, such as those revealed in analysis of our staff questionnaire. Chapter 8 presented some of the school-level practice evidence, in the form of cluster profiles of those schools which we chose as case studies for this book. These can be compared with the pupil performance tables for project schools given in Tables A1 and A2.

As Tables A1 and A2 show, no consistent pattern emerges across the whole sample of project schools in terms of pupils' performance from 2002 to 2004. The profiles of individual schools are more interesting and, by looking at these in association with other sources of data, both qualitative and quantitative, it is possible to make sense of what has happened in these schools. This is what we chose to do (see Chapters 6 and 7).

What has become very clear to us in the course of this study is that the 'intervention' of a development and research project is only ever part of the story of innovation in educational settings, albeit sometimes a highly valued one. As researchers, we needed to stop seeing the project from our end, and instead see it from the point of view of those meeting the ideas in their schools. Success depends crucially on what happens there: on how teachers receive ideas and re-evaluate their existing practices and beliefs, how they experiment with new practices and develop them, how they share them with others, how they are supported in doing this, how school leaders make sense of the plethora of initiatives they are expected to implement, how they make space for dialogue and risk taking, and how they deal with tension and constraint. As Fullan (2001) has consistently pointed out, it is not dissemination and adoption of a single project's ideas that are the issue. The real challenges are concerned with implementation, embedding and continuation in 'real' practice settings. This was the focus of our research.

Quality assurance

Our survey instruments were subjected to extensive piloting and trialling, in an additional ten schools recruited for the purpose, before they were used in project schools. Likewise, interview schedules were also piloted. Coding frames for the analysis of qualitative data were developed in an iterative process drawing on the theoretical insights

Table A1 LHTL project secondary schools: pupils' academic performance: contextual value-added indicators, 2002–2004

School name	KS2→ Core subjects Lev 5+	KS3 Overall points score	KS3→ 5+ A*–C GCSEs	KS4 Capped points score	5+ A*–C in 2004	No passes in 2004 (%)
Ash School	7 **	4 **	94 *	97 *	53	4
Beech School	63	37	70 *	57	64	4
Box Tree Girls' School	9 **	11 **	54	21 **	40	1
Cherry School	50	34	33	67	35	3
Elm High School	84 *	73 *	19 **	76 *	50	6
Fir Tree School for Girls	63	52	51	34	39	2
Garland Tree Science & Technology College	41	51	96 *	74 *	42	2
Hawthorn High School	3 **	3 **	8 **	14 **	84	2
Katsura School	68	42	56	63	51	3

School						
Lime School	70	73 *	88 *	86 *	40	2
Mulberry School	16 **	17 **	41	52	57	2
Nutmeg School	99 *	98 *	90 *	55	56	1
Redwood High School	3 **	1 **	26	28 **	67	1
Umbrella Tree School	92 *	85 *	2 **	3 **	54	3
Vine School	43	66 *	94 *	80 *	33	1
Willow School	79 *	73 *	94 *	76*	52	3
Yew Community School	91 *	91 *	26	19 **	63	1

Notes: Table 10.1 gives raw scores of percentage 5 A*–C passes in GCSE in 2004 and percentage no passes. It also shows value-added from KS2→KS3 and KS3→KS4 as a percentile rank (1 = highest VA; 100 = lowest VA). Stars indicate where performance is significantly different to that expected from a comparison with the progress of 'similar pupils in similar schools' i.e. taking into account pupils' prior attainment (test and teacher assessment results) and a range of pupil and school contextual indicators (gender, ethnicity, SEN, FSM, geodemographic data). Significant differences, to 95% confidence limits, are starred:

* = significantly lower than expected
** = significantly higher than expected

Table A2 LHTL project primary schools: pupils' academic performance: contextual value-added indicators, 2002–2004

School name	KS1→ En Mean NC Level 2004	KS2 En VA NC level percentile rank	KS1→ Ma Mean NC Level 2004	KS2 Ma VA NC level percentile rank	KS1→ Sc Mean NC Level 2004	KS2 SC VA NC Level percentile rank
Alder Primary School	4.5	79	4.4	97 *	4.7	86 *
Birch County Primary School	4.3	84 *	4.7	33	4.7	67
Deodar Primary School	4.5	62	4.7	34	5.1	5*
Fir Tree Primary School	4.4	75	4.5	79 *	4.8	58
Chestnut Primary School	4.4	87 *	4.6	87 *	4.6	96 *
Dove Tree Community Primary School	4.7	25	4.8	33	5.1	18 **
Goldenrain Junior School	3.8	94 *	4.0	82 *	4.0	99 *
Hazel Primary School	4.6	73	4.8	50	4.9	61
Ironwood Community Primary School	3.8	47	4.2	15**	4.5	17**
Juniper Primary School	4.3	65	4.2	89 *	4.5	76 *
Maple C of E School	4.2	71	4.4	59	4.6	55
Oak Infant School	N/A	N/A	N/A	N/A	N/A	N/A

School						
Pine Junior School	4.1	76*	4.2	62	4.5	67
Quince JMI School	4.9	20	5.0	60	5.1	58
Rowan C of E School	4.6	53	4.5	68	4.8	58
Sycamore Primary School	4.2	84 *	4.3	76	4.4	88 *
Tulip Tree C of E School	4.5	82	4.6	87 *	5.0	51
Aspen Infant School	N/A	N/A	N/A	N/A	N/A	N/A
Eucalyptus Junior School	4.7	24 **	4.9	19 **	5.0	27 **
Laburnum C of E School	4.6	52	4.7	44	4.9	46
Pear Tree School	4.7	42	4.7	47	4.9	48
Service Tree Primary School	4.3	50	4.8	4 **	4.9	14 **
Walnut County Primary School	4.5	10 **	4.3	40	4.4	76 *

Note: Table 10.2 shows mean NC level scores for each of the three core subjects (English, mathematics and science) in 2004, and value-added scores as a percentile rank. VA scores were calculated by comparison with all maintained primary schools nationally. Pupils' prior attainment and a range of pupil and school contextual indicators have been taken into account. Significant differences, to 95% confidence limits, are starred:

*   = significantly lower than expected
**   = significantly higher than expected

which had informed the data collection and the evidence that was provided in a preliminary analysis of a sub-sample of responses or observations. These frames were then subjected to reliability trials before being used to code full data sets. Outputs from this analysis facilitated the examination of patterns (qualitative and, sometimes, quantifiable) in the data which were then interpreted by triangulating with other data sources and drawing on theory.

Analyses, working papers and draft publications were tabled for discussion at team meetings and no material was made public without the collective agreement of the team, for every member would need to feel confident in defending it. In the usual way, publications in journals have been, or are being, refereed.

Regular meetings of the whole research team (once a month), the research and development team (including local authority co-ordinators) and the project's advisory group (twice a year), ensured that progress and findings were regularly scrutinised by both researchers and users. Two major dissemination events – one for practitioners and one for policy-makers – also provided opportunities for feedback and refinement of findings.

References

Note: Publications marked with an asterisk are outputs from the LHTL project.

Argyris, C. and Schön, D. (1978) *Organizational Learning: A Theory of Action Perspective* (Reading, MA: Addison Wesley).

Assessment Reform Group (ARG) (2002) *Assessment for Learning: 10 Principles* (Cambridge: University of Cambridge School of Education).

Ball, S. (2003) The teacher's soul and the terrors of performativity. *Journal of Educational Policy*, 18(2): 215–228.

Bassey, M. (2001) A solution to the problem of generalization in educational research: empirical findings and fuzzy predictions. *Oxford Review of Education*, 27(1): 5–22.

Bereiter, C. and Scardamalia, M. (1989) Intentional learning as a goal of instruction. In L.B. Resnick (ed.) *Knowing, Learning, and Instruction; Essays in Honour of Robert Glaser* (Hillsdale, NJ: Lawrence Erlbaum Associates), pp. 361–392.

Black, P., Harrison, C., Lee, C., Marshall, B. and Wiliam, D. (2002) *Working Inside the Black Box: Assessment for Learning in the Classroom* (London: NFER Nelson).

Black, P., Harrison, C., Lee, C., Marshall, B. and Wiliam, D. (2003) *Assessment for Learning: Putting it into Practice* (Maidenhead: Open University Press).

* Black, P., McCormick, R., James, M. and Pedder, D. (2006) Learning how to learn and assessment for learning: a theoretical inquiry. *Research Papers in Education*, 21(2): 119–132.

* Black, P., Swann, J. and Wiliam, D. (2006) School pupils' beliefs about learning. *Research Papers in Education*, 21(2): 151–170.

* Black, P., Swann, J. and Wiliam, D. (forthcoming (a)) Secondary school pupils' beliefs about learning.

* Black, P., Swann, J. and Wiliam, D. (forthcoming (b)) Teachers' beliefs about learning.

Black, P. and Wiliam, D. (1998a) Assessment and classroom learning. *Assessment in Education*, 5(1): 5–75.

Black, P. and Wiliam, D. (1998b) *Inside the Black Box: Raising Standards through Classroom Assessment* (London: NFER Nelson).

Black, P. and Wiliam, D (2006) Developing a theory of formative assessment. In J. Gardner (ed.) *Assessment and Learning* (London: Sage), pp. 81–100.

Boud, D. (ed.) *Developing Student Autonomy in Learning* (London: Kogan Page).

Bransford, J.A., Brown, A. and Cocking, R. (1999) *How People Learn: Brain, Mind, Experience and School* (Washington, DC: National Academy Press).

Bredo, E. (1993) The social construction of learning. In G. D. Phye (ed.) *Handbook of Academic Learning: Construction of Knowledge* (San Diego, CA: Academic Press), pp. 3–45.

Brown, A.L. (1981) Metacognition: the development of selective attention strategies for learning from texts. In M. Kamil (ed.) *Directions in Reading: Research and Instruction* (Washington, DC: The National Reading Conference).

Brown, A.L. (1997) Transforming schools into communities of thinking and learning about serious matters. *American Psychologist*, 52(4): 399–413.

Butler, R. (1988) Enhancing and undermining intrinsic motivation: the effects of task-involving and ego-involving evaluation on interest and performance. *British Journal of Educational Psychology*, 58: 1–14.

* Carmichael, P., Fox, A., McCormick, R., Procter, R. and Honour, L. (2006) Teachers' professional networks in and out of school, *Research Papers in Education*, 21(2): 217–234.

* Carmichael, P. and Procter, R. (2006) Are we there yet? Teachers, schools and electronic networks. *The Curriculum Journal*, 17(2): 167–186.

Castells, M. (2000) *The Rise of the Network Society*. Vol. I. *The Information Age: Economy, Society and Culture*, 2nd edn (Oxford: Blackwell).

Clarke, S. (1998) *Targeting Assessment in the Primary Classroom* (London; Hodder and Stoughton).

Clarke, S. (2001) *Unlocking Formative Assessment* (London: Hodder and Stoughton).

Coffey, J., Sato, M. and Thiebault, M. (2005) Classroom assessment up close – and personal. *Teacher Development*, 9(2): 169–184.

Collins, J. (2005) *Good to Great: Why Some Companies Make the Leap and Others Don't* (New York: HarperCollins).

Costa, A. and Kallick, B. (1993) Through the lens of a critical friend. *Educational Leadership*, 51(2): 49–51.

Dearden, R.F. (1976) *Problems in Primary Education* (London: Routledge and Kegan Paul).

DEMOS (2005) *About Learning* (London: Demos).

Dewey, J. (1966) *Experience and Education* (London: Collier Books).

Dweck, C.S. (2000) *Self-theories: Their Role in Motivation, Personality and Development* (Philadelphia, PA: Psychology Press).

Ecclestone, K. (2002) *Learning Autonomy in Post-compulsory Education: The Politics and Practice of Formative Assessment* (London: Routledge Falmer).

Feinstein, L. (2006) The wider benefits of learning: a synthesis of findings from the Centre for Research on the Wider Benefits of Learning (London: Institute of Education) (mimeo).

Fielding, M., Bragg, S., Craig, J., Cunningham, I., Eraut, M., Gillinson, S., Horne, M., Robinson, C. and Thorp, J. (2005) *Factors Influencing the transfer of Good Practice* (London: Department for Education and Skills).

Fontana, D. and Fernandes, M. (1994) Improvements in mathematics performance as a consequence of self-assessment in Portuguese primary school pupils. *British Journal of Educational Psychology*, 64: 407–417.

* Fox, A., McCormick, R., Carmichael, P., and Procter, R. (2006) Teachers' learning through networks. Paper presented at the annual conference of the American Educational Research Association (Session 41.066 Workplace learning: people and places), 7–11 April, San Francisco.

* Fox, A., McCormick, R., Procter, R., and Carmichael, P. (2007) The design and use of a mapping tool as a baseline means of identifying an organisation's active networks. *International Journal of Research and Method in Education*, 30(2): 127–147.

Frederiksen, J., and White, B. (1997) Reflective assessment of students' research within an inquiry-based middle school science curriculum. Paper presented at the annual meeting of the American Educational Research Association, Chicago.

Fullan, M. (2001) *The New Meaning of Educational Change*, 3rd edn (London: RoutledgeFalmer).

Gibson, J. (1979) *The Ecological Approach to Visual Perception*. (Boston: Houghton Mifflin).

Gorard, S. (2006) The concept of a 'Fair Test' is relevant to all researchers: introducing the Trials in Public Policy Project. *Building Research Capacity*, 11: 6–9. (TLRP Journal).

Hakkarainen, K., Palonen, T., Paavola, S. and Lehtinen, E. (2004) *Communities of Networked Expertise: Professional and Educational Perspectives* (Amsterdam: Elsevier).

Hammersley, M. (2001) On Michael Bassey's concept of the fuzzy generalisation. *Oxford Review of Education*, 27(2): 219–225.

Hargreaves, D. (2003a) *Education Epidemic: Transforming Secondary Schools through Innovation Networks* (London: DEMOS).

Hargreaves, D. (2003b) *Working Laterally: How Innovation Networks Make an Education Epidemic* (London: DEMOS).

Hargreaves, D. (2004) *Personalising Learning: Next Steps in Working Laterally.* (London: Specialist Schools Trust).

Hautamäki, J., Arinen, P., Eronen, S., Hautamäki, A., Kupiainen, S., Lindblom, B., Niemivirta, M., Pakaslahti, L., Rantanen, P. and Scheinin, P. (2002) *Assessing Learning-to-learn: A Framework*. Evaluation 4 (Helsinki: National Board of Education).

HM Government (2003) *Every Child Matters*. CM 5860 (London: HMSO).

Hodgen, J. and Marshall, B. (2005) Assessment for learning in English and mathematics: a comparison. *The Curriculum Journal*, 16(2): 153–176.

James, M. (2005) Insights on teacher learning from the Teaching and Learning Research Programme. *Research Papers in Education*, 20(2): 105–108.

James, M. (2006a) Assessment, teaching and theories of learning. In J. Gardner (ed.) *Assessment and Learning* (London: Sage), pp. 45–60.

*James, M. (2006b) Balancing rigour and responsiveness in a shifting context: meeting the challenges of educational research. *Research Papers in Education*, 21(4): 365–380.

* James, M., Black, P., McCormick, R. and Pedder, D. (2006a) Learning how to learn, in classrooms, schools and networks: aims, design and analysis. *Research Papers in Education*, 21(2):101–118.

* James, M., Black, P., Carmichael, P., Conner, C., Dudley, P., Fox, A., Frost, D., Honour, L., MacBeath, J., McCormick, R., Marshall, B., Pedder, D., Procter, R., Swaffield, S. and Wiliam, D. (2006b) *Learning How to Learn: Tools for Schools* (London: Routledge).

* James, M. and Pedder, D. (2005) Professional learning as a condition for assessment for learning. In J. Gardner (ed.) *Assessment and Learning* (London: Sage), pp. 27–44.

*James, M. and Pedder, D. (2006) Beyond method: assessment and learning practices and values. *The Curriculum Journal*, 17(2):109–138.

Lave, J. (1988) *Cognition in Practice: Mind, Mathematics and Culture in Everyday Life* (Cambridge: Cambridge University Press).

Law, B. (1992) Autonomy and learning about work. In R.A. Young and A. Collin (eds) *Interpreting Career* (London: Praeger).

Leithwood, K. and Aitken, R. (1995) *Making Schools Smarter: A System for Monitoring School and District Progress* (Newbury Park, CA: Corwin Press).

MacBeath, J. (2006) *School Inspection and Self-evaluation: Working with the New Relationship* (London: Routledge).

* MacBeath, J. (2008) Stories of compliance and subversion in a prescriptive policy environment, *Educational Management, Administration and Leadership* (in press).

MacBeath, J. and Mortimore, P. (2001) *Improving School Effectiveness* (Buckingham: Open University Press).

* McCormick, R. and Carmichael, P. (2005) Theorising and researching teacher learning across schools. Paper presented at the ESRC Seminar Series: Knowledge and Skills for Learning to Learn, 15 March, University of Newcastle.

Marshall, B. (2004a) *English Assessed: Formative Assessment in English* (Sheffield: National Association of Teachers of English).

Marshall, B. (2004b) Goals or horizons – the conundrum of progression in English: or a possible way of understanding formative assessment in English. *The Curriculum Journal*, 15(2): 101–113.

* Marshall, B., Carmichael, P. and Brandon, A-M. (2005) Learning about AfL: a framework for discourse about classroom practice. Developing student teachers' powers of observation as an aid to self-reflection. *Journal of Teacher Development*, 9(2): 201–218.

* Marshall, B. and Drummond, M-J. (2006) How teachers engage with

assessment for learning: lessons from the classroom. *Research Papers in Education*, 21(2): 133–149.

Massey, A. (1998) The way we do things around here: the culture of ethnography. Paper presented at the Ethnography and Education conference, 7–8 September, Oxford University.

Moseley, D., Baumfield, V., Elliott, J., Higgins, S., Miller, J. and Newton D. P. (2005) *Frameworks for Thinking: A Handbook for Teaching and Learning* (Cambridge: Cambridge University Press).

Nonaka, I. and Takeuchi, H. (1995) *The Knowledge-creating Company: How Japanese Companies Create the Dynamics of Innovation* (New York: Oxford University Press).

Paavola, S., Lipponen, L. and Hakkarainen, K. (2004). Models of innovative knowledge communities and three metaphors of learning. *Review of Educational Research*, 74(4): 557–576.

Palonen, T., Hakkarainen, K., Talvitie, J. and Lehtinen, E. (2004) Network ties, cognitive centrality, and team interaction within a telecommunication company. In H. Gruber, E. Boshuizen and R. Bromme (eds) *Professional Development: Gaps and Transitions on the Way from Novice to Expert* (Dordrecht:, Kluwer Academic Press), pp. 273–294.

* Pedder, D. (2006) Organisational conditions that foster successful classroom promotion of learning how to learn, *Research Papers in Education*, 21(2): 171–200.

* Pedder, D. (forthcoming) Profiling teachers' assessment practices and values for promoting learning how to learn.

* Pedder, D., James, M. and MacBeath, J. (2005) How teachers value and practise professional learning, *Research Papers in Education*, 20(3): 209–244.

* Pedder, D. and MacBeath, J. (forthcoming) Organisational learning approaches to school management: teachers' values and perceptions of practice.

Perrenoud, P. (1998) From formative evaluation to a controlled regulation of learning processes: towards a wider conceptual field. *Assessment in Education*, 5(1): 85–102.

Phye, G. D. (1997) Inductive reasoning and problem solving: the early grades. In G. D. Phye (ed.) *Handbook of Academic Learning: Construction of Knowledge* (San Diego, CA: Academic Press).

Resnick, L. B. (1989) Introduction. In L. B. Resnick (ed.) *Knowing, Learning, and Instruction: Essays in Honour of Robert Glaser* (Hillsdale, NJ: Lawrence Erlbaum Associates), pp. 1–24.

Rogoff, B. (1990) *Apprenticeship in Thinking: Cognitive Development in Social Context* (New York: Oxford University Press).

Sadler, R. (1989) Formative assessment and the design of instructional systems, *Instructional Science*, 18: 119–144.

Schön, D. (1971) *Beyond the Stable State* (London: TempleSmith).

Sfard, A. (1998) On two metaphors for learning and the dangers of choosing just one. *Educational Researcher*, 27(2): 4–13.

Shulman, L. S. (1987). Knowledge and teaching: foundations of the new reform. *Harvard Educational Review*, 57(1): 1–22.

Stenhouse, L. (1975) *An Introduction to Curriculum Research and Development* (London: Heinemann).

* Swaffield, S. (2007) Light touch critical friendship. *Improving Schools* (in press).

* Swaffield, S. and MacBeath, J. (2006) Embedding learning how to learn in school policy: the challenge for leadership. *Research Papers in Education*, 21(2): 201–216.

van Aalst, H. (2003) Networking in society, organisations and education, in Organisation for Economic Co-operation and Development/Centre for Educational Research and Innovation (ed.) *Schooling for Tomorrow, Networks of Innovation: Towards New Models for Managing Schools and Systems* (Paris, Organisation for Economic Co-operation and Development), pp. 33–63.

Veugelers, W. and O'Hair, M. J. (eds) (2005) *Network Learning for Educational Change* (Maidenhead: Open University Press).

Watkins, C. (2003) *Learning: A Sense-maker's Guide* (London: Association of Teachers and Lecturers).

Weber, M. (1961) *General Economic History* (New York: Collier Books).

Wenger, E., McDermott, R., and Snyder, W.M. (2002) *A Guide to Managing Knowledge: Cultivating Communities of Practice* (Boston: Harvard Business School).

Willis, P. (1983) Social production and theories of reproduction. In L. Barton and S. Walker, S. (eds) *Race, Class and Education* (London: Croom Helm).

Wood, D. (1998) *How Children Think and Learn: The Social Contexts of Cognitive Development*, 2nd edn (Oxford: Blackwell).

Wood, D., Bruner, J.S. and Ross, G. (1976) The role of tutoring in problem solving. *Journal of Child Psychology and Psychiatry*, 17: 89–100.

Woods, P., Jeffrey, B., Troman, G. and Boyle, M. (1997) *Restructuring Schools, Restructuring Teachers: Responding to Changes in Primary Schools* (Buckingham: Open University Press).

Index

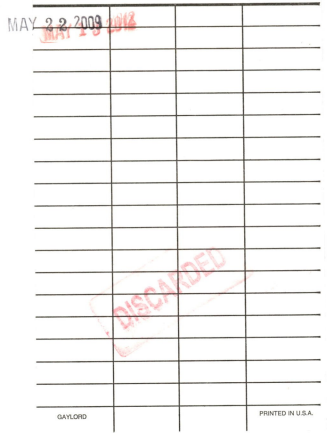